Conflict and Collaboration

Conflict and Collaboration

The Kingdoms of Western Uganda, 1890-1907

Edward I. Steinhart

Princeton University Press

Princeton, New Jersey

Published by Princeton University Press, Princeton, New Jersey
In the United Kingdom: Princeton University Press,
Guildford, Surrey

All Rights Reserved

Library of Congress Cataloging in Publication Data will be
found on the last printed page of this book

Publication of this book has been aided by a grant from
The Andrew W. Mellon Foundation

This book has been composed in VIP Bembo

Printed in the United States of America by Princeton
University Press, Princeton, New Jersey

Contents

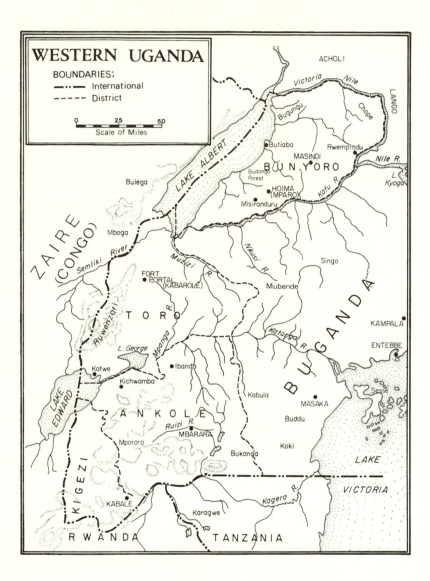

WESTERN UGANDA

BOUNDARIES:
—··—··— International
— — — — District

0   25   50
Scale of Miles

ACHOLI

Victoria Nile

LANGO

Chope

Nile R.

Butiaba

MASINDI

Rwempindu

L. Kyoga

B U N Y O R O

Budongo Forest

HOIMA (MPARO)

Kafu R.

Bulega

Misiranduru

ZAIRE (CONGO)

Mboga

Semliki River

Muzizi R.

Nkusi R.

Singo

FORT PORTAL (KABAROLE)

Mubende

T O R O

Ruwenzori

R.

Mpanga

KAMPALA

Katonga R.

L. George

ENTEBBE

Katwe

Ibanda

B U G A N D A

Kichwamba

Sesse

LAKE EDWARD

A N K O L E

Kabula

MASAKA

Ruizi R.

Buddu

MBARARA

Mpororo

Bukanga

Koki

KIGEZI

LAKE

VICTORIA

KABALE

Kagera R.

Karagwe

R W A N D A

T A N Z A N I A

In the study of response to colonial rule in Africa over the last decade and a half, the subject of African resistance and heroism has at last assumed its rightful place. Until the close of the colonial era it was fashionable to portray Africans as the passive and generally grateful recipients of the benefits of European authority. Independence and liberation movements have had the effect of decolonizing African historiography as well as African territory. In the process, however, some of the complexity and variety of African responses have been hidden in the long shadows cast by the heroes of resistance and the martyrs of rebellion of the early colonial era. It was in the hope of adding nuance, color, and depth to the picture emerging from the shadows that this study of conflict and collaboration was undertaken.

The societies examined in the following pages are not without their heroes and martyrs. But often far more interesting and subtle are the characters and policies of those who chose actively to cooperate with the arrival of European, in this case British, imperialism. By a "controlled comparsion" of the histories of three separate but contiguous and closely related societies,[1] I have attempted to gain insight into the responses of African political elites confronted with a forced interaction with powerful external forces. The means by which these external forces were accommodated to the domestic political scene by the leaders of the local African polity is the process I have called collaboration. It is clear that collaboration as I have used it does not mean submission, defeat, or resignation. On the contrary, it is an active policy of cooperation and compromise. In an African context, freed from the derogatory connotations and nuances of moral corruption as-

[1] See Appendix, "A Note on Method."

sumed by the term in the wake of the European experience of
Quisling and Petain, collaboration can be understood as one
option among several open to African leadership in the situation of crisis and conflict engendered by the scramble for African territory and the colonization of the continent by the
European powers. Our understanding of the role of collaboration in the history of Africa under colonial rule (and of colonial rule in Africa) seems to me to be crucial to our understanding of both Africa's place in the colonial world and of
colonialism's place in the emergence of modern Africa.

Like much recent work in African history, this study de-
pends heavily on the historical memories and perceptions of
Africans as a counterweight to the documentary evidence
provided by the colonial archives and the accounts by the
European participants in the scramble and subsequent colonial era. The gathering of African source material involved a
period of fieldwork in Uganda during which time both written and oral materials were collected. Most important were
the government materials that I was able to consult in the Entebbe Secretariat Archives and the interviews conducted from
June 1968 to February 1969 in the western Uganda area.
These interviews were of two types: extensive interviews
with recognized historical authorities on the politics and
structure of government, and shorter biographical interviews
with the descendants of the most important actors in the
events of the period under study. Fortunately, both the traditional history and the family remembrances proved to be ample, and the historians and remembrancers generous in the
gift of their time and recollections. Occasionally, a participant
in the events of those first exciting years of conflict could be
found who offered not just information but the incomparable
experience of reliving the truly memorable undertakings of
that almost past generation. To these people of western
Uganda, who gave so much of their time, thought, and won-
derful hospitality to yet another ignorant wanderer in their
midst, I offer my sincerest thanks. They above all others have
made this study possible and, I hope, useful.

Having thanked my collaborators, I must acknowledge

how much this work, like any work based on oral sources, is a collaborative effort. Besides the informants themselves, who are the true if often hidden authors of this study, thanks are due to the interpreters and research assistants without whom access to informants would have been impossible. Ezra Barigye, Nebba Mbabazi, and Tomson Joe Kahwa served ably as guides to the languages, the peoples, and the history of the kingdoms. Countless others at Makerere University and various secondary schools who assisted with translations and advice also have me in their debt. Among my mentors, special thanks have to go to Dr. John Rowe of Northwestern University and Dr. Donald Denoon, now of the University of Papua-New Guinea.

Of course, the conduct of field research implies a debt of gratitude to the institutions and agencies that assumed so much of the financial burden. Northwestern University's Council on Intersocietal Studies and Program of African Studies and the University of Texas' Research Institute provided support for two research trips to Uganda. The Makerere Institute of Social Research and Department of History provided invaluable assistance in Uganda, and the African and Afro-American Studies and Research Center at the University of Texas has generously contributed support during the long period of gestation to which this study has been subject. My apologies to those I have offended by omission or by inclusion. The reader may lay the guilt for error and shortcomings at my door only. One further word of thanks is due to all those people in Uganda who, although unconnected with the academic world or with this work, have by their generosity, friendship, and remarkable patience deserved better of me than I fear I have given them.

Conflict and Collaboration

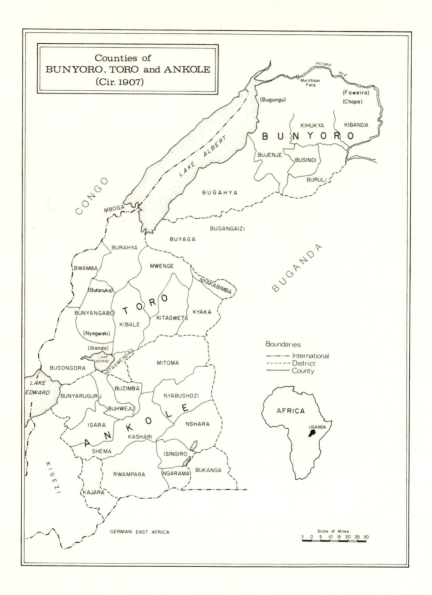

Counties of
BUNYORO, TORO and ANKOLE
(Cir. 1907)

VICTORIA
NILE

Murchison
Falls

(Bugungu)

(Foweira)
(Chope)

KIHUKYA   KIBANDA

B U N Y O R O

BUJENJE   BUSINDI

BURULI

LAKE ALBERT

C O N G O

MBOGA

BUGAHYA

BUGANGAIZI

BURAHYA   BUYAGA

BWAMBA   MWENGE   NYAKABIMBA

B U G A N D A

(Butanuka)

BUNYANGABO   T O R O   KYAKA

KIBALE   KITAGWETA

(Nyagwaki)

(Ibanda)

LAKE
GEORGE

BUSONGORA   MITOMA

KITAGWENDA

LAKE
EDWARD   BUZIMBA

BUNYARUGURU   NYABUSHOZI

BUHWEJU

A N K O L E

IGARA   NSHARA

KASHARI

SHEMA   ISINGIRO

K I G E Z I   NGARAMA   BUKANGA

RWAMPARA

KAJARA

GERMAN EAST AFRICA

Boundaries:
—··—··— International
— — — — District
———— County

AFRICA

UGANDA

Scale of Miles
5 0 5 10 15 20 25 30

CHAPTER I

Nineteenth-Century Background

T H E area around the Great Lakes of East Africa was until the late nineteenth century one of the most remote and least known areas of the African continent. The deep vegetation of the Sudd to the north, the dense Ituri forest to the west, and the desolate thorn bush of the Nyika areas of Kenya and Tanzania kept the high plateau, expansive lakes, and snow-capped mountains of the lacustrine region a matter of legend and mystery. How much more mysterious it seemed when it was learned that along with the Nile source this region contained Bantu-speaking peoples who lived in highly centralized and well-ordered societies under monarchies seemingly uninfluenced by the states and kingdoms of the rest of the world. The discovery of such powerful kingdoms raised a vision of control over a wide area and large population in the minds of early European observers. "What a field and harvest ripe for the sickle of civilization," wrote Henry M. Stanley in regard to Buganda's prospects for Western Christian influence.[1] In the wake of such enthusiasm these kingdoms and their people would soon fall to that sickle, wielded by a congeries of British soldiers, missionaries, administrators, and statesmen. By the first decade of this century a new kind of kingdom and empire would be planted in East Africa among the same lacustrine peoples.

The area itself describes a magnificent crescent-shaped plateau pressed between Lake Victoria on the southeast at an altitude of 3,715 feet and rising to the west to a height of almost 6,000 feet. The western border of the crescent is high-

[1] H. M. Stanley, *Through the Dark Continent*, 2 vols. (New York: Harper and Bros., 1878), 1:194. For a geographical appreciation of the region, see S. J. K. Baker, "The Geographical Background of Western Uganda," *Uganda Journal* 22, 1(1958):1–10.

lighted by the dramatic panoramas of the great Rift Valley. Starting in the north, where the Victoria Nile catapults down to Lake Albert over the breathtaking double falls called Murchison, the Rift Valley is marked by a steep escarpment which falls precipitously to a lake-dotted valley floor. Across Lake Albert the mountains of the eastern province of Zaire break the western horizon. A hundred miles to the south, the Semliki River flows into the lake across a broad plain. The northern fringes of one of Africa's most mysterious and magnificent mountains, Ruwenzori, cuts off this plain to the east and continues the divide between the Uganda and Zaire Republics. Rising to a snow-capped height of 16,794 feet, this uplifted granite horst dominates the landscape of western Uganda for some 60 miles of its length and can be seen on clear days for over 100 miles. Southeast of the mountains, the valley again takes up its course. Again lakes, this time Lakes George and Edward, sit on the valley floor, whereas a majestic escarpment marks its eastern limit. To the south again the plain gives way to the 6,000-foot mountains and highland lakes of Kigezi, whose Swiss-like impressiveness marks the southwestern corner of the western Uganda crescent.

The region's southern boundary is the border of Tanzania and Rwanda, largely a political border but marked by the Kagera River for part of its length. Between the Kagera in the south and the Victoria Nile in the north, the western plateau forms a fairly continuous hilly expanse broken by the Katonga and Kafu rivers. On these hills, people speaking Bantu languages and sharing a common ethnographic term—western lacustrine Bantu—developed the political culture that so impressed the first European travelers. Although some groups who spoke these languages had continued to live in acephalous communities through the nineteenth century,[2] the distinguishing feature of the region was the elaboration of

---

[2] In Western Uganda, the Bakiga, Bakonjo, and Baamba are such exceptions. See B. Taylor, *The Western Lacustrine Bantu* (London: International African Institute, 1962), pp. 72–95 and 114–302; M. Edel, *The Chiga of Western Uganda* (New York: Oxford University Press, 1957); E. Winter, *Bwamba* (Cambridge: Heffer, 1956).

kingship and centralized government among a population compounded of both pastoral and agricultural peoples. Three states in particular—Ankole, Bunyoro, and Toro—interest us, as they would prove central to the development of colonial rule in western Uganda.

The origin of the lacustrine kingdoms is shrouded in myth. Little is agreed upon among historians regarding the processes of state formation in the area. Tradition credits a group of alien gods called Bacwezi with bringing both statecraft and cattle to the region.[3] Although some historians have questioned the existence of such a people, to most the myth has provided confirmation of the suspicion that states were created in the wake of pastoral conquest of a sedentary agricultural population.[4] The conquest theory has been disputed by many close observers of the history of the region, but few dispute the manifest fact that somehow or other pastoral people managed to establish dynasties and dominance in western Uganda from 18 to 22 generations or about four to five centuries ago.[5]

Pastoral dominance reached its extremes in the southern lacustrine regions, especially in Rwanda and Burundi.[6] Among the Uganda kingdoms, Ankole, or more properly Nkore, was the most "cattle conscious" as well as the most southerly. But all three kingdoms that were to undergo British influence were divided into two classes in which status was determined by the ownership of cattle and justified by an elaborate racial ideology and mythology. The dominant class,

[3] R. Fisher, *Twilight Tales of the Black Baganda*, 2nd ed. (London: Cass, 1970), pp. 84–110.

[4] L. Krader, *Formation of the State* (Englewood Cliffs, N.J.: Prentice-Hall, 1968), pp. 43–51. Cf. C. C. Wrigley, "Some Thoughts on the Bacwezi," *Uganda Journal* 22, 1(1958):11–17.

[5] S. R. Karugire, "The Foundation and Development of Western Kingdoms," seminar paper, Makerere University, Kampala, 1972; R. Oliver and G. Mathew, eds., *History of East Africa* (Oxford: Clarendon Press, 1963), pp. 169–187; Merrick Posnansky, "Kingship, Archaeology and Historical Myth," *Uganda Journal* 30, 1(1966):1–12.

[6] M. d'Hertefelt, A. Trouwborst, and S. Scherer, *Les Anciens Royaumes de la Zone Interlacustrine Méridionale* (London: International African Institute, 1962).

called Bahuma (or Bahima in Runyankole), was a strictly pastoral people, owning and herding cattle for their livelihood. In most of the lacustrine kingdoms they probably numbered no more than 5 to 10 percent of the population.[7] The agricultural class, or Bairu,[8] worked their own small land holdings, growing millet, sorghum, maize, matoke (cooking bananas), beans, and vegetables. They were by and large excluded from both political power and from accumulating wealth in cattle and the associated social standing.

The division of society into two classes is underscored by the ecology of the region. The Bairu lived in "villages" (ekyaro) of some 40 to 100 homesteads, "each standing in a holding of between 5 and 10 acres about 100 yards from its nearest neighbor."[9] In contrast to this, the pastoral Bahuma lived in widely scattered cattle kraals often far from any cultivated area and as far from each other as the requirements of water and pasturage demanded. Neither village nor kraal were lineage communities, although the kraal owner was often a "pater familias" over kinsmen and clients in his kraal. In Ankole, where the pastoral-agricultural dichotomy was most pronounced, the countryside was generally divided into areas of pasturage and of agriculture with very little need for social or economic contacts between ecological regions.[10] This ecological independence provided the original basis for the division of society into two distinct social classes with a minimum of friction.

The political organization of the western lacustrine kingdoms reflected the class structure of these societies. Even in Bunyoro and Toro, where the royal lineages were not Huma

[7] Taylor, Western, p. 14. In using words in the Bantu languages of the area, I have tried to limit myself to the use of stems only for adjectives and the prefixes Ba- (Mu-, sing.) for people, Bu- for places, Ru- or Lu- for languages. Titles and proper names follow current usage in the absence of a standard orthography.

[8] The term Bairu originally meant servant and is somewhat despised today, especially in Ankole.

[9] Taylor, Western, p. 15.

[10] Ibid., p. 100; and K. Oberg, "A Comparison of Three Economic Organizations," American Anthropologist 45 (1943):575–587.

herdsmen but an alien dynasty, the domination of the social system by the pastoralists deeply influenced political institutions. Numerous cattle rituals surrounded the kingship, and royal wives were almost invariably drawn from pastoral lineages.[11] The ruler's court was peripatetic, following the need for changing pasturage for the large royal herds. The system of administration relied heavily on the pastoral population as chiefs and tax gatherers. The military system likewise revolved around cattle owners for logistic support and military leadership in all three polities.

These were the basic social and political similarities between the kingdoms. The differences between them were not dramatic but were to prove important in determining the primary reactions to imperial intervention. These differences in social structure, political organization, and ideology were accentuated by developments in each area in the nineteenth century, an era that proved as revolutionary in its impact and influence on many "precolonial" societies as the colonial era itself.

Ankole

The precolonial political system of the Banyankole, like the other social values, was the virtually exclusive preserve of the Hima pastoral class. It was this political system radiating out from the royal kraal that was the chief instrument of control of the Bairu majority by the Bahima. In one view:

Bahima domination of the Bairu arose not only because these racially and economically different people were brought into contact in large numbers by environmental conditions and because it was economically profitable, but because the Bahima were able to dominate. Bahima herdsmen accustomed to protecting their herds from animal and human enemies, were individually superior fighting men. Constant raiding and counterraiding de-

[11] J. Roscoe, *The Bakitara* (Cambridge: Cambridge University Press, 1923), pp. 91–118 and 149–155.

veloped a military discipline which could be expanded
and put to political uses. . . . The unilateral *ekyika* or
lineage offered wider political and military cooperation
than the relatively smaller Bairu *oruganda* or extended
family.[12]

Whatever the tendencies of social organization, by the early
nineteenth century the Bahima had organized themselves into
a strong, centralized kingdom. The monarch was drawn from
a segment of the *Hinda* clan. The Bahinda were one of the
many Hima (pastoral) clans. Positions in the administrative-
territorial hierarchy were the virtually exclusive preserve of
Hima aristocrats selected by the monarch. The extent of this
monopoly of power by Bahima and the converse oppression
of the Bairu is still the subject of considerable debate.[13]

It might be mentioned here that a considerable amount of
study has been done on the mechanics of a similar class domination in the related kingdom of Rwanda. The work of the
anthropologist, Jacques Maquet,[14] has tended to stress the
functional and reciprocal nature of class relations within an
overall framework of the general acceptance of the dominant
class's ideology. This ideology, which stresses the racial
superiority of the cattlekeepers, the superiority of cattle as a
social and economic value, and the superiority of the pastoral
lifestyle can certainly be seen in operation in Ankole as well as
Rwanda. Maquet's estimate of the degree of acceptance of this
ideology by the Bairu (Bahutu) of Rwanda, which is a crucial
factor in estimating the role of ideological as opposed to the

[12] K. Oberg, "The Kingdom of Ankole," in *African Political Systems*,
M. Fortes and E. E. Evans-Pritchard, eds. (London: Oxford University
Press, 1940), pp. 126–127.
[13] E. Steinhart, "Ankole," in *Early States*, H. Claessen and P. Skalnik, eds.
(The Hague: Mouton, 1977). Cf. S. Karugire, "Relations Between the Bairu
and Bahima in Nineteenth Century Nkore," *Tarikh* 3, 2(1970):22–33. Cf.
Interview A/28, Kamujanduzi and Katundu, 28 August 1968.
[14] J. J. Maquet, *The Premise of Inequality in Ruanda* (London: Oxford University Press, 1961); and "The Problem of Tutsi Domination," in *Cultures
and Societies in Africa*, S. and P. Ottenberg, eds., (New York: Random
House, 1960), pp. 312–317.

role of physical domination, has been severely challenged by the work of another anthropologist, Helen Codere.[15] A historical study by DesForges[16] has gone a long way toward reconciling conflicting anthropological data. The question of the degree of ideological congruity between the two classes during the nineteenth century remains both a thorny problem and the key to understanding the structure of the class societies of both Rwanda and Ankole, where a similar controversy exists between the anthropological data of Kalvero Oberg and the historical findings of Samwiri Karugire.[17] At a minimum, a system of class domination by the pastoral Hima population of Ankole existed in the nineteenth century. It was based on the possession of cattle and the superiority of the Hima military organization, the greater social cohesion of the Hima group, and the acceptance of Hima superiority by the Bairu class. This acceptance was in turn based on a combination of fear and reciprocity in social and economic matters tempered by the geographical and social separation of the two classes, which limited the degree of penetration of Hima government and economic prestations into Bairu life.[18] Domination was further tempered by a very slight upward mobility of (especially militarily) talented Bairu. This mobility allowed Bairu to assume positions of authority and eventually to assume the role, if not the "race," of Hima pastoralists.[19]

Structurally, the dominance of the Bahima rested on a set of three hierarchical institutions: the royal administration, the

[15] H. Codere, "Power in Rwanda," *Anthropologica*, series 2, 5 (n.d.), pp. 45–83.

[16] A. DesForges, "The Impact of European Colonization on the Rwandan Social System," conference paper, African Studies Association, Bloomington, Indiana, 1966. Cf. R. LeMarchand, "Power and Stratification in Rwanda: A Reconsideration," *Cahiers d'Etudes Africaines*, 6, 4(1966):592–610.

[17] Karugire, "Relations," and his *History of the Kingdom of Nkore in Western Uganda to 1896* (Oxford: Clarendon Press, 1971), pp. 33–80.

[18] M. Doornbos, "Images and Realities of Stratification in Pre-Colonial Nkore," *Canadian Journal of African Studies* 7, 3(1973):477–487.

[19] E. Steinhart, "An Outline of the Political Economy of Ankole," conference paper, Western Association of Africanists, Laramie, Wyoming, 1973.

clientage structure, and the military system. These institutions gave substance to the cultural domination, which revolved around the complex ideology of racial superiority, the superiority of cattle and cattlekeeping, the Hinda monarchy as a "national" institution, and the religious beliefs of the drum and Bacwezi cults.[20]

Many of the questions raised by class domination in Ankole remain unanswered or controverted. It is essential, however, that we have some image of the realities of the kingdom's complex political and social structure if we are to assess the impact of imperialism on that structure and of the structure on the forces of empire that engulfed it. It is therefore important to bear in mind that the system of pastoral domination, which had evolved from meager beginnings in the fifteenth century, had by the early nineteenth century become one of the most rigid and authoritarian systems of political and social exploitation in the lacustrine region. Based firmly on a social division of labor into pastoral and agricultural sectors, the political system headed by the Mugabe was the exclusive preserve of the Hima elite, despite the occasional exercise of delegated authority by Bairu. A wide range of agricultural activities remained beneath or outside the purview of the Hima aristocrats, but that does not gainsay their real domination of the political apparatus, the military machinery, the strategic goods of cattle and pasturage, and, consequently, of the compound order of the two social classes that comprised Ankole society.[21]

The primary business of the administrative structure was the collection of taxes. Tax or tribute was collected in kind. The Bahima in theory owed all their cattle to the king, who could reallocate or collect them at will. In effect, taxation was part of a broader system of cattle redistribution. Bairu were taxed in labor services and the preparation and supply of millet, beer, and other food goods for royal consumption or redistribution.

[20] Oberg, "Kingdom," pp. 122–125 and 150–157; and J. Roscoe, *The Banyankole* (Cambridge: Cambridge University Press, 1923), pp. 34–58.
[21] Cf. E. Steinhart, "Ankole," in *Early States*.

According to the anthropologist Oberg,[22] tax collection was the responsibility of the Enganzi or favorite chief, later prime minister. This man was selected by the Mugabe (king), and was in effect the chief executive officer of the royal court. He could influence the formation of military policy and the reallocation of booty and was at the apex of the administrative hierarchy. Contrary to Oberg, I contend that his view represents an anachronism created by projecting developments of the colonial era back onto the traditional political system. In this view, the traditional role of the Enganzi was a courtier, a personal attendant, friend and advisor to the Mugabe and not at all the center of administration. The Mugabe himself exercised what powers of appointment and dismissal of chiefs the monarchy possessed, as well as the collection and distribution of cattle and the raising of tax revenues. He was himself the apex of the administrative hierarchy.[23] The usurpation of these powers by a commoner official at the outset of the colonial era is the subject of a later chapter.

Radiating out from the royal court was a territorial administration of chiefs and collectors called *bakungu*. There is some question as to the social origins of the bakungu, but it can be assumed that when on occasion these posts were in the possession of Bairu, it was by Hima delegation, as virtually all the major chiefly posts in the late nineteenth century were held by royal clansmen or Bahima.[24] This is not to deny the possibility of social mobility for the Bairu. There was a degree of intermarriage, and an outstanding Mwiru might be admitted to the ruling class by gaining the favor of the Mugabe, taking a Hima wife, and adopting a pastoral lifestyle. But in so doing, he ceased being a Mwiru and became a person of doubtful social status regardless of his political prominence.[25]

---

[22] Oberg, "Kingdom," pp. 145–150. Cf. D. Stenning, "Nyankole," in *East African Chiefs*, A. Richards, ed. (London: Faber and Faber, 1959), pp. 147–155.

[23] Steinhart, "Outline"; and Karugire, *Kingdom of Nkore*, pp. 110–111.

[24] Oberg, "Kingdom," pp. 146–147.

[25] The question of "racial" origins, affinities, and differences of the two

A system of "counties" under the administration of the leading chiefs already existed in Ankole in 1890. However, boundaries were unmarked, and a hierarchy of subcounty units and authorities was either undefined or totally absent. Rather than a discrete district, a territorial unit centered on the kraal of the most important man of the area, who was appointed chief by the Mugabe and charged with tax collection. It was this system of administrative chieftaincies that proved most adaptable as an instrument of colonial overrule.

Besides the hierarchy of administration, there was another hierarchical system that pervaded Ankole society. The system called *okutoija* or *okutoizha* comes from the verb meaning to bring presents to the king or an important chief.[26] The act of giving gifts to one's superiors is the symbolic basis of a relationship of fealty and service to a superior and of protection from that superior for his gift-giving client.[27] By this contract, cattle passed upwards from Hima herders to the Mugabe and formed the nexus for the personal relations found among the Hima aristocrats. In addition, gift cattle provided revenue for the royal court. This clientage system extended to the Bairu as well as the Bahima and provided an additional structure of class differentiation, as Bahima and Bairu had different services to perform and received different rewards.

Although the Bahima received cattle from the Mugabe or

---

groups is beyond the scope of this introduction and the competence of the author. Although other students of Ankole have described an intermediate class called Bambari as the product of intermarriage (cf. Stenning's evidence in Taylor, *Western*, pp. 99–100, and Oberg, "Kingdom," p. 135), I believe that it is more useful to view the groups as being more ideological than biological. In this sense, the intermediate group represents an area of shadowy social identification. As an example, one of my informants, whose grandfather had been a Mwiru war leader, lived in a traditional Hima pastoral style in the Nyabushozi pastoral heartland. His wife was Muhima. When asked if he was Muhima or Mwiru, he replied that he was "Munyankole only." Interview A/39, Zororwa, 5 September 1968.

[26] M. B. Davis, *A Lunyoro-Lunyankole-English and English-Lunyoro-Lunyankole Dictionary* (Kampala: Uganda Bookshop, 1952), p. 172.

[27] Oberg, pp. 148–149; and cf. E. Steinhart, "Vassal and Fief in Three Lacustrine Kingdoms," *Cahiers d'Etudes Africaines* 7, 4(1967):606–623, for an analysis of comparable systems in Rwanda, Bunyoro, and Buganda.

their clients which became the property of the Hima lineages, no Bairu could own or transfer ownership of cattle. He might for a period of time have the use of a cow or bull, the milk from a live cow, or the meat from a bull that died in his custody. He could, however, never own the offspring of a cow he held for his patron, and most patrons were careful to lend only barren cows or bulls to their Bairu subordinates. Thus, although a limited economic advantage passed to the Bairu, they could never become owners of capital in cattle and thereby enter the ranks of the pastoral class. In addition, menial tasks such as house and fence mending were performed by the Bairu as their part of the clientage contract.

Clientage, whether noble or base, among Bahima or Bairu, also served as an instrument of political subordination. Clients could not do battle, military or political, against their patrons, and were expected to support their patrons in the continual rivalry and maneuver that marked court life for the Hima aristocrats. Thus, the more clients held cattle from the Mugabe, the more Bairu who were dependent on the loan of cattle from a prince or noble Hima patron, the more tightly woven was the network of dependency and fealty, service and subordination. Clientage was a means whereby a man of wealth and pastoral status could build up a personal following, supplement his kinship connections, and become recognized as a leader of men and a power in the land.[28]

The third structure of Hima dominance and political control was the organization of "war bands" (emitwe). Basically a military apparatus that took root in the early nineteenth century, the various war bands were bivouacked on the margins of the country under leaders designated by the Mugabe and supplied with cattle. They provided the defensive framework for the territory and could be mustered and sent on cattle raids by royal command. They were led almost exclusively by Bahima, especially princes of the Hinda clan.[29] The control of this apparatus by the Mugabe and his designated leaders gave

[28] Oberg, "Kingdom," pp. 148–149.
[29] Karugire, Kingdom of Nkore, pp. 54–55; A. Katate and L. Kamugungunu, Abagabe B'Ankole, 2nd ed., 2 vols. (Kampala: East African Literature Bureau, 1967), 1:157–158.

the court an efficient monopoly of physical force, because these fighting groups, especially as developed by Ntare V (d. 1895), were the only repository of trained military manpower in the kingdom.[30]

In addition to the structural supports, Ankole religion and mythology provided an ideological foundation for Hima and Hinda political dominance. Chief among the ideological supports was the "cult" of *Bagyendanwa*, the royal drum. The drum of two stretched cowhides tied with leather thongs at each end of a hollowed and shaped log "acted as a unifying agent" as well as "a concrete power capable of helping men in need."[31] By its singularity and impartiality, the drum was supposed to form a common focus of belief and ritual for the Banyankole, overriding regional and class differences and emphasizing the distinctness of the Banyankole as the subjects of Bagyendanwa from the peoples of surrounding kingdoms.

Beyond this common focus, the drum cult unified Ankole by maintaining particular cultural and political institutions. The drum was a royal drum, identified with the Mugabe and, through its mythological origins, with the founding of Ankole by the Bacwezi.[32] Thus it was the central ritual object in affirming and perpetuating the core political institutions of kingship and pastoral dominance.

Besides the drum cult, other Ankole religious and ritual practices and beliefs functioned to support the political organizations of the kingdom. This is particularly true of the *emandwa* or spirit cult, which derives from the Bacwezi legend. This cult, which crosses political boundaries, is widely known in the lacustrine region and provides a mythological charter for pastoral dominance through much of Uganda, Rwanda, and Burundi.[33] Both Bunyoro and Toro share with Ankole the drum and spirit cults as ideologi-

[30] Personal communication from S. Karugire, and his *Kingdom of Nkore*, pp. 200–235.

[31] Oberg, "Kingdom," pp. 150–157.

[32] Ibid., p. 156; and Karugire, *Kingdom of Nkore*, pp. 138–139.

[33] D. W. Cohen, "The Cwezi Cult," *Journal of African History* 9, 4(1968):651–657.

cal supports to political structures, but to a slightly lesser degree.[34]

Up until the early nineteenth century, the system of social relations described here pertained in nascent form to the small and insignificant statelet of Nkore, located in the southeastern section of what became the Ankole kingdom and district. However, late in the eighteenth century, Nkore began a political and territorial expansion that brought in its train not just increased size and importance but considerable modification in the social and political system of the original statelet. Triggered by drought and related ecological changes, the Hima herders under the leadership of the Hinda dynasty began to expand and intensify their operations into geographical and cultural regions previously only marginal to the Nkore state.[35] Ecological barriers that had restricted contacts between agricultural and pastoral groups were perforated by expanding pastoral clans that forged new relations with previously autonomous agricultural communities and strengthened pastoral dominance over those farmers already contained within the old Nkore social system. The result was an intensification of the hierarchy and pastoral dominance of the new society of Ankole.

This new society began to develop in an international environment conducive to increasing centralization and hierarchy. The southern kingdom of Rwanda was embarked on a similar expansion based on the strength of her cattle-based mobile armies and rigid caste-like social structure.[36] The continuation of Rwandan success through the nineteenth century was a useful example for the state-building forces within neighboring Ankole. Simultaneously, the more tolerant and ag-

[34] Taylor, *Western*, pp. 39 and 64–65. Cf. J. Beattie, *Bunyoro: An African Kingdom* (New York: Holt, Rinehart and Winston, 1960), pp. 25–29, 77–79.

[35] E. Steinhart, "The Kingdoms of the March," in *Chronology in African History*, J. B. Webster, ed. (Halifax: Longman, 1977). Cf. J. B. Webster, "Noi Noi: Famines as an Aid to Dating," in ibid.

[36] K. Rennie, "The Pre-Colonial Kingdom of Rwanda: A Reinterpretation," *Transafrican Journal of History* 2, 2(1972):11–14; and J. Vansina, *L'Evolution du Royaume Rwanda des Origines à 1900* (Bruxelles: Acadamie Royale des Sciences d'Outre-Mer, 1962), pp. 10–16.

riculturally based empire of Kitara to the north was undergoing a period of decline, which facilitated the rise of the Hinda state to prominence in the marcher zone between the Rwanda and Kitara spheres.[37] Most important, Ankole was blessed with two long reigns under monarchs who are remembered for their conquering spirit.

Under Mugabe Mutambuka (c. 1839–1867), Nkore not only expanded geographically to the west and north, but she perfected a new military system that was to improve greatly not only her defensive ability vis-a-vis foreign enemies, but her capacity for internal security vis-a-vis her newly subordinated agricultural masses. The development of standing armies out of the system of royal regiments created prior to the reign of Mutambuka led to a concentration of power in the hands of the monarch that had not previously existed. Moreover, the exclusively pastoral character of these armies, and particularly their situation in the border reaches of the newly acquired territories, meant the creation of a monopoly of force by the dominant class that must have appeared very awesome to the less organized and militarily unprepared agricultural communities. Although the armies were never charged with directly administrative tasks and tended to see their role in terms of the defense of pastoral society from other cattle-keeping and cattle-raiding rivals, it is difficult to imagine that the local peasantry were not impressed with the military might and presence of the once distant and remote Nkore state.[38]

When Ntare V came to power after a long and bitter succession crisis, he inherited a considerable kingdom. Although some territory was lost during his reign to the growing power of Buganda to the northeast, Ntare is remembered as a strong warrior king who helped to expand the kingdom to the north and west at the expense of Bunyoro-Kitara and the former Mpororo kingdoms.[39] Starting with Ganda intervention in the succession war on Ntare's behalf, which was

[37] Steinhart, "Kingdoms of the March."
[38] Karugire, *Kingdom of Nkore*, pp. 200–208.
[39] Ibid., pp. 210–235. Cf. Katate, *Abagabe*, 1:131–139.

instrumental in his accession to power, and despite Ganda expansion into the Kabula region, Ntare's reign saw the development of friendly relations with Buganda at the expense of Ankole's relations with the Kitaran rivals of Ganda expansion. The Ganda-Nkore rapprochement culminated in the warm welcome that Ntare extended to the Christian Ganda refugees of the 1888 civil wars in Buganda.[40] The goodwill this created among the Christian oligarchs, who were by 1889 returned to power in Buganda, redounded to Ankole's advantage.

It was late in the 1880s, when Ntare was at the height of his power, that the monarch had his first dealings with white men and the new imperialism they represented. In July 1889, Henry M. Stanley passed through Ankole en route to the coast after having "rescued" Emin Pasha near Lake Albert. The political and imperial motives behind this humanitarian mission of mercy were such that Stanley was interested in contacting and establishing relations with various of the societies and monarchs through whose territories his column was passing.[41] On the other hand, Ntare was clearly not interested in meeting the great traveler and explorer; in fact, he seemed most anxious not to come face to face with the powerful leader of a considerable military expedition. Whether from superstitious fear of seeing a white face or prudent caution in the face of a potentially hostile force, Ntare chose not to allow Stanley to enter his capital but to send Bucunku, a highly placed but inexperienced Hinda prince, to treat with Stanley. A contract of blood brotherhood was performed, which satisfied the protocol of the day, and Stanley led his heavily armed column beyond the reaches of Ankole toward the coast.[42] With Stanley gone, Ntare continued to exercise as much power as had ever been concentrated in the hands of an

[40] S. Kiwanuka, *A History of Buganda* (London: Longman, 1971), pp. 213ff. Cf. M. Wright, *Buganda in the Heroic Age* (Nairobi: Oxford University Press, 1971), pp. 69–74.

[41] I. Smith, *The Emin Pasha Relief Expedition* (Oxford: Clarendon Press, 1972), pp. 266–270.

[42] H. M. Stanley, *In Darkest Africa* (New York: Scribner's, 1890), pp. 358–383.

Ankole king. Stability and strength based on Hima military and political monopolies and a long, successful reign brought Ankole to the opening of the imperial age well suited to meet its challenges and the disruptions of an uncertain future.

Bunyoro

North of Ankole lay the heart of the empire of Bunyoro-Kitara.[43] Bunyoro, like Ankole, traces its origins to pastoral conquest by a people mythologized and remembered as *Bacwezi*. Following the Bacwezi departure, a new dynasty from the north established itself over an empire that at times claimed to rule what is now virtually all of southwestern Uganda and into Tanzania and Zaire.[44] This *Bito* dynasty, which established itself some 18 generations ago, persisted through the history of the empire, giving Bunyoro both its continuity and its most crucial political feature: a ruling line of different ethnic origin from that of the dominant pastoral class. The Bito dynasty was of Luo origin and thus closely related to groups of Nilotes from the Sudan. The Bito appear to have "invaded" the Bantu-speaking areas some four centuries ago and provided new dynasts to Bunyoro and several other lacustrine kingdoms.[45]

Beneath the Bito dynasty we find a milder replica of the class system of Ankole: a cattle aristocracy and an agricultural

[43] For the early history see A. R. Dunbar, *History of Bunyoro-Kitara* (Nairobi: Oxford University Press, 1965); J. Nyakatura, *Abakama Ba Bunyoro-Kitara* (St. Justin's, P.Q., Canada, 1947), translated as *Anatomy of an African Kingdom*, G. N. Uzoigwe, ed. (New York: Anchor, 1973); K. W., "The Kings of Bunyoro-Kitara," *Uganda Journal* 3, 2(1935):155–160, 4, 1(1936):75–83 and 5, 2(1937):53–69. I shall use Bunyoro and Kitara interchangeably for the kingdom prior to 1890. Only Bunyoro is used to refer to the rump kingdom and colonial district.

[44] Taylor, *Western*, p. 19. The extent of the empire is a matter of some controversy. Cf. M. S. M. Kiwanuka, *The Kingdom of Bunyoro-Kitara, Myth or Reality?*, Makerere History Papers No. 1 (Kampala, Longmans of Uganda, 1968).

[45] J. Beattie, *The Nyoro State* (Oxford: Clarendon Press, 1971), pp. 33–61, and his *Bunyoro*, pp. 25–33. Cf. B. Ogot, *History of the Southern Luo* (Nairobi, East African Publishing House, 1967), pp. 43–47.

peasantry living in relative stability. Here, however, inter-marriage between the Bahuma and Bairu and the laxity of so-cial separation appear to have been far more extensive than in the south.[46] Although this decline in Huma distinctiveness was accelerated by the trauma of the early colonial period, it probably began much earlier and was intensified by the mili-tant "national" policies of the Mukama Cwa II, Kabarega. The blurring of class and ethnic differences during the late nineteenth century is a second distinctive feature of Bunyoro society at variance with the intensified class differentiation of Ankole.

Politically, the Banyoro were organized into territorial di-visions (counties) ruled over by chiefs appointed by the Nyoro king or *Mukama*.[47] The center of the kingdom was found among the rolling hills and lush grasslands of what is now the Mubende district of Uganda. The counties of this area were suited to the pastoral life of the royal court and were closely ruled by royal appointees, often Bito clansmen.

At the southern fringes, chiefs, such as those of Buzimba and Kitagwenda, were often hereditary rulers claiming titles of equal status with that of the Mukama of Bunyoro. How-ever, these petty monarchs were generally required to pay tribute to signalize their allegiance to Bunyoro. Except in times of royal weakness, they seem to have functioned much like the appointive chiefs of the central counties. During peri-ods of weak central government, centrifugal tendencies grew and secession was not uncommon. The authority of the em-pire could then be reasserted only by the dispatch of a military expedition to reduce the rebellious province to its tributary status.

The northern fringes also seem to have been held under a tributary system, but here ethnic factors complicated the pic-ture. Among the non-Bantu speakers north of the Nile, such

[46] Roscoe, *Bakitara*, pp. 7–13; and Taylor, *Western*, p. 21.

[47] The following discussion is based on Beattie, *Nyoro State*, pp. 123–248 and 35–41; Taylor, *Western*, pp. 35–37; Nyakatura, *Abakama*, pp. 159–166; and H. Karubanga, *Bukya Nibirwa* (Kampala: Eagle Press, 1949), typescript translation by A. Katuramu, pp. 13–14.

as the Acholi and Lango, local rulers or headmen would often accept a spear or stool from the Mukama as a symbol of his suzerainty. It is doubtful that this suzerainty implied more than the Mukama's confirmation of succession to the local headmanship and arbitration of disputes along with an economic prestation that may have ranged from preferential trade arrangements to the payment of tribute. In the Bantu-speaking margins south of the Nile, such as Chope and Bugungu, the local population was ruled by royal appointees but did not constitute a homogeneous ethnic group with the Banyoro proper, leading to centrifugal tendencies in these areas of the empire, too. These various centrifugal forces are noted here because, as we shall see, the disruption of the Bunyoro empire by the imperial impact led to massive secession, the loss of many outlying provinces, and the displacement of the center of the kingdom outside its original area into a small corner of its formerly extensive domains.

In his traditional court, the Mukama ruled with the advice of a body of chiefs of his selection known as "crown wearers" (*bajwara Kondo*), who were also delegated household and ritual authority. Members of the Mukama's official family were responsible for the governance of the extensive royal Bito clan. An elaborate court ritual stressed both the uniqueness of the monarchy and its ties to pastoral dominance. Like Ankole, a royal drum served to symbolize monarchical authority, and a myth of descent from the Bacwezi served to legitimize it. The "crown wearers" seem to have operated as ritual leaders in the royal enclosure and the associated cults. The "chief minister" (*Bamuroga*) mentioned in the literature on the Nyoro state appears to have had no political role to play. He seems to have been less influential than Ankole's favorite, the Enganzi, being mentioned only in connection with court rituals involved with the succession rites of the Mukama and never as a responsible territorial or political functionary.[48] None of my informants made mention of anyone bearing this title in reference to the political structure or history of Bunyoro.

[48] Beattie, *Nyoro State*, pp. 95–122, and his *Bunyoro*, pp. 25–35.

There is no evidence of a contractual clientage system such as was found in Ankole. However, an ideology of subordination to authority was keenly developed and provided a strong support for monarchic and chiefly institutions right through the colonial period.[49]

The military system of Bunyoro is particularly crucial for understanding the response to colonialism, for Bunyoro alone of her western lacustrine neighbors adopted a policy of military resistance. Organized through the chiefly hierarchy, the army of Bunyoro was a mass levy of the peasantry. Leadership was open to successful military adventurers of any class. In addition there was considerable reliance on foreign "mercenaries," usually recruited from among the Nilotic populations north of the Victoria Nile. A major military innovation based on the foreign legions of mercenaries and adventurers has been credited to Mukama Kabarega.[50] A special standing army of trained men, mostly armed with guns, was organized during Kabarega's reign. Called *barusura*, these companies were under royal control and were stationed throughout Bunyoro, where they appear to have lived by plunder. Leadership of barusura companies was in the royal gift and tended to be distinct from and often in opposition to the regular administrative chieftaincies.[51] Whether arising from the need for a disciplined force of fusiliers due to increasing availability of firearms or from attempts by Kabarega to bolster royal power vis-a-vis his chiefs, the result was the first experiment with a standing force in this region by an indigenous society, and a military apparatus remembered with awe in Uganda to this day. It was this force and the leadership abilities of Mukama Kabarega that were chiefly responsible for the resurgence of Bunyoro during the late nineteenth century.

Until the reign of Mukama Cwa II, Kabarega (1870–1899),

[49] Beattie, "Democratization in Bunyoro," *Civilisations* 11, 1(1961): 8–20.

[50] G. Uzoigwe, "Kabarega and the Making of a New Kitara," *Tarikh* 3, 2(1970):5–21. Cf. Nyakatura, *Anatomy*, pp. 131–136.

[51] G. Uzoigwe, "Kabarega's Abarusura: The Military Factor in Bunyoro," conference paper, University of East Africa, Kampala, 1968–1969, pp. 1–20. See also his *Revolution and Revolt in Bunyoro-Kitara* (Kampala: Longman, 1970).

the nineteenth century had brought a round of setbacks to Bunyoro that tradition ascribes to a series of weak kings.[52] Late in the reign of Nyamutukura (1786–1835), the weakened condition of the Kitaran empire was manifested by the successful secessionist movement led by the Prince Kaboyo, which stripped the county of Toro to the west of the kingdom's center in Mubende from Kitaran control. This was not the first loss of territory for the Empire. As early as the reign of Duhaga I, Chwa Mujwiga (1731–1782), the Kooki and Bwera districts to the southeast of the kingdom were lost to the expanding Buganda state. During Nyamutukura's reign the tributary states of the southern marches, such as Buhweju and Buzimba, effectively asserted their independence from Kitara.[53] But the loss of the central and rich region of Toro climaxed a precipitous decline in Bunyoro's fortunes. The emergence of a strong ruler in Mukama Kamurasi (1852–1869) began a reversal in Nyoro fortunes, but a new challenge was about to present itself which tended to undo the work of Kamurasi in strengthening the kingdom. It was during Kamurasi's reign that the first Europeans were seen in the Kitaran empire. The presence of European travelers, first from the south via Buganda in the persons of the explorers Speke and Grant and next from the north via Bunyoro's secessionist province of Chope on the Victoria Nile, in the persons of Sir Samuel Baker and his beautiful wife, began the complication of Bunyoro's already difficult international situation, as one of two rivals for mastery of the Nile headwaters.[54]

Kamurasi's work of centralization and resurgence as well as

[52] K. W., "Kings," pp. 57–63; Nyakatura, Anatomy, pp. 91–105. H. B. Thomas, "Gordon's Farthest South in Uganda in 1876," Uganda Journal 5, 4(1936):284–288. A. R. Dunbar, "European Travellers in Bunyoro-Kitara, 1862–1877," Uganda Journal 23, 2(1959):101–117. Uzoigwe, "New Kitara." Contrast M. S. M. Kiwanuka, "Bunyoro and the British," Journal of African History 9, 4(1968):603–619.

[53] Nyakatura, Anatomy, pp. 84–95 and 125–131; Dunbar, History, pp. 38–42; Morris, Ankole, pp. 23–29.

[54] A. R. Dunbar, "European Travellers," pp. 101–117. Cf. H. B. Thomas, "Gordon's Farthest South."

the complex problems of international maneuvering were inherited by his son and successor, Mukama Kabarega.[55] Kabarega brought to these problems a vital and forceful personality and an iron determination to overcome the limits of Bunyoro's power and reestablish its grandeur and that of his dynasty. From the beginning the young contender for royal honors was an innovator, challenging the accepted practices of royal princes. He entered the succession struggle not merely as the candidate of the smaller dynastic and aristocratic faction, but with the open support of the Bairu commoners who were usually considered beneath politics. He secured military support from Bunyoro's northern Nilotic neighbors, particularly the Lango, and from Arab commercial agents, becoming the candidate of a wider imperial mission. His success in defeating Kabigumire, his brother and rival, without the support of the leading Bito or Huma chiefs, was more than a remarkable achievement. It was the beginning of an era of a new politics based on the popular support of Kitara's imperial tradition and the patriotic challenge to the growing power of Bunyoro's neighbors (especially Buganda) that had marked the previous century of decline.

Although Kabarega was never fully able to eliminate the internal opposition of certain wings of the Bito dynasty, he was able to create a strong counterforce to both internal and external threats through his creation and promotion of the barusura military organization. The barusura leadership were often foreign mercenaries and seldom the traditional Huma aristocrats, and thus formed a royal check on the power of the administrative hierarchy, which was dominated by Bito and Huma chiefs. As a factor in foreign affairs, they led the reconquest of Bunyoro's lost territories, sowing a deep respect and often a dreadful fear of Nyoro military might among the tributary and provincial regions in which they were garrisoned or allowed to pillage at will. The reconquest, particularly of the secessionist Toro kingdom, led to a redress in the balance of power in the northern lacustrine region between

---

[55] Uzoigwe, "New Kitara."

the powerful Buganda monarchy and resurgent Bunyoro. In 1886, a Ganda invasion force led by the important chief, Kangao, was defeated, and a temporary stalemate was established between Kabarega, now at the height of his career, and Mwanga, the young and erratic monarch of Buganda.[56] The balance of power would last five years, to be overturned only by the forceful intervention of the European powers in the lacustrine area. The Nile headwaters became a key theater for the enactment of the drama presented by the climax of European imperialism and the inception of African resistance to alien domination.

Toro

The Toro district lies at the foot of the Ruwenzori mountains along the hilly plateau running east from the westernmost limits of the lacustrine zone toward Mubende, once the heartland of the Kitaran empire. By the early nineteenth century, when Toro established its independence from Kitara, the empire was declining and its center shifting northward from Mubende toward the current Bunyoro district. The original secessionist province (Toro) was only a small part of what became the colonial district of Toro with the addition of the Busongora and Kitagwenda marches and the Mwenge and Kyaka pastoral heartlands of Kitara. But the core of Toro was to all intents a child of the Nyoro empire. Its language, Rutoro, is considered as one with the language of the Nyoro court,[57] and the political system can similarly be seen as shared with the parent kingdom.[58] Toro society and polity did not begin to diverge from the Nyoro mainstream until after the secession of Prince Kaboyo in around 1820. The secession and the consequent changes in political outlook and

[56] Uzoigwe, "Kabarega's Abarusura"; and Nyakatura, *Anatomy*, pp. 131–136.

[57] Interview B/43, Rubangoya and Katambarwa, 26 November 1968.

[58] Cf. Taylor, *Western*, pp. 61–62. John Roscoe's monographic series for the Mackie Ethnological Survey includes Toro in the monograph, *The Bakitara*.

proclivities laid the basis for Toro's particular response to the imperial impact.[59]

Toro independence dates from the dispatch of Prince Kaboyo, the favorite son of Mukama Nyakamatura, to Toro in the early 1820s. Kaboyo, hopeful of establishing an independent dynasty in Toro, sounded out local sentiment among the Huma leadership in the pastoral southern regions. Finding a considerable opinion against his father's weak rule, he decided to abscond with one of the royal herds and proclaim himself Mukama while his father still lived. Nyakamatura made half-hearted efforts to reduce Kaboyo's rebellion, but in the battle that resulted, Kaboyo, although defeated, was allowed to escape unharmed. The rebellion was not reduced, and Kaboyo was able to establish his own regime and to pass on his newly created crown to his descendants upon his death in about 1860.[60]

Although in its initial stages the Toro secession seems to have represented a popular and progressive movement, drawing the support of both Batoro agricultural clans and the Bakonjo farmers of the Ruwenzori foothills under the banner of the young prince, this phase of the rebellion was short-lived. Kaboyo quickly came to rely on the pastoral elite who had rallied to his standard from the Mwenge region and entered Toro with him. Following the traditions of the lacustrine states, Toro court and political life became the exclusive preserve of a Huma aristocracy. A replica of the Nyoro court and administration, with many of the same weaknesses and

[59] For the history of Toro from 1820 to 1890, see Kenneth Ingham, *The Kingdom of Toro in Uganda* (London: Methuen, 1975), pp. 21–59; Sir George Kamurasi Rukidi III, "The Kings of Toro," Joseph R. Muchope, trans., Department of History, Makerere University, Kampala, 1969; and various essays by James Wilson, Department of History, Makerere University.

[60] J. Wilson, "Omukama Kaboyo Olimi I and the Foundation of the Toro Kingdom," seminar paper, Department of History, Makerere University, Kampala, 1971, provides the most comprehensive account of the events based on both Nyoro and Toro traditions. See also his "The Foundation of the Toro Kingdom," in D. J. N. Denoon, ed., *The History of Uganda* Vol. 2 (Kampala: East African Publishing House, forthcoming); and Ingham, *Kingdom of Toro*, pp. 21–40.

divisions as the class-ridden mother kingdom of Kitara, was erected in the Toro daughter state.[61] It even appears that following the principles of *matre pulcria filia pulcrior*, the daughter kingdom refined and perfected Kitarian ideology and institutions, coming to despise the uncouth agriculturalists even more than in the Kitaran heartland.

After Kaboyo's long and peaceful reign ended, the kingdom passed into a period of interregnal strife and to a short series of weak or at least unsuccessful monarchs. Power ultimately fell to a usurper (*kyebambe*) named Nyaika, who succeeded in driving a reigning monarch from the throne and establishing his own claim based on descent from Kaboyo and the support of his mother's powerful clan. But civil strife continued under Nyaika and eventually allowed for the success of the Nyoro reconquest under Kabarega. On the pretext of revenge for the theft of a favorite cow, Kabarega, newly established on the Kitaran throne with visions of reestablishing its previous glories, initiated an invasion of Toro in 1876. During the invasion Nyaika died, and his family and court were scattered. Kabarega was able to reestablish a Nyoro administration backed by the power of his barusura armies, reintegrating the secessionist province into a resurgent empire.[62]

While the territory of Toro was being annexed to Bunyoro, the descendants of Nyaika and Kaboyo continued to struggle for their reinstatement as rulers of an independent kingdom. The aid of the rulers of Buganda was sought following the traditions of lacustrine diplomacy. More important, while Bunyoro under Kabarega was undergoing a serious social and political transformation, if not revolution, the Baboyo dynasts, like the Bourbons, learned nothing and forgot nothing. They and their supporters retained an idea of a Toro reconstituted on the basis of the same social and political hierar-

[61] Wilson, "Omukama Kaboyo," pp. 9–12 and 21; Rukidi, "Kings," pp. 6–7. See also J. Wilson, "The Clans of Toro," seminar paper, Makerere University, Kampala, 1972, p. 30.

[62] J. Wilson, "Kaboyo's Sons' Struggle for the Throne of Toro, 1860–1878," seminar paper, Department of History, Makerere University, Kampala, 1973. Nyakatura, *Anatomy*, pp. 123–124, 127–129, 220–221; K. W., "Kings," Part 1, p. 67, gives names of Kabarega's chiefs in the Toro region.

chy and ideology as had existed in the reigns of the Kaboyo and Nyaika. When they were able to return with Ganda and European support in 1891, they were to create a strange new mixture of Toro tradition and the alien ways of their Ganda and British overlords.

The British in Uganda

Having examined the major changes within the African kingdoms of western Uganda in the nineteenth century, we have only to account for the development of European and especially British interest and influence in this area. The history of European involvement in the lacustrine area focused on the kingdom of Buganda. If we are to judge what role external factors played in determining the responses of the western kingdoms to imperial intrusion, a brief review of events in the neighboring Ganda kingdom is needed.

Following up on H. M. Stanley's call for missionaries for Buganda in 1875, representatives of the Anglican Church Missionary Society and the Roman Catholic White Fathers of Algiers reached the shores of Lake Victoria and began their evangelical work in 1877–1878. Within a few years their efforts were being rewarded with increasing numbers of converts from among the courtiers and especially the youthful pages at Mutesa's court at Mengo. When the shrewd and powerful hand of Mutesa was removed by long illness and ultimate death in 1884, the kingdom was thrown into chaos. Although the vast majority of the population had remained true to traditional faith and customs, a growing and important group of converts to Islam and Protestant and Catholic Christianity had emerged at the center of Buganda's political life at court.

The accession to power of Mutesa's adolescent and erratic son, Mwanga, only heightened the crisis as all three religious factions competed with the still powerful traditionalists for the monarch's favor. The murder of the first Anglican Bishop in 1885 and an attempted purge and martyrdom of Christians the following year threw the Ganda converts upon the slender resources of their own faith and the missionaries' uncertain international connections. Ultimately, the resolve emerged among all three religious parties to rid the kingdom of Mwanga and choose a successor themselves. The series of revolutions that resulted in 1888 are too complex to detail here. It is sufficient to note that from the jaws of defeat and exile in Ankole, the two Christian factions were able in 1889 to forge an alliance headed by the monarch they had helped depose and to return to Mengo triumphant. There they established a new Ganda state in which Mwanga reigned, but the Christian oligarchs, both Protestant and Catholic, shared power in an increasingly uneasy condominium. It was this cauldron that Lugard entered in 1890, its fires fed by religious intolerance and a steady supply of firearms from Christian Europe.[63]

Between 1850 and 1890, direct European contacts with the western kingdoms were intermittent and generally superficial in comparison to their impact on the political life of the Ganda state. But they did begin to lay a groundwork of expectation and interaction that would last beyond the period of exploration into the colonial era.

The first element of the interaction that must be emphasized is the remoteness and inaccessibility of the western region to the outside world, which held European penetration to a minimum until the scramble was well underway. There were three possible routes into the lacustrine region from the

[63] K. Ingham, *The Making of Modern Uganda* (London: Allen and Unwin, 1958), pp. 13–43; D. A. Low, *Religion and Society in Buganda 1875–1900* (Kampala: East African Institute of Social Research, 1956); Wright, *Buganda in the Heroic Age*; J. M. Gray, "The Year of the Three Kings of Buganda," *Uganda Journal* 14, 1(1950):15–52; J. A. Rowe, "The Purge of Christians at Mwanga's Court," *Journal of African History* 5, 1(1964):55–71; C. C. Wrigley, "The Christian Revolution in Buganda," *Comparative Studies in Society and History* 2(1959–1960):33–48; For Buganda's place in the diplomacy of imperialism, cf. D. A. Low, *Buganda in Modern History* (Berkeley: University of California Press, 1971), pp. 13–100; Oliver and Mathew, eds., *History of East Africa*, pp. 332–352 and 391–432; R. Robinson and J. Gallagher, *Africa and the Victorians* (New York: St. Martin's, 1967), pp. 307–338. The fullest account remains D. A. Low, "The British and Uganda, 1862–1900" (D. Phil. diss., Oxford, 1957).

African periphery. The east coast route from Bagamoyo or Mombasa via Tabora or Masailand brought one to Lake Victoria's shores and thus into the Baganda sphere of influence in the eastern lacustrine region. This route, which has become the major link between Uganda and the seas, had a profound influence in shaping and even in naming the Uganda Protectorate. But for western Uganda its importance was its indirectness, the fact that it percolated external influences through a filter of Ganda political predominance and ultimately Ganda subimperialism.[64] The second route, from the west coast via the Zaire basin and the dense rain forests of the eastern Congo Free State, was the most arduous. Only a brash and even foolhardy adventurer like Henry M. Stanley would choose such a perilous route to the Nile headwaters and then only with ulterior political motives as an added goad.[65]

The third route, and the one to prove the most significant in the formation of British attitudes toward western Uganda, was the northern route up the Nile River from Egypt. From the days of Mohammed Ali, Egyptian potentates had cast their eyes south in an effort to extend the nominally Turkish province's imperium. Yet it was not until the 1840s that the barriers of sand and sudd, the dense vegetation of the upper Nile, were penetrated by Levantine and European traders in search of ivory. By the 1860s, when the first European explorer used the northern route to reach the lacustrine region, the ivory and slave trade had developed into a booming business for Egyptian and Khartoum merchants. The close association between the northern route and the disruption and anxiety caused in lacustrine society by the Khartoum slave raiders was to prejudice the relationship of the early explorers and the African kingdoms for decades.

One incidental influence of the routes to Uganda was that Ankole and Toro were outside of the main areas about which Europeans expressed concern and interest before 1890.

[64] A. Roberts, "The Sub-Imperialism of Buganda," *Journal of African History* 3, 3(1962):135–150.

[65] Smith, *Emin Pasha Relief Expedition*, pp. 64–84, on Stanley's decision for the west coast route.

Neither the southern nor northern route crossed the territories of either of these states, whereas Buganda sat astride
the southern route and Bunyoro across the northern, making
some of their involvement with European exploration and
advance unavoidable. It was not until Stanley's rescue mission
to Emin, which traversed the Zaire basin from the west and
visited Toro and Ankole in 1889, that firsthand observations
of these peoples were made available to the European reading
public.[66]

Bunyoro was not to be so fortunate. Starting in 1860, a
rapid succession of European explorers, adventurers, and
administrators visited Bunyoro-Kitara, using the northern
route in particular.[67] The net result of these visits was to confirm in the European mind the impression of an African despotism, totally beyond the reach of reason and sympathy,
which had to be broken and reduced if civilization and its
boons were to be extended to the unfortunate inhabitants of
imperial Kitara. Thus while Buganda was blessed by the influences of missionaries and the southern routes perspective,
Bunyoro became the object of European fury, not without
some substantial by-products to the imperial powers.

The first visitors to Bunyoro came merely to look upon the
land, or rather, upon the waters. Speke and Grant, traveling
the southern route, reached Bunyoro in September 1860 on
their legendary quest for the sources of the Nile. They had

[66] Stanley, *In Darkest Africa*.

[67] The following passage is based on several secondary accounts, including
R. Rotberg, ed., *Africa and Its Explorers* (Cambridge, Mass.: Harvard Univer-
sity Press, 1970), pp. 95–173, 223–254, and various articles in the *Uganda
Journal* by A. R. Dunbar, Sir John M. Gray, and H. B. Thomas as well as the
following published sources by visitors to Bunyoro, 1862–1889: J. H. Speke,
Journal of the Discovery of the Source of the Nile (New York: Harper & Bros.,
1864); S. Baker, *The Albert Nyanza*, new ed. (London: Macmillan, 1883); and
Ismailia (New York: Harper & Bros., 1875); Stanley, *In Darkest Africa*; R.
Gessi, *Seven Years in the Soudan* (London: Marston, 1892); C. Chaille-Long,
Central Africa: Naked Truths of Naked People (New York: Harper & Bros.,
1877); W. Junker, *Travels in Africa*, 3 vols. (London: Chapman and Hall,
1890–1892); G. Schweinfurth et al., comps., *Emin Pasha in Central Africa*
(London: George Philip and Son, 1888); G. Schweitzer, comp. *Emin Pasha*, 2
vols. (New York: Reprint, Negro University Press, 1969).

seen the Ripon Falls coming out of Lake Victoria and had stayed some time with Kabaka Mutesa, king of Buganda. Their intention was to follow the Nile downstream to Gondokoro, a seasonal outpost of the Khartoum slavers, where they were to be met by British consular agents before continuing to Egypt and Britain. This combination of intentions and achievements was bound to arouse the suspicion of Kamurasi, the ruler of Bunyoro.

Kamurasi, at war with the rebellious Prince Ruyonga, was encamped near the Victoria Nile in the northernmost reaches of his country. It was here that Speke and Grant found him and where they stayed two months at Kamurasi's insistence. Kamurasi, anxious at the travelers' connections with the rival Baganda and at their expected hospitality from the Khartoumers, who had ravaged the northern parts of his territory and might ally themselves with Ruyonga, held them in some suspicion. Their persistent claims to be interested only in looking upon the river and its lakes was hardly believable. The result was that Speke especially formed a low opinion of Kamurasi's conduct as being unfriendly and unjust. On leaving Bunyoro and reaching Gondokoro in February 1863, Speke was able to transmit his prejudices against Kamurasi and the Banyoro to Samuel Baker, who would be Bunyoro's next sojourner and its most influential and harmful spokesman to the Victorian world.

Baker, an English gentleman of wealth and tropical experience, visited Bunyoro twice during the next decade. His first arrival, in January 1864, was, like his predecessors, as an explorer in search of adventure, reputation, and the sources of the Nile. Speke had failed to see Lake Albert and had been diverted from a section of the Nile to the east of the lake. Baker hoped to bag this small prize by ascending the Nile from Gondokoro. But Kamurasi's suspicions of Speke and of the Khartoumers had intensified. The slavers had paid a most uncourteous call on Bunyoro after Speke's departure, killing and plundering Kamurasi's subjects. Baker's itinerary could hardly have allayed the monarch's fears. Indeed, Kamurasi refused to meet with Baker initially, deputing his brother to impersonate him lest Baker act with the same treachery as had the previous visitors from the north.

Relations between the Nyoro monarch and the Bakers (Samuel had brought his wife with him) were anything but cordial. At one point, Baker drew his revolver on the royal impersonator at an imagined offense to his wife. The main irritants, however, were the Nyoro requests for gifts and for support against the rebel princes. And although Baker eventually raised the Union Jack to protect Kamurasi from the threatened attack of the rebels and their slave-trading allies, they never came to trust each other. During a stay of almost two years, Baker was able to catch his illusive geographical prize, including a glimpse at what he named the Murchison Falls, and his departure in November 1864 came as a relief to both sides.

When Baker returned to Bunyoro in 1872, there had been some changes made, although no other Europeans had reached the country in the interim. By this time, Baker was Sir Samuel, having been knighted for his services to geography and empire. Besides the title he also had an appointment from the Khedive's government in Cairo as Governor-General of the Equatoria Province of the Sudan bordering on what was to become Uganda to the south. So Baker now came to Bunyoro in an official capacity, charged with suppressing the slave trade, encouraging "legitimate trade," and bringing the entire region, which had been ravaged by the Khartoumers, under peaceful Anglo-Egyptian administration.

The changes in Baker's role and status were small compared to the changes undergone by Bunyoro. The country had suffered extensive depredations by the slavers and rebels; Kamurasi was dead and a succession war in which the slavers had successfully supported the now Mukama Kabarega had added to the country's plight. Ruyonga, the rebel prince, was still at large when Baker reached Kabarega's capital at Masindi in April 1872. When Baker refused to support Kabarega in his efforts to dislodge the threat posed by Ruyonga and further exacerbated matters by establishing a permanent garden for his garrison and announcing the annexation of Bunyoro to the Egyptian dominions, the initially friendly relations were scuttled. By June, hostilities broke out when Baker claimed that his troops had been poisoned by tainted beer brought by the Banyoro and his encampment was fired upon by Nyoro soldiers. Several days later, Baker beat a hasty retreat under attack to the Nile despite abortive efforts by Kabarega to restore relations. There he entreated with Ruyonga against Kabarega, and the pattern of enmity between representatives of British imperial expansion and the rulers of Bunyoro was firmly set. Baker himself left at the expiration of his commission in 1873, but his successors, Charles Gordon and his international team of administrators, soon confirmed the hostility toward Kabarega by continuing relations with Ruyonga and Mutesa of Buganda and pressing on Bunyoro's northern frontier with a series of outposts and expeditions.

Despite the presence of garrisons of Egyptians in his territory, despite the voyages and marches of discovery and attempted conquest of Gordon's lieutenants, Bunyoro remained effectively independent of Egyptian control under the dynamic rule of Kabarega. A mutual hostility and confirmed image of implacability were the net result of over a decade of the Anglo-Egyptian mission among the Banyoro.

As if to underline the persistence of the dark image of Kabarega and the Banyoro in the European mind, one European was able to establish cordial if not friendly relations with Kabarega in the period leading up to the decade of the takeover. Emin Pasha, né Eduard Schnitzer, was as exceptional an individual as was his friendliness to the Nyoro state. Before and during his tenure as Governor of the Equatoria Province (1878–1889), Emin not only successfully negotiated an amicable settlement between the Egyptian government and Kabarega's, but developed a warm regard for the virtues of the Nyoro ruler. Unfortunately Emin's high opinion of Kabarega and his reassessment of Baker's jaundiced views of the monarch's temperament and talents never became current. This scholarly and mild-mannered German convert to

Islam did not command the respect or influence of his more narrow-minded and high-spirited predecessor in Bunyoro. The failure of Emin's tolerance to penetrate European consciousness was a preface to the political disaster of the 1890s and decades of declining fortunes for the Nyoro kingdom.

During Emin's tenure in Equatoria, the direction of European interest in Uganda shifted dramatically. The inability of Egypt to control the Sudan through its European agents climaxed in the Mahdist Rebellion and Caliphate, which sealed the northern route to Uganda for over a decade in 1884, stranding Emin in Equatoria until his "rescue" by Stanley in 1889. Meanwhile, the southern route from Zanzibar via Tabora to Buganda had become the main avenue for missionary and European trade entering the northern lake region. The Buganda kingdom became the center of a far more benign and solicitous interest on the part of imperial Europe than that enjoyed by her northern neighbor, Bunyoro. While Buganda became the subject of humanitarian concern on the part of British public opinion,[68] Bunyoro's reputation as an implacable enemy was enhanced by the added hostility of her Ganda rivals. The stage was set by 1890 for a dramatic denouement in both the history of the lacustrine kingdoms and the opening of Africa—a denouement that would also prove midwife to the emerging colonial empire of Britain in East Africa.

Discussion

Before 1890 the area west of Lake Victoria in what was to become the Uganda Protectorate saw the evolution of a unique complex of mixed pastoral and agricultural societies, each with a centralized government under the control of a dominant pastoral class and a royal dynasty. It is in the nexus between the monarchy and its governing class of cattlekeepers that lacustrine politics was located. It is in that same place that the politics of conflict and collaboration would focus. In Ankole, where the monarch was himself a pastoralist, com-

---

[68] Low, *Buganda in Modern History*, pp. 55–83.

pletely identified with the ideology and position of that segment of society, the political elite was narrowly chosen from
the pastoral class. Those few of the agricultural class who
achieved success did so by the thoroughgoing adoption of the
values and perspectives of the herding society. In such a situation of narrowly class-based recruitment to the leading offices
of the state, competition was intense, intrigue was prevalent,
and a ruthless self-seeking was the norm of political behavior.
The imperial authorities would turn these traits of Ankole
politics to their advantage in the decades of conflict beginning
around 1890.

In Bunyoro and Toro, the presence and stature of the Bito
dynasties and the growth of social interaction between the
two economic classes had led to a melioration of the situation
of cleavage and competition to some degree. Especially in
Bunyoro, where class divisions had been more blurred, the
recruitment of leadership into the political elite of territorial
and especially military authorities had broadened considera-
bly. Recruitment to the service of the Mukama was open to
ambitious commoners and to aliens from the margins of the
Kitara empire on the basis of loyalty and achievement unknown in the southern kingdom of Ankole. Despite the conservative political ideology of the Toro monarchs, even their
recruitment of political leadership reflected a little of the
openness of Bunyoro as well as the class bias of the Hinda
kingdoms.

It will be argued that these conditions of recruitment of
political leadership into the ranks of the titled chiefs and military authorities was central to the responses of the three kingdoms to colonial invasion and hegemony, determining, along
with the personalities and perceptions of the actors themselves, the pace and style of accommodation to the imposition
of colonial rule.

CHAPTER II

Lugard and the Western Kingdoms

O<small>N</small> the afternoon of 15 June 1891, the long column of Sudanese and Zanzibari troops looked back upon the ribbon of water and the broad lacustrine plain they had just crossed. Their joy flowed freely, laughing, shouting, and singing, having completed the hundred-mile march and the last difficult canoe crossing, which put them in reach of their objective.[1] The narrow Kazinga channel that they had crossed connects Lakes George and Edward and separated the territory of Ankole from the area of Busongora under the control of Bunyoro's armies. A few miles along lay the village of Katwe with its important salt lake and beyond loomed the towering peaks of Ruwenzori, the Mountains of the Moon. It was against this backdrop of escarpment and mountains in the broad western rift valley that the troops and their British officers were to play out the next episode in the imperial drama.

Commanding the troops in the name of the Imperial British East Africa Company (IBEAC) was Captain Frederick D. Lugard. It was his decision to lead the troops on the long westward march, despite the fact that his cardinal obligation was to secure the Company's foothold in the Buganda kingdom. Lugard's decision, like his appointment to command, would prove controversial and historical. Since Stanley had first visited Buganda in 1875, that kingdom had been considered in England as the key to the entire region. The success of Christian missionaries and their reporting on the troubled state of Buganda had heightened this impression of Buganda's centrality to the future of British interests in the lacustrine basin and the headwaters of the Nile. Thus, although Lugard and his small party of men had succeeded in extracting a

[1] F. Lugard, *The Diaries of Lord Lugard*, 4 vols., M. Perham, ed. (Evanston, Ill.: Northwestern University Press, 1959), 2:245–247.

treaty from the Kabaka and his leading Christian chiefs in December 1890, he lacked the military or political force to guarantee the protection of the kindgom from its external foes or its own seething tensions between rival political and religious factions.

During the 1880s, the work of the missionaries had created a tripartite division within Ganda society among Muslims, Protestants, and Catholics. When Lugard arrived, the two Christian factions had succeeded in ousting the Muslims and were in unrestrained competition with each other for dominance at court. Lacking a sufficient force of his own, Lugard required some scheme for overcoming the divisions within the ruling elite in Buganda and enlisting them in support of his newly negotiated treaty of friendship with the Kabaka. Without the united support of the chiefs or in the face of religious or civil strife, Lugard and the Company force might be overwhelmed and the tenuous hold of Britain on the Lakes region lost.[2]

In order to maintain the Company's foothold, Lugard organized a joint expedition of British and Christian Baganda forces against the Muslim Baganda, who had been expelled from Mengo and found sanctuary on the border with Bunyoro. The expedition succeeded in defeating the Muslim Baganda and their Nyoro allies and at least temporarily paving over divisions among the Christian factions. Lugard had demonstrated the Company's commitment to Buganda and united the Christian Ganda factions. In May 1891, he proceeded to develop a complicated scheme for Buganda's defense, which would take him on a long journey through Ankole, Toro, and Bunyoro and would begin Britain's imperial epoch in western Uganda.[3]

While still at the battlefield in Buganda's Singo county,

[2] For Lugard's experience prior to his Uganda appointment and in Buganda, see M. Perham, *Lugard, The Years of Adventure, 1858–1898* (London: Collins, 1956); on Buganda politics to 1891, see M. Wright, *Buganda in the Heroic Age* (Nairobi: Oxford University Press, 1971), chaps. 1–4.

[3] Lugard, *Diaries*, 2:21–171. Also F. Lugard, *The Rise of Our East African Empire*, 2 vols. (London: Blackwood and Sons, 1893), 2:136–177.

Lugard began to plan in detail an expedition to the western region. He sent back the Ganda armies that had accompanied him and a British representative to remain as resident in the Ganda capital. With his column of troops he set out first to the south through the county of Buddu, then west through the kingdom of Ankole, and ultimately along Bunyoro's western flank until he reached his primary objective: Emin Pasha's abandoned Sudanese army at Kavalli's, west of Lake Albert. Lugard hoped to convince the Sudanese troops to transfer their loyalty from the defunct Anglo-Egyptian government of the Sudan which they had served under Emin's command to that of the IBEAC. Emin and a small group of troops had been "rescued" by Stanley's expedition in 1889. If the abandoned men could be induced to enlist, Lugard would have ample military force to back up his treaty and pursue his adventurous designs against Buganda's enemies. It would be a costly expedition, but to Lugard's thinking, well worth the expense to the Company in strategic terms.[4]

In addition to the Sudanese force, Lugard had several other objects in mind. First, he hoped to induce Ntare V of Ankole to sign a treaty of friendship with him and to impose an embargo on the transshipment of firearms bound for Bunyoro across his territory. Second, he hoped to establish a base for future operations against Bunyoro on their western flank, in the Busongora and Toro region, diverting Nyoro attention from the Ganda frontier. Lastly, he hoped to carry out an investigation of the resources of the western region, which he believed to be extensive, and to secure for the Company the trade and wealth of the area, particularly, the valuable Katwe salt works in Busongora, the nub of a widespread and important commercial network.[5]

Lugard's conception was grand and his ability to lead men,

---

[4] F. Lugard, Diaries, 2:168–169. On Stanley's rescue, see I. Smith, The Emin Pasha Relief Expedition (Oxford: Clarendon Press, 1972).

[5] F. Lugard to IBEAC, 13 August 1891, P[arliamentary] P[apers] C6817 (1892). Cf. Perham, Lugard, pp. 257–259. E. R. Kamuhangire, "Pre-Colonial Trade in Southwestern Uganda," Makerere History Paper (Kampala, 1972), on the extent and importance of Katwe salt trade.

make decisions, and carry them through were equal to that conception. But despite planning, courage, and ability, Lugard vastly misunderstood the situation he was entering and would be affecting. Paradoxically, his ignorance alloyed to his resolution strengthened him and together made the adventure the opening of a new era in British-African relations in Uganda.

Blood Brotherhood and Treaty Making in Ankole

Lugard's first objective after leaving Buganda was to negotiate a treaty with Ankole, which was already entering a time of troubles. In the previous decades, Ankole had been as prosperous and stable as at any time in its history. The long reign of Ntare V saw the petty kingdom of Nkore emerge as a leader in the lacustrine area, a stable polity sought as a refuge by political exiles from Toro and Buganda. Ntare's hospitality may well have laid the basis for future good relations with his neighbors when in the course of time the fortunes of the refugees would turn.[6] For Ankole, however, Ntare's last years would be woeful. Lugard was innocently marching into the midst of a rising crisis.

Lugard was not the first European traveler with whom Ntare had dealings. In 1889, Henry M. Stanley passed through the heartland of Ankole in route to the Tanganyika coast with the "rescued" Emin Pasha. He was met by Ntare's envoy, Bucunku, a young man of the royal line and Ntare's nephew.[7] The meeting seemed to be mutually satisfactory if not quite mutually comprehended as to its significance. For Bucunku the key to the meeting's importance appears to have been the relationship of blood brotherhood into which he en-

[6] Marie DeKiewiet Hemphill, "The British Sphere, 1884–1894," in *History of East Africa*, R. Oliver and G. Mathew, eds. (Oxford: Clarendon Press, 1963), pp. 428–429; and D. A. Low, *Religion and Society in Buganda 1875–1900* (Kampala: East African Institute of Social Research, 1956).

[7] H. M. Stanley, *In Darkest Africa* (New York: Scribner's, 1890), 2:378–380; F. Lukyn Williams, "Early Explorers in Ankole," *Uganda Journal* 2, 3(1935):197–201; and Interview A/43, Muhindi, 9 September 1968. See supra, pp. 17–18.

tered with Stanley. This relationship meant that neither would do the other harm and would provide Stanley with a fictive kinship relation to a prince of the blood (*omwinginya*) and thus a respected position in Ankole society.[8] In Stanley's view, the ceremony appeared to have both political and contractual significance far beyond what Bucunku intended. According to the "treaty" document that Stanley turned over to the IBEAC, Bucunku agreed to cede "all rights of government" over the territories of Ankole and Mpororo to "Bula Matari," a sobriquet for Stanley. Furthermore, Stanley or his representative was granted "the sovereign right and right of government over our country forever." At a stroke, which Bucunku could never have been empowered to make, Stanley had seized in his own name the sovereignty of the kingdom. In return, Stanley offered a guarantee of protection against Kabarega and his armies.[9]

It is doubtful how much Ntare needed protection in 1889, but it is certain that Stanley was in no position to guarantee it. In any case, Stanley did not remain in the country, leaving without actually meeting Ntare and making little impression beyond his blood brotherhood with Prince Bucunku. The "treaty," although it was passed on to the Company, was never used to assert their claims in the region. Instead, Lugard would attempt to negotiate an entirely new treaty of friendship and protection with Ntare just two years later.

Lugard began to send messengers ahead as soon as he approached Ankole's eastern marches. Learning of Lugard's approach, Ntare sent a message of friendship, but refused to offer him hospitality at his capital on the grounds that his cattle had died and he was unable to welcome so distinguished a visitor in appropriate fashion. Lugard suspected that it was either racial fears of meeting a white man or more practical fears of the military potential of his column that lay behind

[8] Cf. F. Lukyn Williams, "Blood Brotherhood in Ankole," *Uganda Journal* 2, 1(1934):33–41, on the significance of this ceremony in Ankole life. Also, Kamuhangire, "Pre-Colonial Trade in Southwestern Uganda," pp. 11–12.

[9] A copy of this "treaty" is found in H. F. Morris, *A History of Ankole* (Kampala: East African Literature Bureau, 1962), p. 14.

Ntare's reluctance to be visited face to face by a European.[10] Although Ntare succeeded in never meeting a European, and it is probable that he also feared Lugard's force, it is equally plausible that the first effects of the rinderpest epidemic that was sweeping through East Africa had indeed reached Ankole and decimated the royal herds of cattle, putting the main food of the Bahima in short supply.

Lugard had to content himself with carrying out negotiations indirectly through his trusted Ganda client, Zacharia Kizito Kisingiri. Representing Ntare was Birere, a youthful paternal uncle, who was presented to Lugard as Ntare's son and heir, as well as his ambassador empowered to conclude binding treaties in Ntare's name. As was customary, a ceremony of blood brotherhood was performed and a treaty statement drawn up and signed. In this treaty, Birere in Ntare's name undertook to recognize British suzerainty, which meant accepting a company flag as a symbol of allegiance to the English as opposed to other European aliens. Birere also agreed to a prohibition on all European entry or settlement in Ankole territory except by consent of the Company's resident in Buganda. Furthermore, Ntare undertook "to prevent the import of arms and ammunition into British territory from the south." Aimed both at the Arab commerce through German territory and at an embargo of Bunyoro, this was perhaps the most important clause of the treaty. In exchange, the Company promised to Ntare and his heirs "the friendship and protection of the said Company."[11]

With the treaty completed, Lugard continued his westward journey toward Busongora. Thanks to his ignorance of Birere's identity and of Ankole tradition, Lugard had secured another vague and easily misinterpreted treaty with a sovereign African kingdom which extended the Company's commitments in the direction of a vast interior empire north of Lake Victoria. With Lugard's column gone, Ntare was free to carry on with the governance of his country unimpeded by

[10] Lugard, *Diaries*, 2:217–225.
[11] Ibid., pp. 226–227. Cf. J. M. Gray, "Early Treaties in Uganda, 1888–1891," *Uganda Journal* 12, 1(1948):25–42.

Britain's vague suzerainty and unprotected from the ravages of disease, misfortune, and war that increasingly befell his realm.

Rendezvous with Kasagama

With the Kazinga channel behind him, Lugard faced the most difficult challenge of his mission to the west. Before him were the barusura armies of Kabarega, the scourge of the entire region. Armed with firearms imported by Arab and coastal traders, the organized standing army of barusura had been the spearhead of Bunyoro's magnificent revival over the past two decades. Not only did Lugard have to invade their territory and face them in battle, but he then had to establish a base of operations in the area to keep the barusura from turning unwanted attentions on Buganda to the east. To accomplish these tasks Lugard had with him two devices calculated to loosen Bunyoro's hegemony over the area that separated him from the Sudanese soldiers at Kavalli's. The first device was a Maxim gun, a prototype of the machine gun. The Maxim was meant to provide Lugard's force with the military means for ousting Kabarega's forces. The political means to keep them out was Lugard's second device: the young Prince Kasagama, son of Nyaika and pretender to the Toro throne. By supporting his claim to rule in Toro, Lugard hoped to gain an ally against Kabarega and access to the rich resources of the western region of Uganda.[12]

The history of Lugard's meeting with Kasagama is important for understanding both Lugard's plans for Toro and the development of imperial rule and future Africa response in that kingdom. In the early 1870s, while Kasagama was still an infant, Kabarega's barusura invaded Toro and drove Mukama Nyaika from the throne. Nyaika died during the invasion and

---

[12] Lugard to IBEAC, 13 August 1891, *PP* C6817; and O. Furley, "Kasagama of Toro," *Uganda Journal* 25, 2(1961):185–186. On the Maxim and Hotchkiss guns in Uganda, see H. Moyse-Bartlett, *The King's African Rifles* (Aldershot: Gale and Polden, 1956), pp. 49–94 passim.

his wife, Kahinju, took Kasagama and three of his brothers with her into exile in Ankole. In Toro itself, Kabarega gradually reasserted his sovereignty, killing Prince Mukarusa, who succeeded Nyaika, and capturing and exiling Prince Mukabirere when he tried to assert Toro's autonomy. Using his barusura as an army of occupation, Kabarega began to appoint new chiefs to administer the territory of virtually all of Toro and Busongora. He drove the Baboyo dynasty of Toro and their supporters from the country and placed a reward on the heads of Nyaika's surviving sons.[13]

Kasagama, led by his mother, Kahinju, fled south and sought refuge with Ntare V in Ankole. Ntare granted them asylum, but his mother, Kiboga, had a score to settle against the Babito Baboyo of Toro for the murder of some of her kinsmen. Kasagama and two of the princes of Toro who had come to Ankole with him had joined a refugee community in Shema county. Kiboga, supposedly at the instigation of Kabarega, invited the princes and their followers to her court. Perhaps suspecting treachery, Kasagama's two older brothers decided to leave their young brother behind. They were both killed and once again Kahinju took Kasagama into hiding. Helped by various Toro refugees and some Banyankole, Kasagama eventually reached Buganda. Here he received the hospitality and help of a distant kinsman named Yafeti Byakweyamba. Byakweyamba was a Mubito from Mwenge county in Bunyoro, who as a courtier to Kabaka Mutesa of Buganda helped introduce the young Kasagama to the Ganda court. When Yafeti was named as a subchief by Kabaka Mwanga, Kasagama and Kahinju joined him at his new post in Kitanda village in Buddu. These associations were to prove crucial for the future of Toro. Kasagama was living at Kitanda with his Bito kinsman when Lugard's ex-

[13] Sir George Kamurasi Rukidi III, "The Kings of Toro," Joseph R. Muchope, trans., Department of History, Makerere University, Kampala, 1969, pp. 14–16; Moses Nyakazingo, "Kasagama of Toro, A Despotic and Missionary King," seminar paper, Department of History, Makerere University, Kampala, 1968, pp. 11–14; O. Furley, "The Reign of Kasagama of Toro from a Contemporary Account," *Uganda Journal* 31, 2(1967):184.

pedition passed there in May 1891 en route to the west.[14] Was this merely a chance meeting, or was there a design hidden in the curious coincidence?

Lugard clearly believed the meeting to be fortuitous and at first was unsure of how to greet the windfall. It was Lugard's Ganda client, Zacharia Kizito Kisingiri, who would guide him in capitalizing on the windfall. Zacharia was a Protestant of chiefly rank and was later to parlay his clientship and association with Lugard and the new powers into a position as a leading chief of Buganda and one of three Regents for Kabaka Daudi Chwa. Both Yafeti Byakweyamba and Zacharia were Protestants, and both pointed out the value Kasagama might have for Lugard's plans. Lugard was soon convinced, and plans were made to attach Yafeti and Kasagama to his column and to install them in a reconstituted Toro kingdom. In Lugard's hopeful words, "Inshallah, this may yet prove a trump card."[15]

Toro tradition also holds that the meeting was fortuitous, granting Lugard even more initiative than he would claim for himself. In this version:

> When Lugard was in Buganda he went around the lodgings of a Batoro community (Kitanda?). There he found a man cooking with salt. He was told the salt was from Toro (Katwe?). He asked who owned Toro and was told "the brown boy." Lugard asked Byakweyamba about "the brown boy" and was introduced to Kasagama, the son of Nyaika. Later they decided to see the land of Kasagama's father.[16]

The role of salt in this tradition can be interpreted as a Toro belief in the primacy of Lugard's economic motive in his alliance with Kasagama. But, along with Lugard's version, it

[14] Rukidi, "Kings," pp. 17–19; Interviews C/29, Rwakiboijogoro, 29 January 1969 and C/9, Komuntali, 15 January 1969. Cf. Interviews C/44 Winyi, 19 February 1969, and C/22 Kabaziba et al., 27 January 1969. See also Nyakazingo, "Kasagama," pp. 14–16.

[15] Lugard, *Diaries*, 2:201. Cf. Rukidi, "Kings," pp. 23–24.

[16] Interview C/13 Mugurusi, 17 January 1969. Cf. Rukidi, "Kings," p. 24.

overlooks the importance of Zacharia Kizito and disregards the role of Buganda's Protestant party.

What Lugard and the Batoro did not realize was that Zacharia Kizito had arranged the "chance" meeting on behalf of the Ganda Christian party led by Apolo Kagwa. Apolo Kivebulaya, the Ganda Protestant evangelist, has entered in his memoirs an account of Kasagama's restoration. He states:

> On this matter of returning to Toro, Kasagama discussed this with the Baganda, wishing to return to their country of Toro, and the Baganda allowed the Kabaka to return to his country of Toro, and they told the Muzungu Captain Lugard, who agreed to return Kasagama to his country. And then Kabaka Mwanga appointed Katikiro Apolo to lead an expedition against the Muslims . . . and they fought with the Muslims and the Katikiro besieged Kabarega and they told Captain Lugard who used the maxim gun. . . . But the Muzungu had talks with the Katikiro Apolo about returning Kasagama to Toro, and the Katikiro agreed, and he appointed Zakariya Kizito to accompany him and they went by way of Rwamatukusa and they got to Budu and there met Kasagama and they set out for Toro in 1891. . . .[17]

Although Kivebulaya believed that Lugard was party to the negotiations for Kasagama's restoration and even initiated it, it is clear from Lugard's own account that the conclave that Kivebulaya understood took place after the Muslim war was a meeting of members of Kagwa's Protestant party. The important places held by Kagwa and Kizito in the Protestant party and the role in the story of Yafeti Byakweyamba, whom Lugard described as a "staunch Protestant,"[18] gives

[17] A. Kivebulaya, Diary, typescript selections, John Bukenya, trans., original in Namirembe Cathedral, Kampala. My thanks to Dr. Louise Pirouet of Makerere University College for making the translation available and to Dr. John Rowe of Northwestern University for pointing me to this information. Personal communication, December 1967.

[18] Lugard, Diaries, 2:201. Cf. Pirouet, "The Expansion of the Church of Uganda,"·Ph.D. diss., University of East Africa, 1968.

rise to the speculation that the purpose of the introduction of
Lugard to Prince Kasagama was the political aggrandizement
of the Ganda Protestants. One may even see in these machinations an early attempt to establish a Protestant client state in
Toro. Such a client state would give Buganda a strategic advantage in the struggle against Bunyoro as well as giving the
Protestants a potential ally against the Muslim and Catholic
parties of Buganda. Regardless of our speculations as to the
Ganda Protestants' motives, the creation of Toro clearly owes
a considerable debt to their goodwill and intervention with
Lugard on Kasagama's behalf. Lugard had his own reasons,
and if Kasagama had aspirations to rule, he was clearly too
young and isolated to have achieved his aims without the intervention of Lugard and his Ganda allies.

So the royal entourage—Kasagama, Byakweyamba,
Kahinju, and some of Kasagama's attendants—left Buddu
with Lugard and proceeded to Ankole. Here, as Lugard had
been led to hope, many Toro refugees still in Ankole rallied
around their young prince. Lugard had his "trump card," as it
became clear that Kasagama was able to draw the support and
loyalty of at least this exiled section of the Toro nation. Here
in Ankole the nucleus of the new Toro state was collected.
Among those who rallied to Kasagama's cause were Rukambuza, Kasami, and Korokoro, later to be chiefs in the counties of Bwamba and Busongora; Kahaibali and Tomasi Kato,
chiefs in Kibale and Nyakabimba; and Mugurusi, later
Kasagama's "prime minister."[19]

Having concluded his treaty making in Ankole, Lugard led
his column to the north and west until he reached the Kazinga
channel. On the morning of 16 July, Lugard's column moved
forward into Busongora "with a strong advanced guard in
readiness to fight." He found the Nyoro chief Rukara
Rwamagigi "in possession." "He fled on our approach," reported Lugard, "but afterwards fired on our outlying pic-

---

[19] Lugard, *Diaries*, 2:201. Rukidi, "Kings," p. 24; Interviews C/29 and
C/38 Rwakiboijogoro, 29 January 1969 and 11 February 1969; Interview C/37
Karamagi, 11 February 1969; Interview C/13 Mugurusi, 17 January 1969,
who states that Mugurusi was with Kasagama in Buddu.

quets. Some shots were exchanged but no harm done on either side." Rukara retreated after this desultory engagement and Lugard remained. A first foothold was established in Busongora and the salt works at Lake Katwe were taken. Lugard's intention was a permanent occupation. "In order to open a road from lake to lake, it would be necessary to annex Busongora and Tora [sic], the southern portions of Bunyoro." For this purpose, Kasagama was a "capital boy," and Byakweyamba a potentially vital agent. "So I brought them with me, together with their following. The Banyoro, hearing of their arrival, knew that my purpose was to reinstate them."[20]

Having built and garrisoned a fort to protect his economic base at Katwe, Lugard led his column first west into the Congo Free State and then back to Katwe and north along the eastern flank of the Ruwenzori mountains. His destination once again was Kavalli's in Bulega, where he hoped to find the Sudanese soldiers needed in Buganda.

Continuing his march to the north, Lugard decided on a site that protected the northern approach to the newly acquired salt work and there built a fort which he named Fort Edward after his uncle, Sir Edward Lugard. From here the word of Lugard's intention to reinstate Kasagama as King of Toro was spread in an effort to rally the Batoro to the cause of the restored Baboyo dynasty.

On 14 August, Kasagama signed a treaty drawn up on the back of the standard Company treaty form. The treaty recognized him as having been restored by the British and ceded sovereignty of "Toro and all its dependencies" to the Imperial British East Africa Company.[21] The treaty articles outline Lugard's major concerns for his Toro client state. First, other Europeans should not settle without Company permission, reflecting his concern over recent German incursions into Uganda and his fear of a revival of German or Belgian interest in the British sphere. Second, Kasagama pledged to prevent

[20] Lugard, *Rise*, 2:167; Lugard to IBEAC, 13 August 1891, *PP* C6817.
[21] Lugard, *Diaries*, 2:282–288. English text of treaty included. Cf. Rukidi, "Kings," p. 25.

the importation of arms and powder into or through his
country and to register all arms that were in the possession of
people in Toro. This was aimed at hindering an invasion of
Buganda by Kabarega and at control of local pro-Nyoro
forces, which at this stage were much in evidence. Third,
Kasagama guaranteed the Company a monopoly on ivory
hunting in Toro and promised to defer the expenses of garrisons, administration, and improvement of the country from
local resources. Lugard still believed Toro to be a potentially
rich area and was interested in insuring the Company's economic position. The last clause outlawed slave raiding. We
may suspect that it was put in by Lugard as an afterthought to
appease certain interests at home. It was, in any event, a
standard part of the treaty-making process.

The treaty, in Swahili and English, was drawn and signed
by Kasagama and Lugard. Yafeti signed as a witness and was
destined to remain an important figure in Kasagama's new
kingdom. Both Yafeti and Mukama Kasagama were extremely cooperative, making gifts of cattle which impressed
Lugard with their sincerity.[22] He could well be pleased, for it
was by gifts of cattle that the people of Toro, like those of
Ankole, signalized their clientage to a great chief. By these
gifts, Kasagama and his guardian, Yafeti, became clients of
Lugard, representing British imperial interests, while continuing as clients of the Ganda Protestants, representing
Ganda imperial interests. Kasagama's loyalties were pledged
to two different and potentially conflicting patrons in exchange for their establishing and protecting him and his client
kingdom.[23] He did not undergo formal installation or corona-
tion as Mukama of Toro for another decade and a half, after
many crises had tried and tested the new monarch's dual
loyalties.

On 26 August, Lugard set out again with a Toro guide in
search of the Sudanese soldiers. Kasagama and Yafeti were

[22] Ibid., p. 294.
[23] E. Steinhart, "Royal Clientage: The Beginnings of Colonial Modernization in Toro: 1890–1900," *International Journal of African Historical Studies* 6,
2(1973):265–285.

left to cope with Rukara's Bunyoro loyalists and to establish
an administration based on Fort Edward and its small garrison. Lugard's column was attacked several times en route by
Nyoro forces, but this did not prevent them reaching the
Sudanese, who were contacted on 6 September, enlisted in
the service of the Company, and were soon following Captain Lugard on the return trek to Kampala in early October
1891.[24]

Before Lugard departed western Uganda, he had one more
service to perform for the fledgling client state of Toro.
Counting wives, children, and other noncombatants, the
Sudanese community that Lugard recruited from Kavalli's
numbered some 8,000, of whom less than 1,000 were armed
men. The total being too large a number to bring into
Buganda, Lugard decided to use some of the Sudanese troops
to protect his Toro dependency from Bunyoro's power. Four
forts were built running in a line roughly from north to south
between Lakes Albert and George. These forts were garrisoned with Sudanese soldiers and their dependents, and a
Toro chief was appointed by Lugard to represent Kasagama
and ensure against raiding into Toro to the west. Instead,
Kabarega's Bunyoro, which Lugard conveniently considered
perpetually hostile, was to provide a target for raids from
which the new recruits could derive both a food supply and
combat discipline.[25]

Before leaving, Lugard placed another Company agent,
DeWinton, "in temporary command at Southern Unyoro,
his role being not to interfere in any way with the Sudanese,"
who were under their own commanders. DeWinton was to
protect the Batoro from Sudanese lawlessness, i.e, slave raiding and foraging, and to help Kasagama restore order by driving out the Nyoro authorities. Kasagama and Yafeti were
instructed to restrict their administration to Toro proper,

[24] Lugard, *Diaries*, 2:300–349. Cf. K. W., "The Kings of Bunyoro-
Kitara," *Uganda Journal* 5, 2(1937):64–65, and Interview C/38, Rwakiboijogoro, 11 February 1969.
[25] Lugard, *Diaries*, 2:350ff; Rukidi, "Kings," pp. 27–29; Lugard to
IBEAC, 11 January 1892, *PP* C6848.

leaving Busongora and other adjacent areas under direct
Company or local authority. Yafeti already seemed to have
his eye on a separate area for himself in Kitagwenda, which
was fair game, being still within Kabarega's dominions. With
the forts erected and Kasagama safely situated behind them,
Lugard was able to leave Toro and return to stage center in
Buganda for the final enactment of the drama of religious war
there.[26]

Lugard and Kabarega's Resistance

The dramatic rise of the "Mountains of the Moon" to peaks
of over 16,000 feet must have provided an awesome backdrop
to the strivings that were to occur in its shadow. On 9 August, at a pass between Lake George and the mountains,
Lugard's advancing army met its first real resistance. The
Banyoro were drawn up en masse across the narrow plain between mountains and lake. These were local levies from the
Toro region, the united forces of seven Nyoro chiefs of the
southern counties, not a barusura regiment. Lugard estimated
them to be between 4,000 and 5,000 "massed like ants." The
Banyoro opened fire, and Lugard's Maxim gun returned the
fire at some 800 yards with devastating effect. Despite their
overwhelming numbers, the Banyoro retreated without
being able to make a determined stand. The undisciplined
Nyoro irregulars were terrorized by the effective range of fire
and fearful din of the gun. They broke ranks and fled from the
field of battle.[27]

[26] Lugard, *Diaries*, 2:420–421. See J. Rowe, *Lugard in Kampala: A Reassessment*, Makerere History Papers No. 3 (Kampala, 1969).

[27] Lugard, *Rise*, 2:121; Lugard, *Diaries*, 2:278–281. The seven chiefs of
south Bunyoro cannot be firmly identified, but almost certainly included
Rukara Rwamagigi (Busongora, east of Lake Edward), Kagambire (Busongora, west of Lake Edward), Ruburwa (Toro), and Mugara (Mwenge).
Ntamara of Kyaka may have been present, but Lugard indicates that only
three of the seven were "Bakungu" or county chiefs (*Diaries*, 2:281). It has
also been suggested that Ireta of Mboga was present, but I would contend
that he was only in the latter engagements involving barusura units. It is also
possible that Rusebe (Buyaga) and Kikukule (Bugangaizi) were present, but

On 26 August, "a large force of Kabarega's regular army . . . as well as a confederation of all the southern Chiefs" again opposed Lugard's progress further north in Toro. The results were equally humiliating, despite the participation of the regulars (barusura) and their estimated 2,000 guns. On 1 September, Kabarega's leading field commander, Ireta, led the Nyoro forces in a skirmish with the column on the banks of the Semliki River as they reached Bulega. This desultory engagement effectively ended large-scale resistance to the expedition. After three encounters Kabarega's armies withdrew, unvictorious.[28]

By force of arms, Lugard had succeeded in reaching Kavalli's and entered into negotiations with Selim Bey and the Sudanese "army" that Emin Pasha had abandoned there. Having secured their allegiance to the Company, Lugard then prepared to bring a sufficient force back to Buganda, leaving the rest to garrison the line of forts he would construct to protect the annexed counties of Toro and Busongora. A line of five forts running roughly from north to south were built to oppose and harass Kabarega's western flank and to inhibit the trade in arms to Bunyoro. Meanwhile, the company officer, DeWinton, and the new monarch Kasagama set about eliminating Kabarega's chiefs and establishing their own behind the protective cordon. By 13 December 1891, DeWinton could report to Lugard in Kampala from Busongora that "a complete ousting of Kabarega's chiefs" had been achieved.[29]

With Lugard's expedition gone, Kabarega found himself faced with a situation unique in the history of Nyoro warfare.

---

there is no traditional evidence of this, nor for including the semiautonomous states of Buzimba, Kitagwenda, and Buhweju in the southern "confederation." Cf. *Bunyoro Church Magazine 1931–1940*, cyclostated selections, Father A. B. T. Byaruhanga-Akiiki, trans., pp. 1–3; K. W., "Kings," pp. 64–65 and J. Nyakatura, *Abakama Ba Bunyoro-Kitara* (St. Justin's, P.Q., Canada, 1947), translated as *Anatomy of an African Kingdom*, G. N. Uzoigwe, ed. (New York: Anchor, 1973), pp. 159–163 and 185–186.

[28] Lugard, *Diaries*, 2:300–301 and 309–311; and Interview B/28 Ireeta, 4 November 1968.

[29] DeWinton to Lugard, 13 December 1891, in Lugard, *Diaries*, 2:478. Regarding the forts, see Lugard to IBEAC, 11 January 1892, *PP* C6848.

A raid had been carried out, but instead of departing with the spoils, the raiders had settled down, seized the land, set up a regime, and continued to despoil his territory and molest his people.[30] The political system, which had been based on territorial chiefs appointed by the sovereign of Bunyoro, was being rooted out by the removal of Kabarega's agents and the appointment of men by the new administrative apparatus. In 1891, Kabarega seems not to have understood the nature of this new challenge to his political authority. Rather, he acted as though he perceived only the military challenge represented by the Sudanese garrisons on his flank. At least, it was this challenge alone that evoked a direct response in the following year, 1892. There is no indication of any attempt to rouse the population of Toro against the intruder or to revitalize the political structure that Kasagama was displacing.

Kabarega's responses to invasion and annexation in 1892 were a combination of diplomatic contacts and military reprisals that failed to either dislodge the invaders by force or to secure a political compromise by negotiation. He dispatched a force under Kikukule to attack the northernmost fort in February 1892, after failing to secure the aid of the Muslim Baganda, exiled to the borderlands of the two kingdoms. The Banyoro force was soundly defeated by the Sudanese garrisons, which lost only one man killed in the engagement, although that man was Ali Bhoket, the garrison's commander.[31]

Faced with a military setback and his country and himself stricken with smallpox, Kabarega attempted once again to settle his dispute with Lugard by negotiation. On 26 March 1892, envoys from Mparo, Kabarega's capital, were received at Kampala by Lugard. "They said they had come to beg for

[30] Contrast Kabarega's experiences with Egyptian imperialism; D. A. Low, "The Northern Interior 1840–1884," in History of East Africa, Oliver and Mathew, eds., pp. 337–339 and 345. Also J. MacDonald, "Report on Uganda Disturbances of 1892," pp. 17–27, E[ntebbe] S[ecretariat] A[rchives] A1.

[31] DeWinton to Lugard, 9 March 1892, in Lugard, Diaries, 3:117. Cf. Lugard, Diaries, 3:71 and 81; K. W., "Kings," p. 65; Nyakatura, Abakama, p. 189.

peace." But Lugard was not interested: "With him alone I don't desire peace. . . . Always hostile, he sends to ask for peace when he fears vengeance is coming." Lugard knew that Kabarega's strength was down; his cattle had suffered from the outbreaks of rinderpest and people were dying of smallpox, which similarly devastated Ankole in 1892. Yet Lugard required an indemnity as the price of peace which he realized Kabarega could not honorably accept. "Hence it is War," wrote Lugard. "And I am not sorry, for when I have time there is nothing I would like better than to turn out the inhuman fiend."[32]

Whatever Lugard's reasons for intransigence—whether guided by the Baganda, by his own reading of Kabarega's record, or merely by his own bellicosity—Kabarega was faced with a difficult decision on which the future of his kingdom could be seen to rest. The Nyoro envoys returned to Bunyoro and a Ganda emissary came bringing Lugard's proposition.

The Ambassador from Kampala, Isaya Mayanja, greeted Mukama Kabarega on behalf of Lugard and Kabaka Mwanga of Buganda. He then told what he had brought: a bundle of cloth and one of barkcloth, a walking stick, a bag, a hoe, and a gun. It was explained that Kabarega was to choose between the gun, which represented war, and the other "gifts," which meant peace. If Kabarega chose peace, he was to send 80 tusks, 600 hoes, and 500 bundles of salt as an earnest of his intentions—indeed, as a tribute and idemnity.[33]

The following morning a closed meeting of Kabarega's advisors was convened. According to a Nyoro historian, Kabarega's mother, Nyangi (Nyamutahingurwa), argued for peace: the tribute could be met from the riches of the country and fighting was pointless. In this she was joined by Nyakamatura of Bugahya county, Ireta, Rwabudongo, the general commanding Kabarega's barusura, and Gutambaki, another barusura leader. On the other side arose Ruburwa

[32] Lugard, *Diaries* 3:120–121. K. W., "Kings," p. 65, reports that Kabarega's messengers were sent to find out "why some parts of his country had been cut off without any consultation with him."

[33] Nyakatura, *Abakama*, p. 191.

and Masura, both county chiefs, arguing against peace with the "treacherous" Baganda. Despite the opinions and arguments of the leading military figures, Kabarega decided to resist. He confronted the ambassador, Mayanja, explaining that he believed Mwanga had been caught by the Europeans and needed the hoes, salt, and ivory as his ransom. Asserting the superiority of Bunyoro ("Mwanga is my son") and the unwarranted desire of Mwanga to stand as an equal or better to his "father," Kabarega challenged the Baganda to fight.[34]

The roles played by the various members of Kabarega's council in advising him at this crucial juncture are instructive. The fact that the leading military figures sided with the queen mother in urging peace seems to reflect their recognition of the stakes and chances of defeat inherent in a military confrontation. On the other hand, Ruburwa, who was the county chief of Toro, had already lost his fiefdom. His intransigence may stem from his expectation that only military victory promised its return. Masura, the county chief of Kibanda and a clan brother to Ruburwa, may have felt safe in his isolated fiefdom in any event. Perhaps clan loyalty among the Banyonza, three of whom were ruling areas directly threatened by the secession, best accounts for both of their stances. We might also suggest that their opposition to a negotiated settlement may have been a reflex of the rift between territorial and military chiefs that the barusura organization had promoted.[35]

Mwanga and the British sent more messengers in 1892, but the decision had been taken and Kabarega appeared convinced of Mwanga's duplicity and desire to betray him to the Europeans.[36] Once again arms would be tried in order to rid the

[34] Ibid., pp. 190–191; K. W., "Kings," p. 65.

[35] G. N. Uzoigwe, "Kabalega's Abarusura: The Military Factor in Bunyoro," conference paper, University of East Africa, Kampala, 1968, pp. 13–17. For other explanations of the decision to resist, Interviews B/14, Kamese, 27 October 1968; B/23 Winyi, 31 October 1968, and B/39 Bikundi, 16 November 1968.

[36] Williams to IBEAC, 22 October 1892, PP C6853. Nyakatura, Abakama,

country of its invaders. Kabarega's hopes of negotiating a British withdrawal seem to have crumbled when the instability and religious crisis in Kampala in 1892 failed to lead to the withdrawal of the Sudanese troops from Bunyoro's southern flank.

Before Lugard left Uganda in June 1892, he took advantage of the relative calm to initiate a new strategy in the west. In May 1892, in order to bring the Sudanese garrisons in contact with the Buganda border and further inhibit the arms trade to the coast, Lugard "wheeled around" the line of forts. Now, instead of a line running from north to south, the southern garrisons were placed in forts running east and west. The effect of this was to sever a larger portion of southern Bunyoro, extend the area of devastation caused by Sudanese garrisons, and put them in a better striking position vis-a-vis both Buganda's "rebellious" factions and Bunyoro.[37]

Kabarega's only response to the new aggression was to continue harassment of the garrisons. He refrained from launching any major offensive actions during the period from mid-1892 to early 1893. The British conducted an inspection of the forts and garrisons in March 1893. The tour indicated that the country around the forts was simply a desert. Kabarega's chiefs were forced from the area of conflict, and nothing was done to try to administer or retain political control over the war-torn region.[38] Kabarega's moderate policy may have stemmed from his quite reasonable hope that the situation in Buganda might lead to a split in the still tenuous Ganda-British alliance and that the withdrawal of the Sudanese might be accomplished by negotiation. With Lugard gone and with the Company under economic and political restraints, Kabarega's hope came close to realization in 1893.

---

p. 192. Cf. A. R. Dunbar, *History of Bunyoro-Kitara* (Nairobi: Oxford University Press, 1965), pp. 82–84; and J. Beattie, *Bunyoro, An African Kingdom* (New York: Holt, Rinehart and Winston, 1960), p. 21.

[37] Lugard, Report #4 to IBEAC for August 1892, *PP* C6848.

[38] Grant to Williams, 25 March 1893, *ESA* A2/1.

Discussion

Within a period of months, Captain Lugard had changed the face and future of western Uganda. His prejudices against Kabarega and Bunyoro, learned from both his readings of earlier British travelers and from the Baganda he had as allies, set British and Banyoro on a course of repeated collisions and conflicts that would end tragically for the African kingdom. His ignorance and sense of self-importance combined with his political purposes to make him the instrument of establishing a pretender monarch to a successionist state in Toro. Lugard's prejudices would normally have had him supporting what he understood as "legitimate" authorities against rebellious and secessionist tendencies. But the fact that legitimacy was with Kabarega, "the inhuman fiend," and secession was with the political interests of his Ganda allies led the Captain to establish a renewed Toro kingdom. His dubious treaty with Birere of Ankole established British friendship with this potentially powerful ally and opened the way for future interventions in Ankole's domestic affairs. Lugard left Uganda in June 1892, having first secured Buganda for the Company at the price of its bankruptcy and, second, vastly extended the area of British influence and interest in what would soon become the Uganda Protectorate. He also established in Ankole, Toro, and Bunyoro a new foundation on which to build British imperial hegemony in western Uganda.

Even at this early stage in the development of responses to the penetration of imperial forces, the influences of the traditional political systems of the respective states are discernable. Despite the gateway position occupied by Ankole on the western trade route to Toro and Bunyoro, her handling of foreign affairs was marked by the aloofness and detachment of her proud and disdainful cattle aristocrats for the mundane world outside the cattle kraal. Ntare's relations with Lugard were preferably conducted at arms length, promising a distant cooperation and assistance rather than yielding to an embrace that might upset the pastoral routine of Hima life.

The response of Kasagama and his adherents to the opportunity presented by Lugard's mission is also indicative of the future. The primacy of a return to power for the dynasty allowed for the acceptance of aid and even subordination to the alien conquerors. This is true not only for Kasagama personally, but even more so for the many Huma herdsmen, especially those in exile, who rallied to Kasagama's standard and returned to power with him. Here the recruitment of Kasagama's elite from among the survivors of his father's reign signals the crucial importance of the nexus between king and chiefs in the establishment of a governing power. Collaboration with the British overlords was made possible by the loyalty to the usurper monarch of his chiefly supporters and functionaries.

The immediate clash of arms between Lugard's column and Kabarega's civil and military leaders leaves no doubt that it was the loyalty of his chiefs on which the Nyoro king would rely in his almost decade-long effort at military resistance that began at Katwe. Without the ability to command the obedience and loyalty of his territorial and barusura leaders, resistance was doomed. Here again, the previous system of elite recruitment on an open and competitive basis, stressing loyalty and personal service to the king, can be seen to underlie the actual reaction of military opposition that keynoted the Nyoro response to Lugard and to each successive British-led invasion of the Kitaran empire.

CHAPTER III

Kabarega and Nyoro Resistance

O N 4 December 1893, eighteen months after Lugard's exit, the military commander of the British forces in Uganda in *baraza* with the chiefs of Buganda formally declared war on Bunyoro and its intractable monarch, Kabarega. Within a few weeks a column of 15,000 men would be driving him from his capital. The negotiations held in 1893 during the brief period when civilians conducted Britain's policy in Uganda were ended. A prolonged period of warfare, which would lead to the collapse of the kingdom and the exile of Kabarega, had begun. Nyoro rulers were forced to respond with new military and political ideas. The resistance movement mounted by Kabarega and his followers was the longest and most tenacious in Uganda's history. It set the pattern for a colonial era in which Bunyoro would always be a trouble spot and for a postcolonial era in which Kabarega would once again be seen as a heroic leader in the struggle for African independence. Whether hero or villain, Mukama Kabarega requires careful study for the role he played in both the history and mythology of African resistance.

Retrenchment and Invasion: 1893–1894

In March 1893, Sir Gerald Portal arrived at Kampala to look into the prospects for substituting Her Majesty's Government for the rule of the financially broken British East Africa Company. His mission was not directed toward resolving the Bunyoro-British antagonism, but the policy of retrenchment urged in Buganda was bound to have implications for the Banyoro. Although Portal's attitudes toward Kabarega retained the basic hostility of his predecessors, the need for restricting government operations led him to conclude that "so long as Kabarega is prevented . . . from raiding

into and overrunning [B]Uganda itself. . . . I can see no object
worth gaining by a forcible subjugation of [B]Unyoro."[1]
Such a view presented for the first time a real opportunity for
negotiating a settlement. But the opportunity would be
missed, and the policy of retrenchment along a turbulent
frontier was doomed to failure.

In order to implement his retrenchment policy in western
Uganda, Portal dispatched Major "Roddy" Owen on a dual
mission to the Sudanese garrisons. Owen's first objective was
the evacuation of the two westernmost forts "as soon as possible." This was planned in order to concentrate the garrisons
in the east for the security of Buganda. Toro was to be left to
its own devices. The second objective was the restoration of
discipline among the Sudanese, who had been left to raid and
pillage indiscriminately since Lugard settled them in
Uganda.[2]

Kabarega seems to have interpreted the retrenchment policy as manifested in the reduction in Sudanese raiding and
preparation for evacuation as a victory for his policy of
harassment and an opportunity to reassert his control over the
southern counties. While Owen, in sympathy with
Kasagama, procrastinated with Portal over evacuating the
protecting garrisons,[3] Kabarega launched an assault on the
diminished forces at Fort Wavertree, the westernmost outpost. The attack was beaten back, but "the Wanyoro [sic]
army . . . then marched south and occupied the road between
Forts Lorne and Briggs, and thus completely severed the lines
of communication" to the western forts, aggravating an already perilous food shortage there.[4]

---

[1] Portal to Rosebury, 24 May 1893, P[arliamentary] P[apers] C7303;
Rosebury to Portal, 10 December 1892, PP C6847.

[2] Portal to Owen, 27 and 29 March 1893, E[ntebbe] S[ecretariat] A[rchives]
A3/1; M. Bovill and G. R. Askwith, comps., "Roddy" Owen (London: John
Murray, 1897), p. 45.

[3] Owen to Portal, 15 and 23 April 1893, ESA A2/1, and Portal to Owen,
22 April 1893, ESA A3/1.

[4] J. MacDonald, Soldiering and Surveying in East Africa (London: Edward
Arnold, 1897), p. 232; Cf. Bovill, "Roddy" Owen, pp. 74–78.

Owen suspected that the Nyoro purpose in occupying the road was to rendezvous with a Nyamwezi arms caravan that was running the gaps between the forts. The impact of the action on the western forts may have been an unintended consequence. In any case, after a successful ambush of a Sudanese detachment in which one Sudanese officer, Ali Shukri, was killed, Kabarega's army withdrew to the north. The pressure on the garrisons was removed and communications restored.[5] Thus, instead of pressing a very real advantage against the forts during the period of evacuation, Kabarega succeeded only in twisting the lion's tail, whetting the desire for revenge, and confirming his image as a villain in the minds of the British personnel in Uganda.

In June 1893, another opportunity to press an advantage against the beleaguered imperial forces presented itself. to Kabarega. At that time, the Buganda kingdom and its would-be protector were thrown into a crisis as a result of continued religious rivalry. On this occasion, the Muslim Baganda, unhappy with their share in the settlement of religious differences the previous year, went into open revolt. British fears of a pan-Islamic revival that would undermine the allegiance of the Muslim Sudanese intensified the situation. An alleged "mutiny" by Selim Bey, commander of the Sudanese soldiers, brought swift action from Major Mac-Donald, the Acting Commissioner, who had replaced Portal as head of the new Uganda Protectorate. Selim Bey was arrested and the Muslim Baganda were successfully driven from Uganda toward the western forts garrisoned by the Muslim Sudanese troops under Owen's command. Owen himself was doubtful of the loyalty of his own Sudanese troops.[6] Once again Kabarega was faced with the theoretical option of trying to ally himself with the Ganda Muslims and the potential fifth column of Muslims within the British lines. According to one author, his failure to do so was "probably because all Baganda, whether pagan or otherwise were the

[5] MacDonald, *Soldiering*, p. 232; and Bovill, *"Roddy" Owen*, pp. 72–78.
[6] Bovill, *"Roddy" Owen*, pp. 89–98.

sworn enemies of the Banyoro."[7] In the light of his later relations with Ganda exiles and Sudanese rebels, this seems doubtful. The "failure" of Kabarega to create a *rapprochement* in 1893 seems more likely to have followed from the Ganda Muslim desertion in 1892 and the recent acts of wanton destruction of his country by the Sudanese. In any case, whatever opportunity for an alliance existed quickly vanished. The Sudanese garrisons did not defect to the Muslim rebels. This doomed the rebels to disaster, and any efforts by the Banyoro to rescue them at this point would have been militarily foolhardy and politically dubious. By 21 July 1893, the rebels had been defeated in battle and Ganda Muslim resistance broken.[8]

The policy of retrenchment in western Uganda had foundered on Owen's qualms over deserting Kasagama and his enthusiasm for the salt lake. With the departure of Portal in June 1893 and the return of military leadership to the Protectorate, the policy of retrenchment was soon replaced by a forward policy which saw the conquest of Bunyoro as only a matter of time. The possibility of negotiating a satisfactory settlement ended and the initiative passed to the military regime in Kampala.[9]

Following the suppression of the Muslim insurrection in Buganda, plans began to be hatched for the invasion of Bunyoro. Kabarega had continued with a mild harassment of the forts, but no major invasion or assault seemed imminent. In September, attempts were made to deprive Kabarega of the allegiance of Kikukule, whose county of Bugangaizi and

[7] A. R. Dunbar, *History of Bunyoro-Kitara* (Nairobi: Oxford University Press, 1965), p. 84.

[8] Owen to Acting Commissioner, 13 July 1893, *ESA* A2/1; MacDonald to Portal, 16 and 26 June 1893, *PP* C7303, and Bovill, *"Roddy" Owen*, pp. 80–106.

[9] Owen to Acting Commissioner, 20 June 1893, *ESA* A2/1; MacDonald, *Soldiering*, p. 296. Strategic considerations regarding Bunyoro and the Nile may also have influenced Owen. Cf. Portal to Owen, 22 April 1893, *ESA* A3/1. Owen also argued that food shortages prevented the precipitate withdrawal. Cf. Owen to Portal, 23 August 1893, *ESA* A2/1.

2,000 guns barred the invasion route from the southeast. The hope was expressed that this important chief of commoner origins might be "seduced" and "cut himself adrift from Kabarega as Kasagama had done."[10] Although Kikukule had agreed to supply food to Owen's garrison in his vicinity, such aid was not, in fact, forthcoming. The failure by the British to understand the differences between Kasagama's aspirations for independent power as a potential dynastic rival of Bunyoro and the simple procrastinations and evasions of a loyal county chief like Kikukule did not, however, long delay the emergence of a strategy for invasion.

The plan for withdrawal of the two westernmost forts was incorporated into the developing policy of aggression. The garrisons removed from Bunyoro's western flank were to be placed in Singo on her eastern flank and there used to sever the southern chiefs and counties from Kabarega's diminishing empire. MacDonald's reluctance to assume the burden of annexing Bunyoro to the Protectorate had checked his designs against the Nyoro monarch. But Colonel Colvile, the new Commissioner, came armed with "instructions to check a suspected Belgian advance into the British sphere and to protect British interests in the Nile Basin. A campaign in the west, therefore, suited his plans admirably."[11] Questions of British interest and spheres provided a convenient justification for the invasion and annexation of Bunyoro, which Colvile set to work planning upon his arrival in November 1893.

In that same month, Kabarega launched his legions, commanded by Generals Rwabudongo and Ireta, against Toro. The western forts having been removed from Toro's borders, Kabarega seized the opportunity to root out the rebellious elements by armed force and to reoccupy and reincorporate these provinces. At the same time, another force of barusura was sent by Kabarega to invade Busoga to the east. Without the trained Sudanese garrisons to oppose them, these barusura

[10] MacDonald to Owen, 29 September 1893, *ESA* A3/1; Cf. Owen to Acting Commissioner, 27 July and 26 September 1893, *ESA* A2/1.

[11] K. Ingham, *The Making of Modern Uganda* (London: Allen and Unwin, 1958), p. 58; MacDonald to Owen, 29 September 1893, *ESA* A3/1.

columns were immediately successful. Kasagama was driven from his home and the British were faced with a reversal of the strategic situation on the ground. The provinces of Toro and Busoga were occupied by Kabarega's military. Suddenly, the flanks of Buganda and not Bunyoro were threatened by hostile forces. Short of men to wage a war on two or three fronts, Colvile decided to gamble and "determined at once to march on Kabarega's capital, and there if possible dictate to him terms of peace."[12]

Before a march on Mparo could begin, Kikukule, whose position and power in Bugangaizi posed a threat to Buganda's security, would have to be encountered. On 17 November, allegedly to punish the Nyoro chief for the murder of "friendly natives supplying us with food" and for his "hostile demonstrations towards our forts," Colvile ordered Owen to attack Kikukule's stronghold from Owen's new position in the forts on the Buganda-Bunyoro borderland.[13]

In late November, Owen advanced on Kikukule's position with a force composed of some 200 Sudanese soldiers armed with Remington rifles, 100 porters armed with Snider carbines, and two other Europeans in charge of a Maxim gun. To oppose this force, Kikukule "was said to possess over 2,000 guns."[14] Colonel Colvile later heard that Kabarega had "reinforced Kikukuri with 4,000 guns. As the usual proportion of guns to spearmen is one to three, this would indicate a force of 12,000 men. . . ."[15] Besides what appears to be faulty arithmetic (Colvile's proportions of guns to spearmen should produce 4,000 guns plus 12,000 spears for a total of 16,000 men), the estimate of the force's size seems exagger-

---

[12] H. Colvile, *The Land of the Nile Springs* (New York: Edward Arnold, 1895), p. 69; J. Nyakatura, *Abakama Ba Bunyoro-Kitara* (St. Justin's, P.Q., Canada, 1947), translated as *Anatomy of an African Kingdom*, G. N. Uzoigwe, ed. (New York: Anchor, 1973), p. 193.

[13] Colvile to Owen, 17 November 1893, *ESA* A3/1.

[14] L. Decle, *Three Years in Savage Africa* (New York: Massfield, 1898), pp. 416–428; E. C. Lanning, "Kikukule: Guardian of South Bunyoro," *Uganda Journal* 32, 2(1968):123–124.

[15] Colvile to Cracknall, 6 December 1893, *PP* C7708.

ated and the entire question of the presence of reinforcements
may be fanciful. Decle, a French traveler who accompanied
the expedition, recorded that they were faced "by an army of
3,000 natives."[16] In the absence of any indication in the
British or Nyoro accounts of the presence of any other commanders besides Kikukule, the rumor of reinforcements appears spurious. In the wake of Owen's triumph, however, the
tendency to exaggerate the size of the fallen foe in dispatches
home must have been considerable.

And there can be no doubt that Owen's force won a significant victory, regardless of Colvile's exaggerations. Arriving
in the early morning after an all-night march, Owen's force
was met by scattered rifle fire, spoiling the hoped-for surprise. Owen then led his troops in a disciplined advance in
formation to the accompaniment of drum and bugle. At a
range of 150 yards, the hastily drawn up Nyoro force bolted
in the face of the advancing Sudanese. Two brief counterat-
tacks were mounted, but Owen had won the day. Nyoro
losses were estimated at some 70 killed, including Kikukule's
son and six minor chiefs. Owen lost only one dead and two
wounded. Kikukule's force scattered in the bush to await the
departure of the victorious raiders, as was the practice in
Nyoro warfare.[17]

Colvile's enthusiasm for Owen's success was unbounded.
Preparations for full-scale invasion began at once and, meeting with the Ganda chiefs on 4 December 1893, Colvile officially declared war on Bunyoro. The next day Kabaka
Mwanga despatched a letter written in Swahili to Kabarega
urging him to come to terms before the impending invasion.
Mwanga's alliance with the British was termed a great friendship with the Europeans in contrast with the Ganda
monarch's filial regard for Kabarega. Preparations went on
for the joint operation of Baganda and British-led Sudanese

[16] Decle, *Three Years*, p. 426.

[17] Owen to Colvile, n.d. *ESA* A2/1 describes the encounter. Also, Decle,
Three Years, pp. 426–428; Lanning, "Kikukule," p. 125; and Interview B/4
Rwebembera, 14 October 1968.

troops. The invading force that was eventually to depart for Bunyoro numbered close to 15,000 combatants carrying an arsenal of more than 4,000 firearms.[18]

Despite Mwanga's warnings of invasion, it appears that Kabarega was caught with his guard down. He sent immediately to recall his barusura, who were still on the offensive in Toro and Busoga, but he was unable to make adequate preparations to oppose the headlong attack that the Ganda–British allies were mounting. Colvile and the Baganda expected that Kabarega would order a determined stand at the Kafu River, which they hoped to be able to overwhelm. Short of that, they hoped that Kabarega would lead a retreat en masse to Mruli on the Nile, where again they hoped he might be encountered and soundly defeated. However, Kabarega appears wisely to have chosen instead to fight a rearguard action, ambushing foragers and the advanced position of the attackers while retreating before the column that moved toward his capital. On 27 December, the Kafu was reached and "only small Parties" of Banyoro were drawn up to contest the crossing, which was effected without difficulty. Any hopes that Kabarega held of regrouping his fighting forces and making a defense of his territory in strength were passed. On 2

[18] Colvile, *Land*, p. 74; Colvile to Cracknall, 2 January 1894, *PP* C7708; Mwanga to Kabarega, 5 December 1893, *ESA* A2/1. The text reads:

Kwa Sultan Kabalega mutotowa Kamulasa,

Nalifulaki sana nilipoona barua yako sababu niliandika barua hii. Mimi mtoto wako Lakini ni rafiki ya WaZungu sana sana. Nilikasirika sana niliposikia kama umeua sukuliafiende nakupiga gubuza nakufakuza Kasagama. Kwa neno hilo wazungu wamekuja Katika inchi yako ukiwa unataka amani katana nao upesi. mimi Sultan Mwanga mutoto wa Mutesa.

To the Sultan Kabarega son of Kamurasi,

I was very pleased when I saw your letter and so I have written this letter. I am your son, but I am the great friend of the white men. I was very angry when I heard that you had killed Shukri Effendi and defeated the general (gabuza?) and chased out Kasagama. For these reasons, the white men have come into your country; if you want peace, meet (agree) with them quickly. I am, Sultan Mwanga, son of Mutesa.

January, the capital of Bunyoro at Mparo Hill was left in
ashes to be occupied by the victorious allies.[19]

The fall of Mparo evoked a new strategy from each side.
Kabarega "had deserted his home without striking a blow,
and now obstinately, but very wisely, refused to give battle."[20] Instead, he withdrew into the Budongo forest to the
north of Mparo, where his bodyguard skirmished with
Ganda-British patrols but where swift maneuver and difficult
terrain provided a modicum of safety from being overwhelmed or captured. The main force of the armies returned
from Toro, and Busoga arrived late and bedraggled and
major offensive operations were probably both impossible
and strategically unwise. At this stage the hit-and-run tactics
adopted by Kabarega's guard were not what we might call
"guerilla warfare," but were rather a continuation of his rearguard maneuvers. Kabarega was buying time with space.
Previous experience suggested that the Baganda would stay
awhile, pillage and cause damage, but given time and the anticipated problems of disease, food supply, and logistic support of an army of occupation, they would soon enough
withdraw and leave the Banyoro free to rebuild, sow new
crops, and restore their power. Despite Kabarega's accurate
anticipation of the problems that would plague the invaders,
experience on this occasion would prove a poor teacher.

On the other side, Colvile was quick to realize the inadequacy for his purposes of simply capturing the razed capital of
Mparo and then retreating. He wrote:

> Kabarega was retiring before us, and knowing that it was
> necessary for the peace of Uganda that his power should
> be broken—a result which would not be brought about
> by a mere punitive expedition—I saw that we must either
> capture him or drive him out of his kingdom.[21]

Colvile therefore sent out forces to pursue Kabarega into the
Budongo forest in an attempt to capture him. Learning that

[19] Colvile, *Land*, pp. 81–116; Nyakatura, *Abakama*, pp. 192–195.
[20] A. B. Thruston, *African Incidents* (London: John Murray, 1900), p. 137.
[21] Colvile, *Land*, p. 119.

Kabarega had dispatched much of the royal wealth in cattle and ivory to Mruli, Colvile attempted to lure him out of the forest by feigning a move on Mruli. A Ganda chief's anxiety for battle spoiled this ploy when he advanced too soon and disclosed to the Banyoro the position of Colvile's hidden army.[22]

Kabarega withdrew again into the forest and his chiefs, including Ireta, drew up a rearguard force to protect him. Surprise was eliminated and with it the hope that Kabarega might be captured by a rapid maneuver. Kabarega sent all but a bodyguard of about 1,000 men back to their homes. A small bodyguard demanding little food and the protective cover of the forest would allow him to thwart his foes until they tired of the pursuit and returned to Buganda.[23]

But Colvile was not to be frustrated so easily. Failing to capture the elusive Mukama, he resorted to a siege. But to besiege Kabarega in the Budongo forest meant to occupy the country around it. Positions were established at Katanwa and Kibiro in late January 1894. It was hardly coincidental that occupation allowed Colvile to send an expedition by boat from Kibiro to Wadelai on the White Nile and an overland expedition to Bugunga in the northwestern corner of Bunyoro. In execution of his Foreign Office orders to forestall a Belgian advance, he succeeded in reaching the Nile and establishing a British presence there. Kabarega's posture of resistance had provided the occasion to execute those orders by the short route of military occupation.[24]

On 23 January, the Banyoro attacked the Sudanese expedition in Bugungu, north of the fringe of the forest. The British-officered troops were "ignominiously surprised," but managed to beat off the attack. Two days later, a night attack was again driven off by the Sudanese and the attackers withdrew to Budongo. An iron boat launched on Lake Albert was also fired on once. On 24 January, at the southern edge of the

[22] Ibid., pp. 130–132 and 142–143; Colvile to Cracknall, 5 February 1894, *PP* C7708.

[23] Interview B/28 Ireeta, 4 November 1968.

[24] Colvile, *Land*, pp. 145–172.

Budongo forest, the Banyoro also attacked the Sudanese at Kitanwa. Still with only a small part of his forces available to fight, Kabarega was ordering his various chiefs to engage the invading armies, presumably in the hope of dislodging them by harassment.[25]

In the face of this resistance, Colvile ordered the Ganda General Kakungulu to seek out Kabarega's camp and attempt to capture him again. On 31 January, a large army of Baganda found three camps on the southwestern edge of the Budongo and managed to inflict upon the Banyoro defenders a severe defeat. Kabarega, who personally led his soldiers, narrowly escaped capture. The Budongo area was, it seemed, no longer a safe refuge. He fled north of the Nile into his first, brief exile.[26]

Colvile had thus altered his expressed strategy from capturing Mparo and dictating peace terms to occupying all Bunyoro, thus destroying any possible basis for a negotiated settlement. A new line of forts from Baranwa on the Kafu to Kibiro on Lake Albert once again cut across Bunyoro territory, but this time they sliced through heartland. A fort at Hoima near Kabarega's former capital became the command post for the occupation force. In Colvile's words:

> Kabarega, the terror of the region . . . has been reduced to the position of a petty chieftain, his chief source of wealth, the salt mines of Kibiro, having been taken from him, while the southwestern portion of his kingdom (i.e., Toro) has been handed over to a confederation of friendly chiefs (under Kasagama) from which he is cut off by our chain of forts.[27]

Cut off from Toro and with the entire south and eastern areas of Bunyoro soon annexed to Buganda, Kabarega was

[25] Thruston, *Incidents*, pp. 144–147; Owen, "Diary of Magungu Expedition," 31 January 1894, *PP* C7708; Colvile, *Land*, pp. 191–199; Colvile to Cracknall, 5 February 1894, *PP* C7708.

[26] Thruston, *Incidents*, p. 149; Colvile, *Land*, pp. 187–188; Nyakatura, *Abakama*, pp. 195–197.

[27] Colvile to Cracknall, 29 March 1894, *PP* C7708.

militarily defeated. Though deprived of his major sources of wealth and with the country ravished by an invading army, even now Kabarega could not be allowed peace and security in his diminished estate. The forts would remain. "Captain Thruston was left in command of Unyoro with three and a half companies of Sudanese. . . ." When the headquarters column recrossed the Kafu and returned to Buganda on 27 February 1894, "the power of Kabarega had been broken and half his kingdom wrested from him."[28]

Occupation and Political Crises: 1894–1895

The situation confronting Bunyoro in 1894 was unique in the history of the kingdom. The entrenchment of an alien authority in the heart of the kingdom represented a challenge to royal power qualitatively different from the challenges of invasion or secession previously experienced. Prior invasions had usually ended with the intruder withdrawing to his own land to enjoy the fruits of victory. Samuel Baker's occupation of 1872 and Lugard's invasion of 1891 were somewhat exceptional. Nonetheless, without external sources of supply and support, even these intruders did not strike at the root of royal power. A policy of harassment had succeeded in driving Baker's force from its fortified camp at Masindi, making such a policy appear to be an effective military strategy in the face of European-led occupation.[29] Toro's severance in 1891 still appeared as an attempted provincial secession backed by the armed intervention of Baganda, British, and Sudanese supporters of the pretender, Kasagama. Again a policy of harassment was adopted by the Nyoro defenders, which seemingly succeeded in bringing about the removal of the Toro forts and garrisons. Invasion and secession had yielded to Kabarega'a military response of harassment and patience.

[28] MacDonald, *Soldiering*, pp. 320–321.
[29] S. Baker, *Ismailia* (New York: Harper & Bros., 1875), pp. 360–424, and A. R. Dunbar, "Early Travellers in Bunyoro-Kitara," *Uganda Journal* 32, 2(1959):109–112.

But would such a response be adequate in the new situation of military occupation and territorial annexation?

In April 1894, the wholesale annexation of all southern and eastern Bunyoro was confirmed. Kasagama, driven out by the barusura invasion and reoccupation of Toro, was reinstated by Major Owen and allowed to extend his domains eastward to include Kyaka and parts of Nyakabimba and southward over Kitagweta and Kitagwenda. The small tributary states of Buhweju and Buzimba were isolated and eventually absorbed into the Ankole kingdom. But the major annexations were those "lost counties" alienated to Ganda chiefs as a reward for their contribution to the destruction of Bunyoro power as well as for reasons stemming from the internal situation of Buganda.[30]

Colvile's annexations of Bunyoro territory were confirmed in 1896 by his successor, Berkeley, and again in 1900 by Sir Harry Johnston, Her Majesty's Special Commissioner. Although the situation within the annexed territories, particularly the treatment of the Nyoro cultivators by the new Ganda overlords, became an important factor in the subsequent history of both Bunyoro and the Uganda Protectorate, leading ultimately to a referendum and re-union in 1965, the direct administration of these territories by Ganda chiefs places them largely outside the framework of royal resistance and chiefly collaboration. However, annexation by Ganda chiefs did not sever the "lost counties" so completely that they did not affect the events within the remaining parts of Bunyoro as the pattern of resistance began to emerge.[31]

Faced with a permanent occupation, Kabarega's chiefs and

---

[30] Nyakatura, *Abakama*, pp. 161–164, and *Bunyoro Church Magazine 1931–1940*, cyclostated selections, Father A. B. T. Byaruhanga-Akiiki, trans., pp. 68–69. For a brief but important account of the "lost counties" issue, see A. D. Roberts, "The 'Lost Counties' of Bunyoro," *Uganda Journal* 26, 2(1962):194–199.

[31] For resistance developments in Ganda-occupied Bugangaizi, see Lanning, "Kikukule," pp. 122–136. On the "lost counties" referendum, see G. S. K. Ibingira, *The Forging of an African Nation* (New York: Viking, 1973), pp. 272–273.

military leaders initiated a guerilla resistance. At this time it becomes appropriate to speak of guerilla warfare as opposed to the harassment of rearguard and defensive maneuvers. Local forces, supported by regular barusura units, began a systematic offensive against the army of occupation by raids on garrisons, foragers, and supply columns. Eventually the scale of actions increased in the classic pattern of rural guerilla warfare. However, without social revolutionary ideology or precedent, the guerilla war was limited to actions under the command of members of the old ruling elite. No noticeable appeal directly to the populace for armed insurrection against the alien rulers was made by the guerilla leaders, who organized and recruited the populace in the traditional manner. It is this limitation on the transformation of guerilla resistance to the full mobilization of a "people's war" that appears to distinguish the "primary" and "primitive" resistance movement of Bunyoro from those twentieth-century rebellions from which our notions of guerilla warfare are usually drawn. The Bunyoro resistance became a guerilla war in tactics and strategy, not in ideology or political direction.

On 6 March 1894, Fort Baranwa on the Kafu was attacked by a Nyoro force under chiefly command. "It appears that the force, stated to consist of 200 guns was under Yabaswezi (Byabacwezi?) son of the chief Youngamata (Nyakamatura?), chief of the county between Kibiro and the Kafu (Bugahya?)."[32] In fact, Byabacwezi had succeeded his father by this time, both as county chief of Bugahya and as leader of the ekibale, a personal regiment of barusura connected with the Bugahya chieftaincy. It was this personal barusura unit that attacked Baranwa.[33]

The following day a party led by Rwabudongo ambushed the headquarters force commanded by Captain Thruston, but no casualties were inflicted. This appears to have begun a pol-

[32] Thruston, Summary of Unyoro Field Force Diary (henceforth UFFD), 21 February to 16 March 1894, ESA A2/1.

[33] Nyakatura, Abakama, pp. 159 and 167, and Interviews, B/1 Muganwa, 3 October 1968 and B/6 Nyakatura, 18 October 1968. There is some question as to the time of Nyakamatura's death, but it was before 1894.

icy of harassing the garrison at Hoima. On 14 March a second attack on Hoima, this time led by Byabacwezi, was repulsed by the Sudanese garrison. In the wake of these sorties, Thruston concluded that Kabarega's general policy was one of harassment aimed at avoiding any "full-scale attacks."[34]

At this time, Kabarega had withdrawn with a small force to Mruli, where he had earlier sent his treasury of ivory, cloth, and cattle. His main forces had been disbanded and sent "home" while he was still encamped in the Budongo forest. This dispersal of forces created a situation in which strong parties of armed men were scattered about the country under their chiefs, "partly with the object of greater security for themselves, and partly so as to be collected together in case an opportunity offered of waylaying . . . caravans and patrols."[35] Coincidently, major units of barusura had their farms and homes in the area of Bugahya between the occupation headquarters at Hoima and the Kafu River crossing, enabling them to disperse and reform readily in a strategic area. That area proved particularly difficult for the British to subdue.

While efforts of harassment continued against the occupation forces, cracks in the wall of resistance began to appear. Thruston rather optimistically reported that there was "a general wish among the peasantry to make peace, but they are prevented by their chiefs who are still influenced by fear of Kabarega."[36] Such an evaluation of the pacific nature of the peasantry and the source of motivation of the chiefs can hardly be accepted at face value. Nonetheless, Thruston was probably correct in seeing the chiefs as the main support of resistance at this time along with the organized military forces of the Nyoro state. The peasantry was certainly not mobilized in opposition to the occupation and may well have desired to be left alone by both the chiefs and the new rulers. Groups of

[34] UFFD, 21 February to 16 March 1894, *ESA* A2/1; Thruston, *Incidents*, pp. 155–156.

[35] UFFD, 27 June to 27 July 1894, *ESA* A2/1, and Nyakatura, *Abakama*, pp. 197–198.

[36] Thruston to Commissioner, 17 March 1894, *ESA* A2/1.

refugees began collecting "under the protection" of the forts, especially at Kibiro and Kitanwa on the Lake Albert periphery of Bunyoro. Those who submitted to the protection of the invaders became subject to raids by the Banyoro still loyal to Kabarega. But the crucial developments began in June 1894, when the first minor chiefs came in to submit to the new authorities.[37]

Rumors reached Hoima of a spirit of conciliation even among Kabarega's closest supporters. Thruston reported: "the prince, Jasi, was reported to have urged on his father the desirability of making peace. . . ."[38] Jasi's close personal friend, Rwabudongo, also appears to have favored a policy of conciliation. Thruston went further in his apparently wishful belief that many chiefs were dissatisfied with Kabarega's "refusal to come to terms."[39]

Whatever the discontents among his followers, Kabarega persisted in directing a partisan resistance, based on small unit actions. In line with another traditional practice of Nyoro warfare, Kabarega sought the support and alliance of the Lango peoples of Bukedi in northern Uganda. The Lango had long served in Nyoro armies. Of necessity, Kabarega continued to work through his chiefs, his barusura, and his traditional allies, such as the Lango. The possibility of rallying the general population to the resistance banner was without real precedent and would in any case have been extremely difficult for a monarch isolated from his people by military force and without even rudimentary organizational tools for rallying such support other than his chiefly hierarchy. It would be anachronistic in the extreme to expect the monarch of a

[37] For example, raids on Kitanwe on 26 June by Rwabudongo (UFFD, 26 May to 27 June) and Butiaba (UFFD, 27 June to 27 July, *ESA* A2/1). Cf. Thruston to Colvile, 25 May 1894, *PP* C7708.

[38] Thruston to Commissioner, 28 March 1894, *ESA* A2/1, reports it as "Kabarega's son," who I take to be Jasi, a leading military advisor to his father.

[39] Thruston to Colvile, 26 June 1894, *PP* C7708. On Rwabudongo, cf. Interview B/14 Kamese, 27 October 1968, and B/39 Bikundi, 16 November 1968.

"primitive state" to engage in the kind of agitation and propaganda among the masses that we identify with modern peasant rebellions and revolutions. In such a situation, Kabarega was thrown upon the slender reed of his traditional chiefly hierarchy, military system, and allies. These would all prove inadequate to the challenge of Western imperialism.

While the Nyoro resistance moved to guerilla tactics, the British and their Ganda allies prepared for a decisive strike. In April 1894, an expedition consisting of over 5,000 Baganda, Sudanese, and Swahili under British officers was sent to attack Kabarega's camp at Mruli. The British hoped to capture him or, failing that, at least to drive him from his kingdom into exile. The possibility of seizing the national treasury of cattle, guns, cloth, and ivory reportedly cached on an island in the Victoria Nile was also recognized. Only one skirmish against a Nyoro force commanded by Ireta and two canoe battles were fought en route to Mruli, which was taken without effective opposition on 4 May.[40]

Kabarega had chosen not to engage the invaders and had escaped without difficulty, taking what treasure and cattle he had to safety with him. Still, the British counted the expedition a success. First, the large force of Ganda irregulars, no doubt anxious for plunder, ravaged the countryside as they foraged and pillaged for food and property. Second, Kabarega was forced to flee across the Nile for protection. Last, Kabarega's failure to oppose the advance with an effective resistance appeared, according to the British "to have made a great impression on the Wanyoro at large. . . ." A dubious moral victory was thereby claimed by the invading allies.[41]

On 6 May Byabacwezi, continuing the harassment of the occupation forces, led an attack on a supply caravan from Buganda. His forces, stationed around the hill known as Musaija Mukuru in Bugahya, constituted a standing threat to

---

[40] Colvile, Land, p. 257.

[41] Ibid., pp. 257–264; Diary of the Mruli Expedition, n.d., PP C7708. For Ireta's presence at Mruli, UFFD, 1 May to 26 May 1894, ESA A2/1.

Thruston's supply lines and foraging parties. The hill itself, a steep, flat-topped natural fortress, had a reputation for being unassailable. On 20 May 1894, Musaija Mukuru's reputation was discredited. The hilltop fortress became a death trap when Thruston led a determined charge of some 50 Sudanese, who reached the crest and scattered and killed the Banyoro defenders. Besides the Sudanese, some Banyoro irregulars under a collaborating chief named Amara also took part in the attack. A son of Kabarega's was killed, whereas Byabacwezi, the Nyoro commander, reportedly "was the first to run away and escaped."[42]

In June and July, Kabarega's chiefs appear to have established armed camps near the caravan routes so as to continue to waylay caravans and harass the supply lines to Hoima. Two such camps were broken up by Thruston. Raids by those loyal to Kabarega on Banyoro who submitted took place, and Thruston recognized the impossibility of "protecting" the population "living outside the immediate vicinity of our forts."[43] The policy of harassment, however, did not cause the British forces to withdraw. Although most of the Baganda levies had left Bunyoro in March, this was primarily due to an outbreak of smallpox. More militant action was required.

In late August 1894, Kabarega dispatched a large force to attack Hoima. The force was commanded by Prince Jasi and included contingents from 12 major chiefs. Ireta and Rwabudongo led their forces despite the objections of the latter to Kabarega's plan. Contingents of Lango and Nyamwezi mercenaries were also sent. Byabacwezi mobilized his forces from his home at Misiranduru, and numerous other local con-

---

[42] UFFD, 1 May to 26 May 1894, *ESA* A2/1; Thruston, *Incidents*, pp. 188–192. If "Amara" was Ntamara, Kabarega's chief of Kyaka, as we at first suspected, he would be the first *county* chief to collaborate actively. The chief Ntamara was a Munyonza by clan, and hence related to Kabarega's queen mother. However, this Ntamara appears to have been loyal to Kabarega as late as September 1894 (cf. UFFD, 29 September to 29 October 1894, *PP* C7708). Thus, Amara's identity remains uncertain at best.

[43] UFFD, 27 June to 27 July 1894, *ESA* A2/1.

tingents arrived at Mparo hill for the attack. In all a force of some 750 guns had collected there on 27 August.[44]

Despite the advantage of numbers, the attack was a failure. Surprise was impossible, and in the frontal encounter across the Hoima stream, Thruston was able to drive the Nyoro gunmen back and turn their flank, after which they retreated, hard pressed by the Sudanese. Losses were as heavy as 200 killed. The large number of spearmen who assembled failed to become engaged, and the Lango apparently withdrew before the battle upon seeing the strength of the Hoima defenses. An attack on Baranwa fort on the Kafu was also repelled at this time. Only Kibiro appeared to be immune from attack and harassment, probably because the inhabitants were said to practice a policy of sending tribute in salt to both sides.[45]

Kabarega appears to have been understandably angered at the failure of this expedition. Upon their return to Kabarega's camp at Rwempindu (Mashudi), Ireta and Rwabudongo were dispatched again to organize raids on the supply caravans. On 29 September a caravan of ivory was attacked. The column was long and "extremely vulnerable," and suffered four killed and four severely wounded, a large percentage of the 40 man armed guard. Forster, the officer in charge, had his donkey "shot dead under him." Reprisals were taken on a "local chief" who supported the attack, who may have been Ntamara, the former county chief of Kyaka.[46]

To this point, the Nyoro response to the foreign occupation was solely military, although political grumblings could be heard from various segments of the elite and the masses. Following this raid, a full-blown political crisis began to develop. Only the Nyonza chief, Ntamara, returned to Kabare-

---

[44] UFFD, 28 July to 28 August 1894, *ESA* A2/1, and Nyakatura, *Abakama*, pp. 200–201.

[45] Thruston, *Incidents*, pp. 205–211. Cf. Nyakatura, *Abakama*, pp. 200–201.

[46] Thruston, *Incidents*, pp. 200–201 (reported out of sequence); UFFD, 29 September to 29 October, 1894, *PP* C7708, pp. 132–134; Thruston to Acting Commissioner, 30 October 1894, *ESA* A2/2.

ga's camp after the attack of 29 September. Byabacwezi, Rwabudongo, and Ireta moved to the south of the forts on the Toro road. This appears to be the first instance of overt insubordination among these leading chiefs, a fulfillment of their earlier threat to sue for peace if Kabarega was forced to flee the country again.[47]

Whereas Ireta quickly returned to active resistance, Byabacwezi and Rwabudongo soon found it to their advantage to collaborate with the British. Meanwhile, they seem to have tried to establish a practical neutrality by removing themselves from the reach of either Kabarega or the British authority in Bunyoro. Rather than submit or resist, they would bide their time.

At the same time, life for the populace was becoming much more difficult. Thruston adopted a "scorched earth" policy of weekly raids along the Hoima-Buganda road to depopulate the roadside and destroy cultivation and villages in the vicinity in an effort to secure his supply lines. Although the Banyoro failed to oppose these raids, they often ambushed and harassed the returning column, causing by these constant engagements a high casualty rate among the occupation forces. Thruston reported "that in twelve months four percent of my force had been killed and six percent wounded. The percentage of ten persons killed and wounded (per hundred) is a much higher figure than any that has recently been experienced in our frontier wars against more formidable foes."[48] Despite the costs, the war of constant raiding and ivory theft with burning of villages and crops put severe pressure on the population and the chiefs to submit in the hope of gaining relief from the devastation.

In November 1894, in a daring surprise raid, Thruston almost succeeded in capturing Kabarega and ending the war. Leaving Hoima on 8 November with over 200 Sudanese, he traveled almost 80 miles to Rwempindu, Kabarega's camp, by forced marches. The attackers managed to overtake the

[47] UFFD, 29 September to 29 October 1894, *PP* C7708, and Interview B/14 Kamese, 27 October 1968.

[48] Thruston, *Incidents*, pp. 218–219.

messengers sent to warn the Mukama and arrived at 3 a.m. on 11 November, after a continuous march covering some 35 miles. They entered the camp in silence and were discovered going from hut to hut in search of Kabarega. The Banyoro started firing and quickly vanished into the countryside. When the firing ceased, "Kabarega had fled, leaving behind his clothing, his cattle, his ammunition, his ivory, cloth and household goods and the superstitiously venerated insignia of his office."[49] The Banyoro started a fire in an effort to destroy much of the valuable booty. Nonetheless, all these goods were lost to Kabarega's kingdom. Kabarega fled across the Nile again and Thruston, after leaving a note in Arabic requesting Kabarega's submission, began to withdraw.[50]

The Sudanese column was ambushed several times as it withdrew towards Hoima, losing at least three killed and several severely wounded. Thruston himself was nicked in the chest by one shot.[51] However, the damage done by the raid to Kabarega's prestige and his ability to continue in resistance could not be reversed by such harassment.

In the closing days of 1894, after a month-long lull, Kabarega dispatched an emissary to Hoima to sue for peace. As Thruston had predicted, the embarrassment and defeat at Rwempindu and especially the flight into exile had caused Kabarega to "lose hold over his Chiefs. . . ."[52] Under such circumstances he was compelled to seek terms, if only to buy time. Thruston was unable to set definite terms for want of the Commissioner's approval. He offered instead a three-month truce and an outline of likely conditions, including Kabarega's settlement at Hoima and agreement to accept British "advice on any matter suggested" and possibly an idemnity in ivory. Kabarega's emissary seemed agreeable to

[49] Ibid., p. 227.

[50] Ibid., pp. 220–228; Thruston to Commissioner, 21 November 1894, *ESA* A2/2; Nyakatura, *Abakama*, pp. 201–202, and K. W., "The Kings of Bunyoro-Kitara," *Uganda Journal* 5, 2(1937):66.

[51] Thruston, *Incidents*, pp. 229–231.

[52] Thruston to Colvile, 21 November 1894, *PP* C7708.

these terms as long as Kabarega had only to recognize British and not Ganda sovereignty over Bunyoro.[53]

But the truce was to be short-lived. Although Rwabudongo, Ireta, and Byabacwezi may have resented being sent to fight Kabarega's battles, it appears that they were willing to raid on their own account against Bunyoro's enemies. In January 1895, Kabarega sent to Rwabudongo requesting 50 tusks as a contribution to the expected indemnity. Rwabudongo "replied that he was not a woman" and would not make peace. Instead he launched a raid to the south against Mwenge.[54]

Calling Rwabudongo's action a raid may be understating the event. Rwabudongo's ample forces were joined by Ireta's. Kikukule of Bugangaizi also participated, and about 1,300 guns made up the attack force. It struck Butiti, Mwenge, on 16 January 1895. Byakaweyamba, the Mwenge county chief, was forced to flee and call for British protection. Two of his subchiefs were killed. In addition to the attack on Mwenge, the road south was opened and contact made with an arms caravan from Karagwe. Successful in all these engagements, Rwabudongo retreated to Misiranduru, his headquarters.[55]

To the British, Rwabudongo's raid meant the end of the truce. Kabarega's envoy, no doubt fearing recriminations, stealthily departed Hoima on 23 January. At first the British officers were unaware of the "wildcat" nature of the strike and proposed a dual counterattack on Misiranduru and Kabarega's position in Chope, the northeastern corner of Bunyoro. On 12 February, a raid on Rwabudongo's failed to catch an Arab caravan believed to be trading there. Some prisoners who were taken said that Rwabudongo had at-

[53] Postscript and Summary dated 28 December in Thruston to Colvile, 26 December 1894, *ESA* A2/2. In his book Thruston indicates that the emissary arrived at the end of November and he offered a four-month truce. Cf. Thruston, *Incidents*, pp. 232–233.

[54] Cunningham to Commissioner, 9 February 1895, *ESA* A4/1.

[55] J. P. Wilson to Commissioner, 2 February 1895, and Cunningham to Commissioner, 9 and 18 February 1895, *ESA* A4/1.

tacked Mwenge without royal sanction and that "Rabadongo and the other chiefs would no longer obey KabaRega."[56]

In the absence of a negotiator from Kabarega, an attack was ordered on his position in Chope. The force consisted of four and a half companies of Sudanese regulars and some 2,000 Ganda and Nyoro levies under four British officers. Two separate columns proceeded to the Nile, where they found Kabarega's barusura entrenched on Kajumbera Island, north of Mruli. The barusura had built stockades and trenches all along this section of the Nile to defend the various crossing points. One crossing being as well defended as the next, a direct assault on Kajumbera Island was planned for the morning of 2 March 1895. A platform for two Maxim guns was built to allow them a free line of fire across the Nile at the white-robed barusura manning the fortified positions.

> It was a cold misty dawn when the five canoes carrying the Sudanese under Cunningham, Dunning and Ash-burnham pushed out. . . . Meanwhile Vandeleur was straining his eyes from the platform to get a glimpse of the opposite shore. At last the air cleared, the canoes paddled out into the stream and the maxims opened fire. . . .[57]

Kabarega's soldiers were alert and prepared. They opened a heavy fusillade on the canoes, capsizing two of them and forcing the others to retreat. Both Dunning and Cunningham were severely wounded in the attack, and Ashburnham's helmet was pierced by a shot. Several Sudanese were killed or wounded; the Banyoro were completely victorious. Dunning later died of his wounds. All the attacking force could do was hastily retreat to Hoima to lick its wounds.[58]

[56] Cunningham to Commissioner, 18 February 1895, *ESA* A4/1. Cf. Jackson to Cunningham, 18 January 1895, and Dunning to Commissioner, 15 February 1895, *ESA* A4/1. Also, S. Vandeleur, *Campaigning on the Upper Nile and Niger* (London: Methuen, 1898), p. 53.

[57] F. I. Maxse, *Seymour Vandeleur* (London: National Review Office, 1905), p. 57. Cf. Vandeleur, *Campaigning*, pp. 57–59.

[58] Cunningham to Commissioner, 23 March 1895, *ESA* A4/1; Vandeleur, *Campaigning*, pp. 57–62; Nyakatura, *Abakama*, p. 204.

During the following weeks, while a new attack force was being collected to avenge the humiliation suffered at Kajumbera, the situation in Bunyoro was perilous for the invaders. Harassment was increased by the Banyoro and it was impossible to venture far outside the forts without protection. But the Banyoro had not the strength to push their advantage to the point of victory, and by April the British and Baganda were prepared to advance again. In the words of one young officer, "The fiat had gone forth 'Kabarega delenda est.' "[59]

The second expedition united the military forces of the British in Bunyoro and Buganda with those of the Ganda kingdom. On 15 April, the convalescent Cunningham arrived at Mruli, opposite Kabarega's stronghold at Lukungu, with four companies of Sudanese and 200 irregulars. On 20 April, Major Ternan, in command of the expedition, arrived from Kampala with another company of Sudanese. With him came Apolo Kagwa, the Katikiro of Buganda, with an enormous army of Ganda levies totalling 20,000 men. On 22 April, a sixth company of Sudanese under Mr. Grant and 400 Baganda under the Ganda general, Kakungulu, reached Mruli from Lake Kyoga in 123 canoes. This force, armed with Hotchkiss field pieces and Maxim guns, was undoubtedly the largest and best-armed force Kabarega had ever faced.[60]

While the attacking force collected on the Nile banks, the Banyoro busied themselves with preparations to repulse another attempted crossing. The Nyoro began to dig trenches. When Cunningham took to firing on the diggers with a Maxim gun, work was stopped only to be resumed at nightfall. The Banyoro guarded all the possible crossings for some distance down the river, and the swampy foliage was "cut down to the water's edge to give the defenders a clear field of fire. . . ."[61] But against overwhelming numbers, these precautions and the courage of the defenders would prove insufficient.

[59] Vandeleur, *Campaigning*, pp. 65 and 62–64.

[60] Cunningham to Jackson, 7 June 1895, *PP* C7924, and Maxse, *Vandeleur*, p. 58.

[61] Vandeleur, *Campaigning*, p. 66. Cf. Cunningham to Commissioner, 20 April 1895, *ESA* A4/1.

The attack began on the afternoon of 22 April when, under cover of Maxim and Hotchkiss guns, "the canoes suddenly advanced across the river in line, and the cliff opposite was wreathed in smoke where the Wanyoro were firing from their entrenchments. It was a strong position and in places there were two or even three tiers of fire."[62] The Ganda and Sudanese attackers managed to wade ashore, regroup, and storm the central stockade. The Banyoro fell back, pursued by the Baganda irregulars. Some 41 Banyoro were killed defending the trenches, and the attackers marvelled at their courage in remaining "at their post till the last."[63]

It took three days to ferry the pursuit column across the Nile. This time Kabarega was not to be allowed sanctuary in the territory north of the Victoria Nile. He withdrew from his position opposite Kajumbera Island and, while one column under Cunningham moved along the left bank of the Nile to prevent him recrossing into Bunyoro, the main force pursued the fleeing monarch into the country of the "Wakedi" (Lango) starting on 27 April.[64]

On 3 May, a flying column of two Sudanese companies and 7,000 Baganda made contact with a Nyoro rearguard that had been charged with keeping Kabarega's royal herd of cattle. The Banyoro herders offered only light resistance against the enormous column, and over 1,000 head of cattle were captured by the column and driven back to Mruli and eventually to Buganda. On 6 May, the main column under Ternan reported the capture of a royal party that included Kabarega's mother, a son, and a daughter. The capture of the queen mother was considered "a most important factor," both as a blow to Kabarega's prestige and an inducement to other notables and chiefs to submit to the new authorities. Thus, while Kabarega himself evaded capture, the capture of mem-

[62] Vandeleur, *Campaigning*, p. 67.

[63] Ibid., p. 68. Cf. Cunningham to Commissioner, 22 April 1895, *ESA* A4/1.

[64] T. Ternan, *Some Experiences of an Old Bromsgrovian* (Birmingham: Cornish Bros., 1930), pp. 182–189; Vandeleur, *Campaigning*, pp. 68–70; Nyakatura, *Abakama*, p. 204.

bers of his family and the loss of a large proportion of the royal herd of cattle were severe setbacks.[65]

The expedition had two other consequences of enormous political import. First, the destruction that followed in the wake of this vast army, living off the country on both sides of the Nile, is difficult to overestimate. The hostility of the Lango was increased as Baganda were constantly attacking and being attacked by the villagers among whom they moved. On 11 May, a large party of Baganda were virtually exterminated in a series of Lango ambushes. Although the hostility was initially directed at the invaders, disruption of the country north of the Nile would eventually turn Kabarega's sanctuary and protectors against him.[66]

Second, the expedition turned the disaffection of Kabarega's chiefs into an active and growing tendency to submit and enter into collaboration with the imperial powers. On 4 May, Rwabudongo himself, having suffered another raid by Baganda at his place at Misiranduru, gave himself up to the British authorities in Toro. He announced his willingness to turn in his arms and to settle and serve under Kasagama of Toro. Some 300 of his followers surrendered with him. The problem of retaining the allegiance of the chiefs had reached crisis.[67]

By June, the British occupation force had returned to Hoima and new posts were built at Mruli and Masindi in northern Bunyoro to keep Kabarega a fugitive and pacify the surrounding area. Meanwhile, the southern counties of Bunyoro remained in a disturbed state. Contributing to the "disturbed state" of this area were the chiefs Kikukule of Bugangaizi and Muhenda of Buyaga, two counties that were ceded to the Baganda. The inruption of Baganda Catholics and White Fathers into the western region led to the estab-

[65] Cunningham to Commissioner, 17 May 1895, *ESA* A4/1; Vandeleur, *Campaigning*, pp. 72–74, 77, and 83; Jackson to Kimberley, 1 July 1895, *PP* C7924; Ternan, *Experiences*, pp. 189–191; K. W., "Kings," p. 66.

[66] Vandeleur, *Campaigning*, pp. 74–79.

[67] J. P. Wilson to Commissioner, 4 May 1895, *ESA* A4/1, and Vandeleur, *Campaigning*, p. 83. Cf. Interview B/14 Kamese, 27 October 1968.

lishment of a fortress-mission station at Bukumi in Bugangaizi in early 1895, displacing Kikukule and his followers across the Kafu into Bugahya. Here they continued as a threat to Bukumi and, in January 1895, aided Rwabudongo in raiding Mwenge and making contact with a caravan bringing arms up from the south.[68]

In June 1895, Lieutenant Vandeleur led a raiding party from Hoima into the southern districts to attempt to capture an Arab trading party and initiate regular patrolling of the conquered southern provinces. The Protectorate government had issued a proclamation to all trading caravans to report to the various forts to be inspected for contraband, "the British Government being at present at war with Kabarega."[69] Word of illicit caravans had reached Hoima on 15 June, and Vandeleur set out to intercept them with a column of 250 men. Raids on Kikukule's and Muhenda's camps were successful in surprising the traders and capturing a great deal of loot, including "bales of cloth, coloured silks, cowries, twenty-four tusks of ivory, guns, percussion caps, and thirty-three kegs of gunpowder."[70] En route back to Hoima, the column stumbled upon and surprised another caravan, capturing the Arab leaders and giving the *coup de grace* to the arms trade to Bunyoro. A policy of "careful watching and patrolling until Muhenda and Kikukuli have come in or been caught" was adopted in the wake of these successful raids.[71] The British pressure on Kabarega's chiefs both north and south of the Hoima fort was growing, and there seemed little that Kabarega could do to prevent the collapse of his regime.

The success of the British military victories was almost immediate. Around the new post at Masindi the population

---

[68] Lanning, "Kikukule," pp. 130–134; Interviews B/4 Rwebembera, 14 October 1968, and B/5 Nyamayarwo, 16 October 1968; Nyakatura, *Abakama*, p. 203.

[69] Proclamation, 1 April 1895, *ESA* A5/1.

[70] Vandeleur, *Campaigning*, pp. 87–89.

[71] Pulteney to Commissioner, 1 July 1895, *ESA* A4/2; Vandeleur to Cunningham, 1 July 1895, *ESA* A4/2, and H. B. Thomas, "Imperatrix v. Juma and Urzee," *Uganda Journal* 7, 2(1939):70–72.

was "becoming decidedly friendly," while in the south the Banyoro were "so tired of bolting into the bush that they remained in front of their houses and did not stir."[72] Not only was the population accommodating to the new situation, but the policy toward the chiefs was beginning to pay off. The plan regarding chiefs loyal to Kabarega's regime was "the same as proved successful with Rabadongo—continued patrols to their places and burning of their houses."[73] In this way, various petty chiefs began to sue for peace in July 1895. It might be added that the policy pursued with regard to Rwabudongo included magnanimous treatment once the chief had submitted. Rwabudongo himself was made a county chief in Toro briefly in June 1895. Others would be left in peace, and often left in authority, once they demonstrated their willingness to cooperate.[74]

During July, Byabacwezi sued for peace at Hoima and Ireta came into Masindi. Kikukule and Muhenda after a raid in Nyakabimba sent messages saying that they wished to come in. On 30 July, word was sent to Hoima by Kabarega asking for peace. "Unconditional surrender was the reply. . . ."[75] It appears that the southern chiefs, Kikukule and Muhenda, were merely buying time. Byabacwezi, on the other hand, was actually sent to Hoima by Kabarega to discover what the conditions for Kabarega's restoration and peace would be. There is evidence that Kabarega envisioned having his chiefs submit so that they might operate from within as a pressure group for his restoration and to prevent the Baganda from being installed as rulers throughout his kingdom. Nonetheless, the submission of Byabacwezi and Rwabudongo in mid-1895 were the death knell to the first phase of organized resistance to imperialism in Bunyoro.[76]

[72] Cunningham to Commissioner, 10 July 1895, *ESA* A4/1.

[73] Ibid.   [74] J. P. Wilson to Jackson, 19 June 1895, *ESA* A4/1.

[75] Cunningham to Commissioner, 30 July 1895, *ESA* A4/2; Cunningham to Commissioner, 17 July 1895, and Pulteney to Commissioner, 18 and 19 July 1895, *ESA* A4/2.

[76] Nyakatura, *Abakama*, p. 204. Interviews B/5 Nyamayarwo, 16 October 1968, and B/1 Muganwa, 3 October 1968.

Regardless of Byabacwezi's original motive for coming to Hoima, he was placed in a delicate and contradictory position. If he served Kabarega well as a fifth columnist, it meant securing the confidence and support of the occupation authorities. This could only be done by opposing those chiefs who continued to fight for Kabarega directly. When in fact Kikukule and Muhenda camped in his territory of Bugahya in August, Byabacwezi sent to the new British headquarters at Masindi for help in expelling them. Although this served to gain the confidence of the British commanders, it also helped to establish Byabacwezi's independent claim to authority. At some point it seems that Byabacwezi discovered the advantages of collaboration. It is possible but unlikely that despite Kabarega's trust in him, he intended from the outset to make the most of his ambivalent position. Whether as fifth columnist or collaborator, Byabacwezi did a great deal of work in cooperation with the Europeans to settle the affairs of a large part of Bunyoro. This ambivalence is perhaps the most personal and direct example of the dichotomous position of the collaborator. As agent of both imperialism and the struggle to retain a semblance of traditional authority in African hands, Byabacwezi emerges as an archetype of the African chiefly collaborator.[77]

"Unceasing Wars" and Defeat: 1895–1899

From mid-1895 until his capture in April 1899, "unceasing wars took place between the Europeans and Kabarega."[78] The political process of collaboration set in motion by the British occupation continued to sap the strength of Bunyoro political institutions and traditional loyalties, while the military forces of empire assured that Kabarega could not effectively interfere with the creation of a new order. Kabarega's

[77] Madocks to Commissioner, 3 September 1895, *ESA* A4/2; Nyakatura, *Abakama*, p. 204. Nyakatura's account is notably hostile to Byabacwezi, but recognizes that he did not initially collaborate, but was sent by Kabarega "to assure them (the people) not to worry."

[78] K. W., "Kings," p. 66.

resistance began to dwindle from a national war to a minor
rebellion and finally to the personal struggle of a deposed
monarch and his entourage in exile. During the almost four
years until his capture, Kabarega remained implacably opposed to his victorious enemies and at every opportunity attempted to thwart their designs and regain his country.

Acting through his loyal chiefs, Kabarega engaged in
hit-and-run warfare. Kikukule—after being chased from
Bugahya—returned to Nyakabimba, where the population
remained "entirely submissive" to himself and Kabarega. In
September, Kikukule mounted a raid against the area occupied by the Roman Catholic Baganda near Bukumi and in
the following month was himself dislodged and defeated in a
raid by a Sudanese patrol. This brought about Kikukule's surrender at Hoima in October and his temporary settlement in
his old territory. He even assisted in attempting to capture
Muhenda, his former comrade-in-arms, during December
1895. Briefly rearrested in December 1895 and released again
in March 1896, Kikukule remained quietly under the British
occupation until 1898.[79]

Muhenda held out and continued resistance during 1895
until he was captured in January 1896. His capture, along
with the cooperation of Rwabudongo and Kikukule in pacify-
ing southern Bunyoro, effectively ended resistance in the
south. Muhenda remained in Bunyoro for only a few
months, then fled to Kabarega's side in July 1896.[80]

The main scene of battle then shifted to the north and the
Nile frontier. In November 1896, punitive expeditions
against the three subchiefs in Busindi county were reported in
which one chief was killed. Bikamba, a county chief who had
befriended the British, assisted in punishing his subordinates.

[79] Pulteney to Ternan, 9 September 1895, *ESA* A4/2; Pere Achte to Ternan, 26 September 1895, and Ternan to Commissioner, 19 and 26 October
1895, *ESA* A4/2; Madocks to Commissioner, 25 November and 5 December
1895, *ESA* A4/3. For a fuller account of Kikukule's struggles, see Lanning,
"Kikukule."

[80] Ternan to Commissioner, 5 January 1896, *ESA* A4/4; Pulteney to
Commissioner, 31 July 1896, *ESA* A4/5.

A party of barusura attacked an outpost to the northwest of Mruli in January 1896, but were repelled. A fort on the Nile was then proposed and later erected to prevent Kabarega from raiding for food and to force the inhabitants of northern Bunyoro to settle on one side of the frontier or another.[81]

The pattern that commonly emerged in the northern region was for people to attempt to make peace with both sides, professing friendship to the British and allegiance to Kabarega simultaneously. Chiefs particularly worked both sides of the street; Bikamba who aided the British in suppressing dissident subchiefs was suspected of trading arms to Kabarega. The captive queen mother, Nyamutahingurwa, in particular, played a double game. At first, she aided the British by actively encouraging submission and collaboration, but by September 1895, she had proven "a disquieting influence" and "the means by which news is transmitted . . . to Kabarega."[82] She was sent to Buganda with several of the royal children for safe-keeping.

The rest of 1896 was spent dispelling empty rumors. In August, rumors were rife of an alliance between Kabarega and the Lango and Madi supported by forces from the Mahdi of the Sudan. In an effort to raise rebellion, Kabarega sent a messenger with a sword around Bunyoro to his chiefs to tell of the coming invasion. The British response to the rumored attack was to send an expedition to Bugungu in the northwest, and in October 1896 they established more forts along the Nile as a "cordon sanitaire" against Kabarega's arms and influence.[83]

Meanwhile, the military operations carried out by Kabare-

[81] Madocks to Commissioner, 25 November and 5 December 1895, *ESA* A4/3; Ternan to Commissioner, 25 January 1896, *ESA* A4/4, and Pulteney to Commissioner, 12 April 1896, *ESA* A4/5.

[82] Madocks to Commissioner, 3 and 28 September 1895, *ESA* A4/2; Pulteney to Commissioner, 1 July 1896, *ESA* A4/5. For her earlier collaboration, see Jackson to Kimberley, 1 July 1895, *PP* C7924.

[83] Pulteney to Ternan, 30 August 1896, *ESA* A4/5, and 15 September 1896, *ESA* A4/6; Ternan to Berkeley, 26 September 1896 and 27 November 1896, *ESA* A4/6.

ga's forces were limited to skirmishes against patrols and raids for food. Efforts were also made to hinder the supply of food to the garrison at Masindi. A new supply of arms, including a supply of Remington rifle ammunition, had been received by the Banyoro via a black market operated by some Baganda to the dismay of the British officials.[84]

The rumors of alliances seem to have been entirely fanciful. Efforts were made to establish contact with the Mahdists at various times, including an expedition under the former county chief of Toro, Ruburwa, in 1897. The expedition was attacked by hostile Africans, and disease and hunger decimated the scattered Banyoro, only a handful of survivors returning to tell of it. As for alliances with the Lango, Kabarega was unable even to prevent them from attacking him and his supporters as Lango hospitality began to wear out.[85]

When Captain Thruston returned to Bunyoro in May 1897, after some 16 months absence, he learned that Kabarega was a refugee among the Acholi and that Ireta was in exile among the Madi. They were kept out of Bunyoro by a string of forts running from Pajao at Murchison Falls on the Victoria Nile to Masindi Port and Mruli near the Lake Kyoga end. In general, he could report, "The country is quiet. Most of the chiefs have submitted."[86]

Only the northern fringe of territory, within easy striking distance of external guerilla bases across the Nile, was still troubled. Jasi, Kabarega's oldest son and a respected military leader, was stationed near the eastern end of the "cordon sanitaire." In early May 1897, he led a raid against some Banyoro traders engaged in carrying hoes to Busoga along

[84] Pulteney to Ternan, 7 September 1896, *ESA* A4/5, and Ternan to Berkeley, 11, 13, 14, 15, and 18 October 1896, *ESA* A4/6.

[85] Pulteney to Ternan, 30 August 1896, *ESA* A4/5, and Ternan to Berkeley, 20 October 1896, *ESA* A4/6; L. O. Katyanku and S. Bulera, *Obwomezi Bw'Omukama Duhaga II* (Kampala: Eagle Press, 1950), pp. 19, 20; Cf. J. M. Gray, "Kabarega's Embassy to the Mahdists in 1897," *Uganda Journal* 19, 1(1955):93–95.

[86] Thruston, *Incidents*, p. 290. Cf. Madocks to Commissioner, 10 May 1897, *ESA* A4/8; Nyakatura, *Abakama*, p. 205.

the river routes. At the same time, Kabarega was reported moving south from Acholi to join Jasi, and the British feared an attempt to reenter the country.[87]

Kabarega's harassment also appeared on another front. On 29 May 1897, the collaborating county chief of Bugungu, Amara, died despite the medical services of a visiting British physician. Kabarega immediately claimed to have accomplished his demise by "witchcraft." There is evidence that Kabarega did cause Amara's death, with poison as the agent of his "magic." An arrest of a minor chief on charges of aiding Kabarega in Amara's death was attempted. But the chief, named Ichoma, was killed together with 20 followers while resisting. Thruston hoped that this summary justice would "make other chiefs less ready to become agents of Kabarega's medieval methods of diplomacy."[88]

During the remainder of 1897, Jasi was to continue his "aquatic ambuscades" and his raids on "friendly" Nyoro villages and chiefs along the Nile in Chope, which made the roads between the forts in Chope quite insecure. At the same time, Ireta had begun raiding along the Nile in Kihukya county, disturbing that stretch of the northern Bunyoro frontier. Amara's death in Bugungu created a state of disorganization that completed the picture of turbulence along Bunyoro's northern periphery. When in late 1897 Mwanga's rebellion and the Sudanese mutiny erupted in other parts of the Protectorate, fears among the British officers that Kabarega would rendezvous with Jasi and somehow link up with the mutineers and Ganda rebels were added to the already troubled situation.[89]

The situation worsened in January 1898, when British

---

[87] Thruston to Commissioner, 14 May 1897 and 31 May 1897 (#297 and #298), *ESA* A4/8.

[88] Thruston to Commissioner, 17 June 1897, *ESA* A4/8; Thruston to Commissioner, 31 May 1897 (#297) and 1 June 1897, *ESA* A4/8; Cf. W. J. Ansorge, *Under the African Sun* (London: Heinemann, 1899), pp. 169–170.

[89] Thruston to Commissioner, 1 and 17 June 1897, *ESA* A4/8; Dugmore to Commissioner, 20 October and 2 December 1897, *ESA* A4/9; and Dugmore to Commissioner, 10 December 1897, *ESA* A4/10.

power in Bunyoro reached a nadir. A young officer, Lieutenant Dugmore, had replaced Thruston as Officer Commanding Bunyoro when the latter was called away for service against the mutineers. Dugmore, new to his command, felt that the failure of the British to reduce the rebellion and mutiny elsewhere was upsetting his own soldiers in Bunyoro. He sent for help, fearing that if the mutineers reached Bunyoro, the loyalty of the Sudanese garrisons there would be tenuous at best. Meanwhile, Kabarega had not been waiting, but had been active in agitating for a rising among the Nyoro chiefs in support of his planned reentry into the country south of the Nile. Most of the chiefs seemed to be wavering or perhaps "fence-sitting." By January, the situation was so insecure that a small military movement, such as the removal of a Hotchkiss gun from the Pajao fort, exacerbated what the British officer described as a "feeling of distrust . . . among the Banyoro, who seem to think it is a prelude to our abandoning the whole district."[90]

Violence erupted at Masindi on the night of 17 January. A Sudanese sergeant was speared near the enclosure of the county chief Bikamba, alleged "to be in league with Kabrega,"[91] and the garrison panicked. Suspecting an attack by Kabarega and insurrection by the local Banyoro, the Sudanese began firing at shadows. Bikamba, apparently trying to get to the fort to quiet things, was seized and killed outside his enclosure. Disorder reigned for two hours, and several Banyoro were killed and wounded. The Sudanese sergeant later recovered from his spear wound.[92]

Word of the Masindi disturbances reached Hoima and led

[90] Dugmore to Commissioner, 6 December 1897, *ESA* A4/9; Dugmore to Commissioner, 30 December 1897 and 17 January 1898, *ESA* A4/10. Cf. Ansorge, *African Sun*, pp. 158–159, and Dugmore to Commissioner, 11, 12, and 13 January 1898, *ESA* A4/10.

[91] Dugmore to Commissioner, 18 January 1898, *ESA* A4/10.

[92] Dugmore to Commissioner, 20, 23, and 27 January 1898, *ESA* A4/10. Cf. Ansorge, *African Sun*, pp. 159–164; Interviews B/6 Nyakatura, 18 October 1968, B/9 Mugenyi, 20 October 1968, and B/21 Munubi, 31 October 1968.

to an attack on Byabacwezi's enclosure by the Sudanese, who were without British officers. Byabacwezi fled, but his house was burned, and many women were seized by the Sudanese. Despite the tensions and disturbances, Kabarega did not invade, and his call for a general rising received little response among the populace, who seem to have followed a "wait-and-see" policy. Some chiefs wavered until the arrival of reinforcements in February returned them to loyalty or at least quiescence.[93]

In the wake of the disturbances, military operations by both sides were increased. Kikukule, who was at Masindi for medical treatment during the incident, immediately left, and after almost two years of collaboration, raised the flag of resistance once again. Meanwhile, Ireta had crossed the Nile into Kihukya and intensified his operation there. From January to June 1898, raiding by Banyoro forces under Ireta and Kikukule along with rebel Baganda under Mwanga and mutinous Sudanese kept Bunyoro in constant turmoil. But the British had been reinforced in Buganda, and now larger numbers of British officers and troops brought from India were available to reduce both the resistance and mutiny.[94]

In May, Mwanga rendezvoused with Ireta's forces, and in July crossed the Nile to join Kabarega, his former enemy. They were further reinforced by the remaining Sudanese mutineers. Despite the coalition, by July the military initiative had passed to the British as forces composed of loyal Sudanese, Somali, and Baluchi soldiers took the field against the scattered Nyoro, Ganda, and Sudanese resisters.[95]

---

[93] Fowler to Commissioner, 27 February 1898, *ESA* A4/10; Dugmore to Commissioner, 23 January 1898, *ESA* A4/10; and Ansorge, *African Sun*, p. 165.

[94] Dugmore, "Report," n.d. (#228), *ESA* A4/10; Martyr, "Intelligence Report," 26 June 1898, *ESA* A4/11; Cf. various letters in *PP* C8941, pp. 21–35 passim and C9123, pp. 7 and 33.

[95] Fowler to Commissioner, 20 May 1898, *ESA* A4/11; Martyr to Commissioner, 26 July 1898, *ESA* A4/11; Interview B/28 Ireeta, 4 November 1968; Price, "Report," n.d. (#534) and Martyr, "Report," n.d. (#540), *ESA* A4/12. Cf. Nyakatura, *Abakama*, pp. 205–211.

On 3 September, the Sudanese garrison at Hoima having been withdrawn, a party of Banyoro led by Kikukule attacked the fort, which was defended only by Nyoro "friendlies" and Ganda irregulars. Byabacwezi, in charge of the post, fell back and made no attempt to oppose the force. The fort was destroyed, but the victory was more an embarrassment than a real setback for the British. Reinforcements drove the Banyoro out on 7 September.[96]

Ireta, defeated on 23 August in an ambush, remained in the Budongo forest and tried to hold a line severing Bugungu from the south and east. He continued to raid the area between Masindi and Pajao on the Nile until as late as March 1899. Meanwhile, in December 1898, Bilal Amin, the leader of the Sudanese mutineers, had been killed by a British patrol. The end of the resistance was drawing near. It came on 9 April 1899, when a column under Colonel Evatt and the Ganda general, Semei Kakungulu, surprised Kabarega and Mwanga in the early morning hours at their camps in Lango country, north of the Nile.[97]

The capture has been vividly described by Prince Bisereko (later Mukama Andereya, Duhaga II). Kabarega's army had been sent to oppose a British column thought to be advancing on them further south in Bukedi. A small group of royal clansmen and chiefs remained behind with Kabarega.

On the following morning, the 9th April 1899, we discovered that the enemy had played a trick on us. Their army came following a Lango named Kuturu, who was a spy, and had betrayed the Mukama to the Europeans. As we were speaking to some visitors and while some of us were still asleep, having had a sleepless night, and before the army had gone very far, we heard guns sounding from behind us. We thought perhaps it was our Sudanese

[96] Broome to Commissioner, 1 October 1898, *ESA* A4/13; Berkeley to Salisbury, 6 October 1898, *PP* C9232.

[97] Martyr to Berkeley, 25 August 1898, *PP* C9123; Evatt to Commissioner, 17 March 1899, *ESA* A4/16; Evatt to O. C., Unyoro, 8 and 10 April 1899, *ESA* A4/16.

shooting an animal. It turned out to be the army that
Lango Kuturu had led to attack us. We had no time to
defend ourselves. As the Europeans reached us many
people escaped into the bush only to die of hunger afterwards or to be killed by the Lango as they escaped.[98]

Prince Jasi was shot in the chest and later died of his
wounds. Prince Rwahwire and two of Kabarega's brothers
were also killed, and two of his daughters were wounded in
the battle. Kabarega continued firing as he withdrew into a
swamp. He was hit in the leg and hand before he dropped his
weapon. Prince Bisereko went to his side and they were captured together. When Kakungulu recognized the fallen
Mukama, he was apparently struck by sorrow at Kabarega's
condition. Kakungulu refused to kill him, not wanting to be
considered a regicide.

Kabarega was taken to Kampala and eventually deported to
the Seychelles, where he remained in exile until 1923. After
his capture, Ireta surrendered on 11 May with all of his followers including 27 Sudanese mutineers.[99] Kikukule followed suit on 27 May, surrendering to a party of Baganda
sent to bring him in. He showed "signs of age and of having
experienced hardship for some time." He died of fever as a
prisoner a few months later on 10 September 1899.[100]

[98] Katyanku, *Duhaga II*, pp. 26–29. Cf. Nyakatura, *Abakama*, pp. 211–213,
and Dunbar, *History*, pp. 95–96.

[99] Evatt to Commissioner, 13 May 1899, *ESA* A4/17; Evatt to Commissioner, 30 May and 3 June 1899, *ESA* A4/17. Ireta's surrender followed orders sent by Kabarega and was at first opposed by his followers. He went to
Masindi and submitted there, turning in his guns. He was arrested and sent to
prison in Kampala. He remained in prison for eight days, was released and
provided with a cook and allowed to send for his own (two) wives. Eventually brought to trial, he won the case. It was argued that he was a saza chief to
Kabarega and was not "sent into the country," which implies that he was
entitled to treatment as a prisoner of war and not a "rebel" who could be
shot. He remained in Buganda, received land there, and was baptized as Stanley. Ireta died in 1910. He was never a chief again after his surrender. Interview B/28 Ireeta, 4 November 1968.

[100] Evatt to Commissioner, 30 May and 3 June 1899, *ESA* A4/17; Grant to
Ternan, 10 September 1899, *ESA* A4/20. Cf. Lanning, "Kikukule," p. 144.

Indeed, all of Bunyoro had "experienced hardship for some time." Cattle were all but exterminated to provide food for the thousands of invading soldiers and poverty became Bunyoro's most characteristic condition. The impact on Bunyoro's population will never be known accurately, but war, famine, and disease took an enormous toll in lives and suffering during the decade of conquest and after. How does one balance these costs against the acts of heroism and determination of a king and his people struggling to retain their independence and their heritage? In 1899 resistance was ended and a new colonial order was being created.

Discussion

Bunyoro's resistance was not only the most lengthy, costly, and arduous of the armed reactions to British intrusion in Uganda, it was also the one most characteristic of what can be termed royal resistance. Not only was the resistance led and directed by Mukama Kabarega, it was fundamentally a movement to retain sovereignty in the hands of the monarch and the ruling dynasty. In many ways the resistance owed its military and political character to the monarchical system that generated and sustained it. Kabarega's singular role as decision maker and inspirational focus suggests the central role of the kingship in organizing the national energies to resist. The indivisible loyalty to the monarch that sustained the Nyoro state served to unite chiefs and people in resisting the threat to their sovereignty. Once the king had defined the threat as one that endangered the state's sovereignty, he implied that breaches of loyalty were not mere political advantage seeking, but treasonable. But if the monarchy served to unite the Banyoro against alien intruders, we are left with the task of accounting for the failure of resistance and in breakdown of that unity.

From the weight of evidence, we must conclude that the failure of Nyoro resistance was due to the overwhelming military and technological superiority of the attacking forces. In the face of continual defeats and few victories, the resistance was bound to be broken. The inability of Kabarega to mount

offensives from exile or to negotiate a settlement meant the
ultimate military defeat of Nyoro armed resistance. But military defeat alone did not mark the decline of resistance. Fis-
sures began to appear in the fabric of Nyoro society which
indicated that there was a collapse rather than a mere defeat of
resistance. These weaknesses were not military or technological, but social and political in nature.

The first weakness to emerge in Kabarega's resistance was
the inability to judge the strength and purposes of his opponents. It is difficult to estimate the effectiveness of Kabarega's
intelligence and espionage systems. Misjudgments of enemy
intentions in 1892 and 1893 seem to be due not to the ade-
quacy of information available but rather to the tendency to
evaluate this information on the basis of irrelevant and mis-
leading precedents. Kabarega's tendency to follow the advice
of his territorial as opposed to his military chiefs despite the
latter's better access to strategic information seems to have
contributed to his inability to organize an effective military
answer to the challenge of invasion.

A more serious weakness of the resistance was the inability
of the monarch to formulate an answer to the challenge of occupation. Such an answer must have involved the ability to
arouse and sustain popular support from the commoners
(bakopi) which might have transformed the limited guerilla
war into a mass insurrection or people's war. Even these drastic tactics might have proven unavailing against superior military and organizational strength. But such tactics were never
really attempted.

Instead Kabarega chose to rely on tried and proven instru-
ments of royal power: his chiefly hierarchy, his barusura military units, and his traditional allies and diplomatic supports.
This reflects the habits of rule of a well-established monarch
of a well-organized state. Although Kabarega has been por-
trayed and is remembered as a man of the people, he remained
a monarch, remote from his people and reluctant to call upon
them to mobilize and participate in a new kind of war, which
was necessary (if not sufficient) to save his kingdom. On the
adverse side, it should be clear that the people were not forth-

coming, that the common man generally remained remote from politics, preferring to sit out the war, minding his own parochial interests. The absence of a patriotic fervor or of a monarchical call for mass support must be counted as another failure of the Nyoro resistance.

However, the crucial weakness of the resistance lies in neither Kabarega's character nor his policies nor in the lack of a popular response. Kabarega attempted to rely on his chiefs; the people were expected to follow these traditional leaders. The chiefs were thus the vital ingredient in sustaining the military effort and popular attachment to the cause of the monarchy. It is the defection, submission, and eventual active collaboration of Kabarega's most important chiefs that ultimately undermined both the military resistance and the structure of the Nyoro kingdom. The collaboration of the chiefs allowed for the establishment of a new regime in Bunyoro, rising from the ashes of Kabarega's kingdom.

CHAPTER IV

Kasagama and Toro Clientage

In March 1899, Stephen Bagge, the new British officer in charge of the kingdom of Toro, assured Mukama Kasagama through a missionary interpreter that "In the future the King is to have the whole power in his hands and Mr. Bagge will act with him and do all he can to establish him in his country, but he [Kasagama] is to act fair and do all he can to make progress."[1] Thus after almost a decade of maneuver, uncertainty, and conflict, an arrangement of colonial dependence was affirmed by the British authorities and the hope for peaceful, constitutional progress of the kingdom as part of the Uganda Protectorate was proclaimed. The youthful and willful monarch, a pretender to a disputed throne, had established himself as a royal client and not merely a royal puppet through a series of political crises both within his kingdom and between it and the "protecting" British authorities. The first crisis for Kasagama came on the heels of his establishment as Mukama by Lugard in August 1891.

Clientage and Conflict: 1891–1894

When Lugard left Toro in 1891, he left behind him two checks on the authority of his puppet monarch. The first was the string of Sudanese garrisons that separated Toro from its hegemonic and hostile overlord, Bunyoro. As long as the Sudanese guarded the fledgling kingdom from being overrun by the more powerful Nyoro armies, Kasagama was bound to be beholden to British policies. Second, he left a British officer in charge of civil affairs in "southern Unyoro," meaning both Kasagama's kingdom and the autonomous regions around its periphery. He was explicitly in charge of the valu-

[1] Roscoe to Baylis, 12 April 1899, C[hurch] M[issionary] S[ociety] G3A7/01.

able salt works at Katwe.[2] Even DeWinton, the British officer, had no authority over the Sudanese troops, who were thus able to precipitate the first crisis in Toro's colonial history.

The Sudanese had long supported themselves by cultivating food crops in their exile at Kavalli's. In Toro, however, they were told to secure their living by raiding across the "border" into Kabarega's Nyoro territory. A certain lack of discipline was to be expected from these troops, but it is unlikely that Lugard anticipated the extensive depredations caused by the garrisons raiding into Toro as well as Bunyoro. In January 1892, DeWinton reported that the troops were causing considerable trouble by theft and looting of the populations near the forts, and local memories are strongly outspoken against the "Banubi," as the Sudanese are called, as perpetrators of rape, torture, and wanton murder.[3] DeWinton's powerlessness vis-à-vis the garrisons greatly hampered attempts to restore discipline. His death in early 1892 removed any hope that local British control might mitigate the disruption caused by the Sudanese soldiery. By 1893 missionary and government officials in Buganda were beginning to pass on the complaints of the Batoro against British protection to Sir Gerald Portal's commission.[4]

Instead of Kasagama, the Sudanese and their garrison commanders had become the major power in "southern Unyoro." Despite their propensity to pillage and disruption, they were a crucial military factor, repelling an invasion of Toro by a Nyoro army in January 1892. In order to relieve the

[2] F. Lugard, The Diaries of Lord Lugard, 4 vols., M. Perham, ed. (Evanston, Ill.: Northwestern University Press, 1959), 2:420–421.

[3] Lugard to IBEAC, 2 March 1892, P[arliamentary] P[apers] C8648, reporting DeWinton's letter of 31 January 1892; Sir George Kamurasi Rukidi III, "The Kings of Toro," Joseph R. Muchope, trans., Department of History, Makerere University, Kampala, 1969, pp. 29–30; Moses Nyakazingo, "Kasagama of Toro, A Despotic and Missionary King," seminar paper, Department of History, Makerere University, Kampala, 1968, p. 18.

[4] Grant to Portal, 28 March 1893, PP C7109; Bishop Tucker to Portal, 27 March 1893, E[ntebbe] S[ecretariat] A[rchives] A2/1, encloses complaints recorded by CMS missionary Ashe.

depredations by the garrisons in the Toro area and place them in more direct opposition to Bunyoro and in closer touch with the Buganda headquarters, the southern two forts in the string of four were wheeled about to the east in May 1892. They now ran from west to east to the north of the main route connecting Toro with Buganda. While looting continued, a real crisis was averted and attempts by Kasagama to entrench his control behind this "protective" screen were able to proceed.[5]

Kasagama officially invested his first hierarchy of subordinate county chiefs in December 1891 at Nsorro. There were to be 14 appointees, including Yafeti Byakweyamba as county chief in Mwenge, his home district, and Yoswa Rusoke, an elderly retainer of his father's regime, as Katikiro or "prime minister." Many of this list of chiefs were drawn from the group of exiles in Ankole, returning to power after many years as refugees. They may have had some claim to support among the populace, but before that would be evinced, the remains of Kabarega's regime had to be uprooted and driven from the country.[6]

The main obstacle to the effective operation of Kasagama's new chiefs was the continued operation within the Toro region of Kabarega's old administration and his armies. In November 1892, Rukara Rwamagigi, who had opposed Lugard near Katwe the previous year, was still operating behind the Sudanese forts in Toro. Although DeWinton's instructions were specifically "to drive out the remaining Chiefs" of Kabarega, his illness and untimely death left this unfinished task to the Sudanese. It was not until January 1893 that Lugard was able to report on Rukara's ouster and the end of Kabarega's political system in Toro.[7]

The main threat to Kasagama's new state in these early

[5] Lugard to IBEAC, Report #4, March–August 1892, pp. 76–77, *PP* C6848.

[6] Rukidi, "Kings," p. 30; Interviews C/29 Rwakiboijogoro, 29 January 1969; C/38 Rwakiboijogoro, 11 February 1969, and C/39 Mubirigi, 11 February 1969.

[7] Lugard to IBEAC, Report #3, 11 January 1893, *PP* C6848.

months came neither from the Banyoro resisters nor from the Sudanese protectors. It came rather from his own mentor and collaborator, Yafeti Byakweyamba. From the outset Byakweyamba harbored visions of establishing his own rule over some territory and perhaps his own dynasty. To understand his role in the political intrigue of the Toro kingdom, we must know something more of this dynamic man's background, his position in Toro society, and his claim to authority.

The central, if somewhat ambivalent, element in Byakweyamba's background was his Babito lineage. He was Mubito by clan, the large and widespread group from whom the rulers of Bunyoro and Toro had been drawn for generations. But although of the royal clan he was of the Baitwara lineage, the descendants of Mukama Itwara of Bunyoro, who had long since ceased to be eligible for succession to royal office in either kingdom. Nonetheless, although Byakweyamba lacked status as a member of a royal lineage, he remained a thoroughgoing aristocrat in the lacustrine tradition—this despite a checkered career involving captivity and menial labor in a foreign land.[8]

As a boy, Byakweyamba had been captured by Ganda raiders and taken from his home in Mwenge county in central Bunyoro. He was brought before Kabaka Mutesa of Buganda as a bondsman and, thanks to his Babito clanship and a prepossessing appearance, he was selected by the Kabaka as a personal retainer and attendant at court. He was assigned the honorific duties of "inspector of the beds of the king's wives." It was from this post that he began his gradual ascent through the Ganda chiefly hierarchy until he became chief of the village of Kitanda (meaning bed), where Kasagama had joined him and Lugard "discovered" them in 1891.[9]

[8] Nyakazingo, "Kasagama," p. 14. Interviews C/22 Kabaziba et al., 27 January 1969, C/44 Winyi, 19 February 1969, and C/1 Nyakazingo, 20 March 1968.
[9] Nyakazingo, "Kasagama," pp. 15–16. M. M. L. Pirouet, "The Expansion of the Church of Uganda," doctoral diss., University of East Africa, 1968, p. 59.

During his rise to power in Buddu, Byakweyamba had become thoroughly Ganda in lifestyle and had raised Kasagama as best he could in like manner. As a court retainer, he had been exposed to the teachings of missionaries at Mengo, the Ganda capital, and he became an early convert to Christianity. He was a reader at the Protestant mission and was baptized as Yafeti (Japheth) into the Anglican Church. He may well have suffered martyrdom for his religion during the purge of Christians by Kabaka Mwanga in 1886. Whether at the hands of Mwanga's executioners or earlier as a bondsman and household servant to Mutesa, Byakweyamba was castrated and "crippled."[10] This alone would have made him ineligible for royal honors under lacustrine rules of disability. Nonetheless, his handicap neither limited his operations as a member of the Protestant chiefly hierarchy in Buganda nor apparently did it limit his ambitions once he took himself to Toro as Kasagama's sponsor and guardian.

On the western trip, Lugard consulted with Byakweyamba regularly, seeking his advice on matters of Toro's annexation. At one point he planned to leave Byakweyamba in sole charge of the prized salt works at Katwe. It was clear that the older man was as crucial to Lugard's scheme as was the young monarch and stood to be invested with considerable authority in the puppet state that Lugard hoped to establish. Even at this stage, however, Byakweyamba was angling for an independent fiefdom in Kitagwenda, free from subordination to Kasagama and his Batoro chiefs.[11] Given his Bito heritage, his seniority, and his powerful position vis-à-vis both Lugard and the Ganda Protestants, it is surprising that Byakweyamba did not become Katikiro (prime minister) or at least a regent to the young Kasagama, a role likely envisioned for him by his Anglo-Ganda patrons. From the start, however, he re-

[10] Nyakazingo, "Kasagama," pp. 14–15; J. A. Rowe, "The Purge of Christians at Mwanga's Court," *Journal of African History* 5, 1(1964):55–71; A. B. Lloyd, *In Dwarf Land and Cannibal Country* (London: T. Fisher Unwin, 1899), p. 155.

[11] Lugard, *Diaries*, 2:420–421, and O. W. Furley, "Kasagama of Toro," *Uganda Journal* 25, 2(1961):185ff.

sented being second to the king, refusing to come to court to pay homage and demanding a division of the kingdom between them as equal sovereigns.[12]

In his bid for autonomy, Byakweyamba relied on his personal following of Protestant Baganda who had come with him from Buddu. These men quickly earned for themselves and their patron the displeasure of the Batoro, who appear to have resented the Ganda intruders and their overbearing manner. A crisis was averted when Selim Bey, commander of the Sudanese garrisons, arrested Byakweyamba and his Ganda clients and sent them back to Buganda for a brief period in mid-1892.[13] However, this was not to be Byakweyamba's last attempt at secession.

While these problems kept Toro in turmoil through 1892, another crisis was brewing elsewhere that would not reach Toro until the following year. In April 1893, Major "Roddy" Owen arrived in Toro bringing the news that would force Kasagama to abandon his kingdom and uproot the Toro state by Kabarega's vengeful forces. The expenses incurred by the Company in administering its Uganda territories had led them to threaten withdrawal even while Lugard was still extending the Company's responsibilities. In 1892, a Commission was appointed under Sir Gerald Portal to proceed to Uganda to investigate the possibility of Her Majesty's Government assuming responsibility in place of the Company.[14] Portal allowed that Britain must assume responsibility for Buganda, but was loath to accept the burden of defending the western regions. Thus when Major Owen arrived in Toro in April, it was in order to withdraw two of the Sudanese garrisons for use within the Buganda protected area. Owen's orders were to remove Forts #1 and #2 on the

[12] Rukidi, "Kings," p. 33. Cf. Nyakazingo, "Kasagama," pp. 22–23.

[13] Ibid. Cf. Interview C/1 Nyakazingo, 20 March 1968, and A. Tucker, *Eighteen Years in Uganda and East Africa*, 2 vols. (London: Edward Arnold, 1908), 2:50.

[14] G. Portal, *The British Mission to Uganda in 1893* (London: Edward Arnold, 1894), and Africa no. 2 (1894), "Reports relating to Uganda by Sir Gerald Portal," *PP* C7303, are the official and very complete reports relating to this mission.

western end of the chain and to encourage Kasagama "to remove himself and his people to some district under the protection of the (remaining) forts." To Kasagama's mind the
removal of the Sudanese "would be like taking the lock from
his door."[15]

The news must have been doubly disillusioning, for
Kasagama had just appealed to Bishop Tucker for Christian
teachers, probably in an effort to bolster his regime's prestige
and possibly to avert criticism raised by Byakweyamba of his
alleged anti-Christian stance. The second motive stems from
the tendency of many British residents to interpret any anti-
Baganda attitudes as being anti-Christian thanks to the close
identification of the spread of religion with the spread of
Ganda Christian teachers. Unfortunately, Portal interpreted
Kasagama's request as an attempt to prejudice his settlememt
of the religious divisions within Buganda and, despite
Owen's reluctance to enforce them, the original removal orders stood.[16]

While in Toro, Owen took Kasagama on tour with him to
Ft. George and the salt lake to the south. In Busongora, the
local chiefs asserted their independence of Toro and their hostility to Kasagama while swearing direct allegiance to the
British regime. Owen was swayed, much to Kasagama's displeasure, and decided to deny Kasagama a monopoly of ivory
hunting in the region.[17] So despite Owen's support of
Kasagama's desire to remain in Toro, his actions in Busongora were not calculated to assure Kasagama of British backing for his territorial and political claims. Later in 1893, despite Owen's efforts to establish Fort Gerry (now Fort Portal)
to protect the fledgling kingdom, the Sudanese troops were
withdrawn and the door to Toro stood open.

[15] M. Bovill and G. R. Askwith, comps., "Roddy" Owen (London: John
Murray, 1897), pp. 46 and 55, and Africa no. 8 (1893), "Further Papers Relating to Uganda," pp. 4–6, PP C7109.
[16] Portal, Mission, p. 216, and Pirouet, "Expansion of the Church," pp.
59–111 passim, especially pp. 66, 81, 86–89.
[17] Bovill, "Roddy" Owen, pp. 61–62.

Owen left Toro to begin military operations against Bunyoro in November 1893. Major MacDonald, Portal's successor as Commissioner, ordered the complete abandonment of the Toro region for tactical reasons. Nonetheless, Kasagama decided to remain and was given some 200 guns, but no Sudanese to fire them. Even the guns, Kasagama complained, were without a sufficient supply of ammunition.[18] With the garrisons gone, Kabarega was able to dispatch an army which drove Kasagama from his capital. He sought refuge on the slopes of Ruwenzori among the Bakonjo people. The suffering he endured with his followers was quite severe, several people succumbing to exposure and hunger on the chilling mountainside. In December 1893, the British and Ganda allies launched their offensive, causing Kabarega to recall his armies and bringing relief to the tattered survivors of Kasagama's stand against invasion. In February 1894, Owen was ordered to return to Toro with a small Sudanese detachment to reinstate Kasagama (and Byakweyamba) under British suzerainty.[19]

Owen and Kasagama proceeded to make a new treaty to replace the original document signed by Lugard for the Company. The theoretically strict control of the Company over the chief sources of revenue, salt and ivory, were slightly liberalized by the new arrangement, but still left wide areas for complaint and disagreement on both sides. But Kasagama had more to complain about than a fair share of the profits. The treaty that Owen proposed established Kasagama as head of a "confederacy" that included Byakweyamba as ruler of Mwenge and another Mubito Mutwara named Kijagiri as ruler of Kyaka on the east of Mwenge. Busongora to the south of "Toro proper" was also loosely attached to the con-

[18] Furley, "Kasagama," p. 189, and J. MacDonald, *Soldiering and Surveying in East Africa* (London: Edward Arnold, 1897), p. 299.

[19] Nyakazingo, "Kasagama," p. 19. Official Diary, Unyoro Expedition, p. 28, *PP* C7708. Colvile to Owen, 18 February 1894, *ESA* A3/2. Cf. Rukidi, "Kings," pp. 36–39, for Kasagama's military operation during the invasion of Toro.

federacy, as was Kitagwenda on the Ankole border, despite
resistance to their subordination to Kasagama expressed by
the local chiefs.[20]

At this juncture, Kasagama's confidence in the protective
capacity of his British overlords ought to have been profoundly shaken. Despite the fact that the new arrangements
concluded with Owen provided for "a monopoly over the
ivory and salt trade of the district" and the reestablishment of
the protective Sudanese garrisons,[21] Kasagama was aware
that strategic or economic considerations might at any time
cause his protectors to withdraw and leave him again at the
mercy of Kabarega's armies. When J. P. Wilson, Owen's replacement as Government representative, set up his headquarters at the salt lake in Busongora, thereby lending support to
the claims of the separatist chiefs there, Kasagama must have
been disconcerted. Although Wilson's choice of headquarters
was motivated by a desire to supervise closely the salt revenue, its political overtones were disturbing nonetheless, given
the state of latent hostility between Busongora and Kasagama's Toro.[22] Kasagama must have been highly motivated to
provide for his own security and to seek allies with a firmer
commitment to his regime. The only possible partners were
those whose machinations had helped put him on the throne
in 1891—the Ganda Protestants. But they too were to prove a
mixed blessing.

In May 1894, at the request of Yafeti Byakweyamba, four
Baganda Protestant teachers arrived in Toro. Petero
Nsubuga, who had taught Byakweyamba in Buganda, settled
with him in Butiti, Mwenge. Marko Luyimbazi settled at
Kabarole, Kasagama's new capital.[23] Kasagama, although not

[20] Owen to Commissioner, 8 March 1894, *ESA* A2/1, and Owen to Colvile, 4 March 1894, *PP* C7708. Cf. D. A. Low, "The British and Uganda,
1862–1900," D. Phil. diss., Oxford, 1957, pp. 386–387.

[21] Bovill, *"Roddy" Owen*, pp. 170–171.

[22] J. P. Wilson to Commissioner, 21 August 1894, *ESA* A2/1, and 26
November 1894, *ESA* A2/2; S. Elliot to Commissioner, 2 August 1894, *ESA*
A2/1.

[23] Pirouet, "Expansion of the Church," pp. 66–67, and Rukidi, "Kings,"
p. 40.

yet a Christian himself, began to encourage the new religion and to create a Protestant party in Toro similar to that of Buganda. When the Roman Catholic mission arrived later in 1894, Kasagama was thrown into antagonism with the competing doctine and with the British authorities, who held a different view of the role of religion in an African state from that of the independent-minded monarch.[24] The religious antagonism developed slowly and eventually would be coopted into the colonial political system. But the same problems of secessionism and insubordination that had disrupted Toro prior to Owen's treaty reached crisis proportions all too quickly in the months that followed.

The Crises of 1895

The first crisis was a brief one, but it left a bitter legacy within Toro. On 16 January 1895, Mwenge was invaded by a Nyoro military force. Byakweyamba was forced to flee, and the church at Butiti, his capital, was destroyed. The purpose of this Nyoro expedition was to meet an approaching arms caravan, and it was led by Rwabudongo, the commander of the royal barusura regiment. It appears that this raid did not have Kabarega's sanction.[25] However, it demonstrated both the inability of the Batoro to resist invasion alone and their precarious dependence on British arms.

The raid also exacerbated the growing rift between Kasagama and his kinsman, Byakweyamba. The latter was distressed by the success of Rwabudongo's force and the deaths of two of his subchiefs. He wrote to Apolo Kagwa, Katikiro of Buganda, and to the British Commissioner of his continued weakness and danger:

> My brother Kasagama although repeatedly called upon for help did not come quickly. Kasagama ignored all appeals. All news was sent to him by many messengers.

[24] Low, "British," pp. 388–390.
[25] S. Vandeleur, *Campaigning on the Upper Nile and Niger* (London: Methuen, 1898), p. 53; G. Wilson to Commissioner, 1 and 2 February 1895, and Cunningham to Commissioner, 18 February 1895, *ESA* A4/1.

When I was given Mwenge . . . I was told to occupy
Mwenge not under Kasagama but under Kampala.
Kasagama demands my allegiance to him. I refuse and
tell him I obey the Europeans. In the division of territory
altho' I was told to occupy Mwenge, he appropriated the
larger portion and left me the smaller. These are my
words. Keep me as I was promised.

> I am,
> Bakiombo Yafet
> King of Mwenge[26]

One of the interpretations to which Owen's confederacy
was open can be demonstrated by Byakweyamba's assumption of royal title in his signature to this letter. The exact constitutional relations between the outlying "counties" and
"Toro proper," as it came to be called, were a considerable
vexation. Although Byakweyamba had affiliated his "county"
of Mwenge to the Toro confederacy, his view of his position
was not one of subordination. Rather, he saw himself as the
head of his own Protestant client kingdom in Mwenge, his
county of origin. Secessionist tendencies vis-à-vis Kasagama
were inherent in this view and had already erupted once in
1892, leading to Byakweyamba's arrest by the Sudanese
commander, Selim Bey. The center of secessionism then had
shifted to the southern counties of Busongora and Kitagwenda during Owen's tenures of 1893 and 1894. In April
1895, Kakyentuli, the regent of Kitagwenda, had recognized
Her Majesty's Government, but still would not acknowledge
Kasagama's claim to sovereignty.[27] However, this issue re-
ceded as the center of secessionist controversy shifted back to
Byakweyamba's eastern domains.

Following Rwabudongo's raid, a second crisis was precipitated by the death of Kijagiri, Byakweyamba's clansman
(Mubito Mutwara), who ruled in Kyaka. J. P. Wilson, the

---

[26] Byakweyamba to Commissioner, 1 January 1895 (translated by G. Wilson), *ESA* A4/1.

[27] J. Wilson to Commissioner, 20 April 1895 (#2), *ESA* A4/1, and Interview C/23 Bitamazire, 27 January 1969.

British officer in charge of Toro, moved to fill the vacuum. He succeeded in placing an important Mubito Mutwara named Kagoro in the chieftaincy in April 1894, but "not without a good deal of trouble and opposition from Yak- wiamba."[28] Byakweyamba, on learning of his kinsman's death, sent a force from Mwenge to occupy Kyaka and sup- port the claims of Nyama, Kijagiri's young son. Although the struggle was between two members of the same lineage (father's brother versus father's son),[29] from Byakweyamba's perspective the distinction between the candidates was clear. First, Kagoro was not *his* candidate but that of the British administration in Toro. He was, therefore, neither a client nor in any way subordinate to Byakweyamba. This is under- scored by Kagoro's conversion to Roman Catholicism, and his allegiance, therefore, to the opposition political faction. Nyama, on the other hand, was to become a Protestant parti- san. He was young and would need a regent, which would make him pliable. Moreover, as Kijagiri's son, he had a strong claim to the succession.

Wilson appears to have been swayed by these considera- tions. He acknowledged Nyama's claims, but set him up under the regency of Kagoro, his uncle, which made Nya- ma's succession valueless for Byakweyamba. Byakweyamba then sent to the British officer in Nyakabimba, to Kyaka's east, and asked for Nyama's removal. Pulteney, the Officer- in-Command there, briefly exceeded his jurisdiction and re- moved Nyama from Kyaka in June 1895. Wilson resented this interference in his responsibilities for the Toro district and reappointed Nyama in early July with the support of Kasagama.[30]

Byakweyamba's interference in the succession dispute did not go unnoticed. Pulteney sent accusations against him to Cromer Ashburnham, who replaced Wilson in Toro in July 1895. Byakweyamba was arrested and fined, and his removal

---

[28] J. Wilson to Commissioner, 20 April 1895 (#1), *ESA* A4/1.

[29] Interview C/14 Isingoma and Kato, 18 January 1969.

[30] J. Wilson to O. C. Nakabimba, 14 June 1895, and J. Wilson to Commis- sioner, 5 July 1895, *ESA* A4/2.

from his chieftaincy was suggested by Ashburnham on 22 July with Kasagama's concurrence.[31]

In September 1895, Byakweyamba was arrested again and this time sent to Buganda for trial. The charges ranged from collecting illicit tribute (a sign of his claim to independence) to slaving. Byakweyamba's second removal to Buganda temporarily reduced the secessionist tension. He had failed to gain control of the eastern region and, despite its own contradictions, the colonial administration had demonstrated its power to intervene powerfully in local affairs. Ironically, Byakweyamba's removal allowed his rival, Kagoro, to move with his own following to Mwenge and replace him as chief. Nyama was left in control of his patrimony in Kyaka under the regency of Louis Tibagwa, Kasagama's appointee. The crisis would arise again only when Byakweyamba was released by the British for want of evidence. Meanwhile, the would-be kingdom of Byakweyamba in Mwenge was no more. But a greater challenge to the Kingdom of Kasagama of Toro was in the making.

Rwabudongo's raid in January had precipitated yet another minor crisis in Toro affairs. His surrender in May 1895 set off the chain of events that ended in a major confrontation between Kasagama and the British authorities. When Rwabudongo first made his submission with about 300 followers, he "agreed to acknowledge Kasagama" as his overlord and surrender his guns to the British.[32] When it was discovered how important a man Rwabudongo was in Bunyoro, the British were anxious to have him collaborate with the Toro regime. As an example of the generous treatment offered to defectors, he was briefly made Mukwenda, the county chief of Bunyangabo, before he was sent to Buganda.[33]

[31] This account is based on Ashburnham to Commissioner, 22 July and 5 September 1895, *ESA* A4/2, and 23 November 1895, *ESA* A4/3, and the interpretation of Isingoma and Kato in Interview C/14, 18 January 1969.

[32] J. Wilson to Commissioner, 4 May 1895, *ESA* A4/1.

[33] J. Wilson to Jackson, 10 June 1895 (#2), *ESA* A4/1. Cf. Rukidi, "Kings," p. 41.

Unfortunately, Kasagama's head appears to have been turned by the size of the fish he caught. Encouraged by his Ganda Christian teachers, Kasagama mistreated his new chief, who complained against his childishness. Adding injury to insult, Kasagama ran afoul of the new British officer, Ashburnham, on charges of stealing guns, cloth, and women belonging to Rwabudongo. By this time, Rwabudongo was away from Toro in Kampala, where his future role was being deliberated by the British. Ashburnham, acting on his own initiative, imprisoned Kasagama on 11 September 1895, demanding a heavy fine and the return of the looted goods.[34]

The arrest of the monarch was no slight act, and much of the blame must fall on the inexperience and isolation of Ashburnham. But underlying the conflict were two fundamental problems. First was the constitutional ambiguity of the Owen treaty. Did the British have the right to accept Rwabudongo's submission and name him as Kasagama's chief without Kasagama's approval? Although Kasagama may well have been too readily influenced by his Ganda teachers, as Ashburnham believed, were they not justified in supporting Kasagama's royal prerogatives? Second, a heavy burden of tribute, especially in ivory, had been placed on the monarch. Although the Owen settlement had regularized the division of salt revenues, it continued Lugard's heavy demands for the only export commodity and revenue producer, ivory. J. P. Wilson had already had trouble collecting the tribute, and Ashburnham's impetuosity made of it a *cause celebre* before the end of 1895.

The troubles caused by Rwabudongo's submission were not yet over when Kasagama was released on 14 September upon payment of the fine.[35] In Kampala, Rwabudongo requested that he be resettled on the eastern side of Kyaka in what later became Kitagweta. This request was granted by the Commissioner, and Ashburnham was informed of the decision. Kasagama immediately raised the objection that this

[34] Ashburnham to Commissioner, 11 September 1895, *ESA* A4/2, and Commissioner to Ashburnham, 15 August 1895, *ESA* A5/1.

[35] Ashburnham to Commissioner, 14 September 1895, *ESA* A4/2.

was the chieftaincy of Nyama and could not be expropriated. Ashburnham, moreover, misunderstood the ambiguous decision to resettle Rwabudongo in Kyaka as meaning that Rwabudongo was to be a chief there. He forwarded Kasagama's complaint and began to send Rwabudongo's people to settle in Kyaka.[36] Nyama did not wait for the complaint to be acted upon in Kampala. Instead, he ordered his people to fight, which resulted in the murder of one of Rwabudongo's subchiefs. Nyama was arrested and detained at Fort Portal by Ashburnham, but was later cleared of responsibility for the murder. Meanwhile, Rwabudongo's people were removed from Kitagweta.[37]

Meanwhile, Ashburnham was being driven over the brink by Kasagama's growing intransigence. In recounting the events leading up to the crises, Ashburnham shows his own paranoia and his inability to handle relations with the monarch diplomatically.[38] Kasagama began to apply pressure to the young officer by refusing to supply food and, when summoned, refusing to appear. Fined for his failure to cooperate, Kasagama refused to pay the tribute in ivory that was required. This was followed by complaints of stealing women made against Kasagama and counter charges that Ashburnham was undermining royal authority. In November, Ashburnham again ordered Kasagama's arrest, and on this occasion had him shackled and flogged together with his Katikiro, Yoswa Rusoke, and his treasurer, Mikaeri Rusoke.[39] Even this might have been forgiven, but Ashburnham, still trying to gain mastery of the young king, could not ease up.

In December, Ashburnham ordered his Sudanese gendarmes to search Kasagama's house for gunpowder, which he

[36] Berkeley to Ternan, 27 September 1895, *ESA* A5/1, and Ashburnham to Commissioner, 21 October 1895, *ESA* A4/3.
[37] Ashburnham to Commissioner, two letters, 15 December and 22 December 1895, *ESA* A4/3.
[38] Ashburnham to Commissioner, 26 December 1895, *ESA* A4/3.
[39] Namasole (Kahinju) to Commissioner, n.d. Enclosed in G. Wilson to Commissioner, 15 November 1895, *ESA* A5/1; Berkeley to Ashburnham, 2 December 1895, *ESA* A5/1, and Rukidi, "Kings," pp. 41–42.

hoped would implicate the monarch as an illegal "powder-runner." Learning of the raid, Kasagama fled to Bukonjo in the Ruwenzori foothills, leaving his property with trusted friends. Not to be outmaneuvered, Ashburnham ordered the arrest and interrogation of several chiefs and two Ganda teachers, including the evangelist, Apolo Kivebulaya. One of the chiefs was whipped and died as a result. Ashburnham recommended that the refugee Mukama be called to Kampala for trial.[40] Before the orders arrived, Kasagama took it upon himself with the advice of the Catholic missionary, Pere Achte, to depart for Kampala to register his own complaints and avoid being sent to Kampala in chains.[41]

What lay behind this confrontation was again the vital question of sovereignty. Although Kasagama was willing to accept patronage from his powerful British and Ganda backers, this was not seen as inimical to his status as an independent ruler. Indeed, the traditional contract of clientage as understood by the client required the patron to support his client vis-à-vis those who might threaten his independence. Kasagama required support from the British and Baganda against the claims of both the Banyoro and his own subordinate chiefs. In exchange for this support, Kasagama was willing to guarantee certain economic privileges to the British as enumerated in the treaty.

To Ashburnham, on the other hand, sent to "administer" Toro for the Protectorate, there was no question of Kasagama's subordination to British sovereignty. Thus Kasagama's independent actions appeared to him as insubordination. Stockpiling of arms and defiance of Ashburnham's authority to exact tribute and obedience were Kasagama's methods of showing his independence and thereby delimiting Ashburnham's authority and restricting the relationship to the terms of the clientage arrangement. Ashburnham's diplomatic fail-

[40] Ashburnham to Commissioner, 12 and 13 November and 18 and 31 December 1895, *ESA* A4/3, and A. Luck, *African Saint* (London: SCM Press, 1963), pp. 64ff.

[41] Rukidi, "Kings," p. 42. Ashburnham to Commissioner, 11 December 1895, *ESA* A4/3.

ure stems, then, from his attempting to answer the question of sovereignty in favor of the Protectorate. Instead of governing Toro within the ambiguous framework of royal clientage, which allowed for an uncertain sovereignty, it became a question of who ruled Toro.

The confrontation between the British officer and the royal client was further exacerbated by the absence of a mediator in the figure of a "great commoner." Kasagama, despite his youth, was fully capable of handling his own foreign affairs and had dispensed with the services of Byakweyamba or any other subordinate who might have acted as power broker. All of Kasagama's chiefs, including his Katikiro, were accorded the same treatment by Ashburnham and enjoyed the same subordinate status under Kasagama. Ashburnham failed to find an intermediary in his dealings with the king over the question of sovereignty and fell back on the use of force to secure what he felt to be the necessary subordination of the sovereign. Confronted with force applied by his patron's agent, Kasagama wisely accepted Achte's advice and appealed directly for support to his patrons in Kampala.

Achte's advice was a small contribution to Kasagama's success in Kampala compared to the aid that he received from the Protestant party. The Ganda teachers proved reliable allies, hiding him and his property from Ashburnham's Sudanese gendarmes. And no less a figure than the Protestant Bishop Tucker forwarded Kasagama's bill of grievances to the Protectorate government. Ashburnham's fear of collusion between the missionaries and Kasagama, although justified by events, could not excuse his harsh and ill-advised treatment. The role the missionaries played in securing Kasagama's exoneration and reinstatement in Toro with a reduced tribute burden must have put the young king in their debt.[42] Before returning from Kampala, Kasagama began to repay his missionary friends. He sought instruction and on 15 March 1896

[42] Tucker to Commissioner, 27 November 1895, *ESA* A6/1. Ashburnham to Commissioner, 18 December 1895, *ESA* A4/3. Rukidi, "Kings," pp. 42–43; Tucker, *Eighteen Years*, 2:39; Interview C/9 Komuntali, 15 January 1969.

was baptized as Daudi (David) into the Anglican Church.[43] He returned to Toro to usher in a new era by establishing a Christian kingdom.

The first crises had been weathered by the Toro client state. Having been conceived and delivered by the cooperative efforts of the Ganda Protestants and British empire builders, Kasagama's kingdom was from the outset obliged to offer up loyalty and service to the protecting powers. In the times of trouble that plagued both client and patrons, the system of patronage had been found wanting. But the crisis created by Kasagama's independent will and strivings against the abuses of his patrons, instead of ending in rupture, had strengthened his resolve to collaborate with his patrons when they had vindicated his loyalty by removing Ashburnham, the offending officer, lightening his burdens, and offering him the full support of religion in his efforts to establish his kingdom in Toro.

Church and State in Toro: 1896–1899

With Kasagama's return to Toro in April 1896, the work of spreading the gospel became the chief instrument for creating the new Toro polity. Acceptance of Christian religion became the equivalent of a loyalty oath to the monarchy. Indeed, the conflict between Protestant and Catholic adherents can best be understood in terms of competing political ideologies of the ruling party and loyal opposition, respectively. The intensity of the political competition between the religious factions led to clashes between Kasagama and the British overlords. The ultimate effect of this religio–political struggle was to create a framework of competition for political power acceptable to all the parties, especially the colonial officials, and to pave the way for the full establishment of a colonial regime in Toro.

Shortly after young King David returned to Kabarole, Bishop Tucker, who had baptized him, made a pilgrimage to visit the monarch and assure him of the Church's goodwill. This goodwill was especially evident when it came to sup-

[43] Tucker, *Eighteen Years*, 2:40.

porting Kasagama's effort to spread the faith. Even before their arrival in Kabarole, Bishop Tucker and Reverend A. B. Fisher were involved in a "row with the Papist," the Catholic chief, Sirasi Kagoro, who was still chief at Butiti, Mwenge, in Byakweyamba's absence.[44] Once at Kabarole, the work of proselitization began in earnest. The Bishop reviewed the work of the Ganda native evangelists and assigned two teachers to each of seven outstations. Fisher was assigned to Toro and a mission site was selected for him. To top it off, 15 new converts were baptized. These included Kasagama's mother, now Vikitoriya Kahinju, and his wife, Damari.[45] The queen, who was married to Kasagama by Christian rites on 4 May, was one of 11 of the king's wives. All the others were allowed to remarry as an earnest of the young monarch's devotion to the Christian faith. Orders were given to destroy the shrines of the traditional religion and for people to learn to "read."[46]

As part of his new devotion, Kasagama also adopted a policy of appointing and promoting those chiefs who were not only Christian, but shared the king's Protestant denomination. With the arrival of Captain Sitwell as district officer at the end of May 1896,[47] the question of "freedom of religion" emerged as the central issue of state in Toro. The question was not one of conscience so much as of political principles. Should the king's leading chiefs have their religious allegiance subsumed under their allegiance to the throne? Kasagama hoped to promote the Protestant cause, not merely in the interests of religion, but in order to establish a stable political system based on personal loyalty to the monarch. In addition, he wanted to repay his debt to his Protestant patrons. For these reasons, a Protestant monopoly of chiefly power was sought. The fact that the Roman Catholic mission had its greatest success among the agricultural Bairu population in-

[44] A. B. Fisher, "Diaries," entry for 28 April 1896. Microfilm, Makerere University Library, Kampala.
[45] Tucker, *Eighteen Years*, 2:51.
[46] Fisher, "Diaries," entry for 4 May 1896, and Nyakazingo "Kasagama," pp. 31ff. Interview C/40 Binyomo, 12 February 1969.
[47] Captain C. H. Sitwell, "Diary for May 1895–May 1899," pp. 96–144.

tensified this policy. Chieftaincy in Toro was virtually the exclusive preserve of Bahuma, and the appointment of Catholic Bairu to these posts would have been "untraditional" and seriously resented by Kasagama's Huma supporters.[48] In contrast, the responsibilities of the new British officer, Sitwell, ran counter to Kasagama's policy of religious monopoly. Sitwell was charged with preserving an atmosphere of free competition between the two Christian missions in line with the established policy of division in Buganda. In brief, "Kasagama had very different ideas of the function of religion in society from those of the Administration."[49]

By June 1896, Kasagama and Sitwell were at loggerheads, with Sitwell contemplating the king's deposition. Fisher, the Anglican missionary, consistently supported the monarch against the administration, whereas Achte, the Catholic priest, was the main critic of the Protestant king, adding to the sectarian atmosphere. The return of the Protestant Byakweyamba to Mwenge further inflamed religious feelings. The Catholic Kagoro was once again sent to rule in Kyaka. The Protestant, Samwiri Nyama, was given the Kitagweta area of Kyaka to rule as a separate county.[50] This division of Kyaka may have eased the political competition there by allowing for two chiefs where there had been only one, but the religious question at the center would not permit of so simple a solution.

When Sitwell showed support for the former secessionist, Kakyentuli, the regent for the Catholic Edward Bulemu, and other minor chiefs in the matter of their religious independence vis-à-vis the king, Kasagama went so far as to threaten to abdicate.[51] Fisher, continuing to back the monarch, even supported the king's refusal to build some shelters for the

[48] Fisher, "Diaries," entries for 24 and 28 May 1896. Cf. Nyakazingo, "Kasagama," pp. 24–26.

[49] Low, "British," p. 390. Cf. Pirouet, "Expansion of the Church," pp. 79–80.

[50] Achte to Ashburnham, 30 April 1896, Ashburnham to Commissioner, 4 May 1896, Sitwell to Commissioner, 1 June 1896, ESA A4/5. Fisher, "Diaries," entry for 28 May 1896.

[51] Sitwell to Commissioner, 28 June 1896, Sitwell to Commissioner, 1 and 10 August 1896, ESA A4/5. Cf. Interview C/12 Mujasi, 17 January 1969.

Catholic mission despite orders from Sitwell. According to
Fisher, "You cannot expect a protestant king to build shelters
for the Catholics."[52] Moreover, Fisher believed that Sitwell
failed to treat Kasagama as was due his rank.

By October, Sitwell was again preparing to remove
Kasagama from the throne. Complaints against Kasagama
from the Bairu were added to those of the Catholic missionaries and chiefs. Kasagama continued to refuse to build
roads or to help the Catholic chiefs in any way. In December
1896, Sitwell warned Kasagama that he would be removed
unless there was a change.[53] In January 1897, the situation
showed some improvement. Much to Sitwell's satisfaction,
Reverend Fisher left on home leave and was replaced by A. B.
Lloyd, who was not so anti-Papist and uncritical in his support of the royal prerogative as was Fisher. By February, Sitwell was able to report that "Kasagama appears at last to wish
to do better."[54] He had his people working on roads and was
paying fines imposed on him for his previous lassitude. The
old question of division of the salt revenue from Katwe was
under review again in March and was eventually settled by
Sitwell to Kasagama's advantage.[55]

Once again it was the "staunch Protestant," Yafeti
Byakweyamba, who emerged as a thorn in the side of British
overrule, Kasagama's client state, and religious peace.
Jealousy remained a constant factor plaguing relations between Kabarole and Byakweyamba's capital at Butiti,
Mwenge.[56] Despite his own arrest and removal, Yafeti had
managed to see the chieftaincies of eastern Toro filled by
members of his own branch of the Babito clan.[57] The presence of his Ganda Protestant followers was a constant re-

[52] Sitwell to Commissioner, 1 August 1896 (#197), *ESA* A4/5. Fisher,
"Diaries," entries for 10 June and 10 November 1896. Cf. Interview C/7
Balya, 13 January 1969.
[53] Sitwell, "Diary," pp. 143–144; Fisher, "Diaries," entry for 3 December
1896. Sitwell to Commissioner, 1 and 27 October and 6 December 1896,
ESA A4/6. He identifies the Bairu with the Luganda term bakopi.
[54] Sitwell to Commissioner, 10 February 1897, *ESA* A4/7.
[55] Sitwell to Commissioner, 19 April 1897, *ESA* A4/7.
[56] Sitwell to Commissioner, 6 December 1896, *ESA* A4/6.
[57] Interviews C/14 Isingoma and Kato, 18 January 1969, C/22 Kabaziba et

minder of Byakweyamba's role in securing Ganda patronage of the Toro kingdom and a basis for his independent stance vis-à-vis Kasagama. Complaints of religious persecution in Mwenge against Byakweyamba were first heard by Sitwell in February 1897. Sitwell imposed a fine and admonished Byakweyamba by reminding him of his lesser rank as a county chief compared to Kasagama's royalty. Yafeti refused to appear to pay his fine, and Kasagama, in a surprisingly magnanimous gesture, delivered the fine himself, excusing Yafeti by pleading illness on his behalf.[58] One suspects that the illness Byakweyamba suffered was in part rancor, resulting from his continually being thwarted in his bid for royal power and attempts to create a Protestant kingdom in Mwenge.

In July 1897, Kabaka Mwanga rebelled against his British overlords in Buganda and attempted to raise an army to throw them from the country. Shortly after, several companies of Sudanese soldiers, who formed the military backbone of British power in Uganda, mutinied and British rule in Uganda received its severest challenge.[59] While this double-edged crisis developed elsewhere, Toro remained a quiet backwater. The Sudanese garrisons in Toro were not disarmed and continued to serve under Sitwell's command without incident. Kasagama, despite Sitwell's long absence from Fort Portal on service against Mwanga, continued to carry out the functions of his office, and no excessive religious zeal or political opportunism was evidenced. A. B. Lloyd commented, "Of the troubles reported above (Mwanga's rebellion), we in Toro were practically ignorant."[60] Indeed, in May of 1898 when Sitwell returned, the rebellion and mutiny

---

al., 27 January 1969, C/23 Bitamazire, 27 January 1969, C/34 Basigara, 31 January 1969, and C/44 Winyi, 19 February 1969.

[58] Sitwell, "Diary," pp. 159–160 and 166. Kasagama's motives are unclear. He may have delivered the fine to avoid a crisis and protect Byakweyamba or merely to appear to Sitwell as the conduit of Mwenge's obeisance.

[59] J. V. Wild, *The Uganda Mutiny 1897* (London: Macmillan, 1954). M. Wright, *Buganda in the Heroic Age* (Nairobi: Oxford University Press, 1971), pp. 159–197.

[60] J. Gray, "Toro in 1897," *Uganda Journal* 27, 1(1953):14–27. Cf. Lloyd, *Dwarf Land*, p. 234.

having been contained, he was able to record: "Everything correct after four month and two day absence."[61]

The only untoward incident during this period was again the doing of Byakweyamba. When word of Mwanga's rebellion reached Mwenge, he left presumably to join the rebels and reclaim his old chieftaincy (or a new one) in Buddu.[62] On arrival in Buganda, he found that the Protestant Ganda oligarchs had refused to the man to join the rising and that his old chieftaincy was not to be reclaimed. Presumably despondent at this final thwarting of his designs and troubled by his now painful physical disability, Byakweyamba shot himself, ending his eventful career and his life. It was not until January 1899 that Sitwell officially reported that Byakweyamba had committed suicide in July 1897.[63]

The elimination of Byakweyamba did not end the religious conflict. Division and rivalry in religion were to remain a feature of Toro political life throughout the colonial period. Following Byakweyamba's death, however, the conflict appears to have subsided and been contained within constitutional bounds.

From the latter part of 1897, Sitwell and Kasagama were able to collaborate effectively in settling the religious questions that vexed the country. When the Church Missionary Society considered returning A. B. Fisher to Toro, Sitwell strongly objected on the grounds that "since his departure the religious question has almost ceased, owing in a great way to the help I have received from the Rev. T. Buckley and Mr. Lloyd."[64] If Fisher were allowed to return, Sitwell asked that he might be relieved of his command. Fisher was posted elsewhere. The only other religious question involved an attack on Kakyentuli, the regent of Kitagwenda, led by Nasanaeri Mugurusi, Kasagama's Protestant Katikiro, in Oc-

[61] Sitwell, "Diary," p. 284.

[62] Interviews C/22 Kabaziba et al., 27 January 1969, and C/44 Winyi, 19 February 1969.

[63] Sitwell to Commissioner, 30 January 1899, ESA A4/5, and Sitwell, "Diary," pp. 193–204 passim.

[64] Sitwell to Commissioner, 19 July 1898, ESA A4/12.

tober 1898, when Sitwell was away from the capital. Although the attack was tinged with religious motivation, as Kakyentuli was regent for the Catholic chief, Edward Bulemu, it was essentially political, resulting from the looting within Kitagwenda of a safari carrying guns into Toro from German territory. Kasagama was fined for his part in the raid on Kitagwenda and his collusion in the illicit gun-running.[65]

The reason for the melioration of religious conflict, however, lies deeper than questions of mission personnel or the removal of one or two overzealous chiefs. The question of religious freedom had become unimportant largely because it was resolved *de facto* in favor of the monarch. Despite the continued tenure of a few prominent Catholic chiefs, Kasagama had overwhelmingly succeeded in keeping the chiefly hierarchy within the hands of his own Protestant followers.[66] In December 1898, the first Toro Church Council was formed to give independent direction to the Anglican Church in Toro. Three of Kasagama's county chiefs, the Katikiro, Mugurusi, and three subcounty chiefs had seats on the Council. "The composition of the council illustrates the close connection between the Anglican Mission and the Toro Kingdom Government."[67] As long as the Catholic party remained a small group outside the main halls of power, it was not worth the risk of alienating the administration to try and eliminate them.

Lest the impression of harmony in religion be created, it should be pointed out that two of the four Catholic chiefs were removed during the coming years. Louis Tibagwa was accused of plotting the assassination of Kasagama and dismissed. Tibagwa had emerged as the leading Catholic chief and was considered for the post of "Catholic Katikiro," a

[65] Sitwell to Commissioner, 9 October 1898, *ESA* A4/13.

[66] There were three Catholic Chiefs in 1898: Kagoro, Bulemu, and Tibagwa (Interviews C/3, C/5, C/7, C/10, C/12, C/14, C/28, C/32, C/34, and C/40). There were also two pagan chiefs loyal to Kasagama: Koro Koro in Buruli and Rukambuza in Nyagwaki. They were still pagan in 1906 when their counties were reduced to gombololas (Interviews C/8, C/29 and C/38).

[67] Pirouet, "Expansion of the Church," pp. 84–85.

chieftaincy modeled on the Buganda arrangement.[68] The young Catholic chief Edward Bulemu was put in the charge of Nikodemu Kakurora, a Protestant client of Kasagama. Bulemu was accused by Kasagama of drunkenness, was arrested in 1900, and finally deposed in 1907.[69] A final note of disharmony was the continuing sectarian struggle for control of Mwenge. From the point of view of the Catholic mission, Mwenge remained an area of religious persecution of Catholics, even after Byakweyamba's removal by his own hand. Complaints by the mission against Kasagama seem to have led only to the removal of the offending Catholic missionaries.[70] From Kasagama's point of view, however, Mwenge's troubles were of another sort. The county remained a hotbed of secessionism and a rival power center.

With Byakweyamba gone, power fell temporarily to one of his Babito Baitwara kinsmen, who continued to rule Mwenge without reference to Kabarole. In December 1897, Kasagama sent out a man named Sirasi Kijerre to take over the government of Mwenge. Kijerre was a member of the Babopi clan and a native of Mwenge. The Babopi were the clan of Kasagama's mother, Kahinju, and therefore, Kijerre occupied a special place of trust. In any case, he was not a Muitwara and hence broke the hold that this subclan held over eastern Toro. Kijerre remained for almost a year, but a growing spirit of independence on his part led Kasagama to dispatch a force led by Nasanaeri Mugurusi, the Katikiro, to remove him.[71]

[68] Toro Report, December 1902, *ESA* A12/3; Nyakazingo, "Kasagama," pp. 23–24; Interview C/40 Binyomo, 12 February 1969 and C/32 Kutambaki, 30 January 1969.

[69] Toro Report, November 1902, and J. P. Wilson to Commissioner, 31 December 1902, *ESA* A12/2. Interviews C/12 Muyasi, 17 January 1969, and C/40 Binyomo, 12 February 1969. Cf. G. Wilson, Minute of 6 July 1907, *ESA* SMP 850/07.

[70] Achte to Ternan, 20 July 1899; Roche to Bagge, 23 June 1899, *ESA* A6/6. Bishop Streicher to Ternan, 21 October 1899, *ESA* A6/7.

[71] Interview C/45 Mukonjo, 19 February 1969; C/30 Kagoro, 30 January 1969; C/44 Winyi, 19 February 1969; C/31 Mugungu, 30 January 1969. Sitwell, "Diary," p. 241. By this time, the territory of Nyakabimba in the extreme east, which had been loosed from Bunyoro, was being drawn into the

In January 1899, a suitable replacement for Byakweyamba was found. Byakweyamba's adopted "son" wrote to Sitwell in Kampala, asking "to be put back in Mwenge."[72] Although the oral sources credit Kasagama with the initiative in this appointment, it seems probable that this reflects a tendency to credit all acts of government to the person of the monarch. Moreover, it seems unlikely that the monarch would have been pleased to see the Baitwara "dynasty" regain their hold on Mwenge after almost two years out of power. But Nasanaeri Kagwahabi, the nephew of Byakweyamba, proved an effective and loyal functionary and held his post for over a decade.[73] The clash between the two branches of the Babito clan and the overt secessionism of the eastern region ceased to be a serious factor in Toro politics with Kagwahabi's appointment.

The End of Client Status: 1899–1900

When Kagwahabi came to take up his post in Mwenge in March 1899, he brought with him, as had his uncle Byakweyamba, a considerable number of Ganda Protestant followers.[74] By this time, the question of religion was largely moot, but the problem of Ganda-Toro relations had become a major political issue. The patron–client situation that was created by Zacharia Kizito Kisigiri on behalf of the Ganda Protestant chiefs in 1891 had persisted and grown during the years to 1899. The influence of the Baganda at court was second only to their influence in the church.[75] Ganda teachers were the backbone of the church, and Ganda subchiefs were

Confederacy. The chief was one Samwiri Kato, a Mubopi, but essentially independent of kinship ties to Toro. Interview C/26 Katemba, 28 January 1969; C/44 Winyi, 19 February 1969, and C/31 Mugungu, 30 January 1969.

[72] Sitwell to Commissioner, 30 January 1899, *ESA* A4/15.

[73] Interview C/44 Winyi, 19 February 1969; Interview C/41 Mutazindwa, 17 February 1969.

[74] Bagge to Ternan, 22 September 1899, *ESA* A4/21.

[75] Lloyd, *Dwarf Land*, pp. 161–162; Pirouet, "Expansion of the Church," pp. 58–89, especially p. 81; Nyakazingo, "Kasagama," p. 45.

important supports in introducing Buganda-style government, particularly the regular hierarchy of titled chieftaincies. In cultural matters, Kasagama's early education in Buganda was an important influence, and Byakweyamba's thoroughgoing Ganda-philia was crucial to the growth of both church and state in Mwenge and Toro alike. After the crises of 1895, the ties to Buganda were drawn tighter, symbolized by the fact that it was Zacharia Kizito who became Kasagama's godfather in March 1896.[76] This was the high-water mark of Ganda patronage and influence in Toro, for the dialectic of Ganda subimperialism was about to evoke a reaction of Toro "nationalism."

The growth of Toro's independence from Buganda patronage proceeded on several fronts. In March 1897, Zacharia Kizito visited Kasagama on the occasion of the first anniversary of his baptism. Part of his mission was to suggest to Kasagama on behalf of the Buganda Lukiko (Council) that he abandon Toro's nominal independence in favor of the annexation of Toro as a county within Buganda, ceding sovereignty to Kabaka Mwanga. His offer was both rejected and resented.[77] It may even have propelled Kasagama into a more cooperative policy toward Sitwell and British overrule. This gesture made it clear that Ganda influence, while a valuable aid to the growth of the church and systematic government, was not without its dangers.

Ganda influence at court came under serious attack by a member of the royal household, Kasagama's sister, Bagaya, who began a campaign against the prevalence of Ganda custom, language, and influence in Toro.[78] Bagaya was Mukama Nyaika's firstborn. As a young woman she had been given in

[76] Nyakazingo, "Kasagama," p. 27.

[77] Report on Special Inquiry into Circumstances of Assassination of H. St. George Galt, 30 July 1905, ESA A12/6; and Pirouet, "Expansion of the Church," p. 70.

[78] The material on Bagaya is drawn mainly from Nyakazingo, "Kasagama," pp. 45–50, and Interview C/9 Komuntali, 15 January 1969. See also E. Steinhart, "Royal Clientage and the Beginnings of Colonial Modernization in Toro, 1891–1900," *International Journal of African Historical Studies* 6, 2(1973):276–279.

marriage to Mukama Kabarega of Bunyoro to cement a peace treaty. When Bunyoro was invaded by the British and Ganda allies in 1895, Bagaya was captured and plans were made to repatriate her to Toro. Kasagama dispatched an envoy to escort her back to his capital. On arrival in Toro, Bagaya was greeted in Luganda by her brother's chiefs and messengers. She was soon to discover that Luganda was the language of court, government, and church. Thus, the language of her captors and her husband's enemies appeared to be the new language of her native land. Moreover, before her meeting with her brother, she was persuaded to burn her traditional religious symbols and objects as they were heathen and Kasagama was now a baptized Christian. Food was prepared in the Ganda style, hymns were sung and prayers read in Luganda. Indeed, Toro custom, which was essentially the same as that of Bunyoro where Bagaya had lived, was virtually absent from the capital, having been banished as pagan and "primitive." Bagaya was highly displeased by these developments and became a staunch supporter of Toro tradition and customs. She began her attack with an assault on Ganda cooking, escalating ultimately to supporting royal polygyny.

It should be borne in mind that Bagaya was not merely kin to Kasagama, but upon her return had become "Batebe" or Royal Sister and assumed the title and office of "Mugoli wa Bulera," generally rendered as "The Duchess of Bulera." As such she was an official personage of considerable importance in Toro government. She succeeded in winning the support of many important women of the Babito clan, and this together with her age, size, and temperament, made her a force to be reckoned with in political life. Bagaya became a focus of popular anti-Ganda feeling, which culminated in the elimination of Ganda custom and the restoration of various Toro customary practices at court.

Parallel to Bagaya's role in opposition to Ganda cultural dominance at court was the role played by the CMS missionary Henry Maddox in opposition to Ganda linguistic and ecclesiastic dominance. Maddox was a mission specialist in language, and his approach to Ganda-Toro relations was novel from the outset. When Bishop Tucker visited Toro in 1896, he found it remarkable that Luganda was spoken only in a small circle of great chiefs and courtiers,[79] so prevalent was the commitment of the Anglican Church to Ganda evangelists and hence to Ganda translations of Church books. After his second visit to Toro in September 1898, it was noted that the Toro Church was financially independent: "not only do they pay their own teachers . . . but also the Baganda teachers who are lent them."[80] At this time, it was decided to expand the work and include a linguist. Maddox arrived to fill this post in February 1899. The need for Batoro teachers was immediately evident to him in order "to remove one tremendous obstacle in the way of the conversion of the peasants."[81] Maddox is now chiefly remembered as the missionary who translated the Bible into Rutoro. The possibility of adopting Christian religion and British overrule without Ganda language, culture, and subimperialism became a possibility only when the work of translation was effected and the written language of state could be Rutoro.

In December 1899, Maddox wrote what he considered a highly opinionated letter to his superiors in the CMS. He began by praising the transformation the country had undergone since his arrival, crediting first the efforts of the Britih administration in adopting "a consistent policy of giving the king every possible assistance and teaching him how to rule."[82] He went on: "Another great change has taken place: Uganda influence has decreased enormously, and in matters of state is now almost of no account." Here he again first credits British policy and second "The desire of the king and people to maintain the integrity of their own kingdom." This is a reference to the reaction to Zacharia's mission of 1897. Maddox strongly believed that the rejection of Ganda influence had a salubrious effect on government and hoped to ac-

[79] Tucker, *Eighteen Years*, 2:52.
[80] Roscoe to Baylis, 26 September 1898, *CMS* G3A7/01.
[81] Maddox to Baylis, 11 April 1899, *CMS* G3A7/01. Minutes of Finance Committee, 24 September 1898, *CMS* G3A7/01.
[82] Maddox to Baylis, 4 December 1899, *CMS* G3A7/01.

complish the same in church affairs. The reaction of Arch-deacon Walker, an old guard Ganda-phile, was to assert that "Mr. Maddox will find out gradually that the influence of the Baganda chiefs in Toro is for the good of the Toro people."[83] The association in the minds of most British missionaries be-tween Luganda, Christianity, and progress would die hard. But the end of Ganda cultural and linguistic dominance that accompanied the transformation of Toro from a client state into a colonial dependency was ordained. The transformation in government that Maddox had described in his controver-sial missive was nothing less than the end of Anglo-Ganda pa-tronage.

The Transformation to Colonial Dependency

In March 1899, Stephen Bagge arrived in Toro to replace Sitwell as the district officer (titled Collector). Bagge was to prove far more thoroughgoing than Sitwell in supporting Kasagama's authority. This support by civilian officials be-came the key to effective collaboration. In part this reflects the trend in Administrative policy toward promoting "loyal cooperation" with strong local authorities championed by George Wilson, the chief architect of Uganda's "native pol-icy."[84] At another level, the change in policy reflected a change in the nature of the nexus between Kasagama and the Protectorate authority. Under the clientage relationship, Kasagama had persistently attempted to assert his independ-ence by acts that he understood to be within the royal pre-rogative, such as "raiding" for the purpose of exacting tribute from his weaker neighbors and subordinates. This persistence can be understood as Kasagama's necessary efforts to develop independent bases of power in support of his claim to sovereignty. These same efforts were interpreted by the

[83] Walker to Baylis, 17 December 1899, *CMS* G3A7/02.
[84] D. A. Low, "Uganda: The Establishment of the Protectorate, 1894–1919," in V. Harlow and E. M. Chilver, eds., *History of East Africa* II (Ox-ford: Clarendon Press, 1965), pp. 64–66, 81–84; Low, "British," p. 495, and Bagge to Commissioner, 17 March 1899, *ESA* A14/6.

British as a spirit of insubordination and became the source of
constant friction between the patron British authorities and
their client king. Having secured a relatively strong hold on
his kingdom, Kasagama was able to relax his pressure on the
colonial administration. In response to Kasagama's new
flexibility, the British were able to adopt a policy of consistent
support for the authority of the Toro monarch. This policy
had the effect of transforming the relationship from one of
royal clientage with its attendant tensions into one of royal
collaboration within the framework of Toro's sovereignty
under the Uganda Protectorate.

In particular, the new policy worked to Kasagama's advantage on numerous occasions. In July 1899, Bagge recommended "that the Salt Lake business be handed over to
Kasagama with the government to receive one third in taxation."[85] In August, Bagge reaffirmed the status of Kitagwenda within the Toro Confederacy and insured the payment
of tribute to Kasagama. Two days later, Kasagama was presented with a medal for his service during the Sudanese
Mutiny. Further financial remuneration was provided by the
ivory-hunting monopoly, which was in the hands of
Kasagama's chiefs.[86] Perhaps the most important decision
was Bagge's verdict in support of the king in his investigation
of Roman Catholic mission complaints of interference and
favoritism. Bagge stated:

> I have personally every reason to be pleased with
> Kasagama's conduct, he is ever ready to comply with
> any request I make and I consider he is administering his
> country's affairs in a most praiseworthy manner, law,
> order and general improvement being manifested
> daily.[87]

In September 1899, Toro was exempted from paying a
tribute to Buganda that was imposed on both Ankole and

[85] Bagge to Commissioner, 17 and 24 July 1899, *ESA* A4/19.
[86] Bagge to Commissioner, 12 August 1899, *ESA* A4/20; Bagge to Commissioner, 14 August 1899, *ESA* A4/20; Meldon to Bagge, 16 August 1899,
ESA A4/20.
[87] Bagge to Commissioner, 20 August 1899 and 22 September 1899, *ESA*
A4/21.

Bunyoro. This was not only an economic advantage to Toro, but signified the Toro kingdom's complete independence of Buganda's suzerainty. In domestic matters, Bagge's report on land tenure tended to support the legitimacy of Kasagama's position as sovereign and the claim of his chiefs to hold office without administrative interference in those decisions made by "the majority of the principal chiefs."[88] As an earnest of cooperation, a fine that had been imposed by Sitwell against Kasagama and had remained unpaid due to administrative confusion was cancelled by the order of Sir Harry Johnston, Her Majesty's Special Commissioner.[89] Johnston had come to Uganda to settle upon a system of government for the Protectorate in the wake of the rebellion of 1897 in Buganda and the Sudanese Mutiny. His efforts in negotiating the Buganda Agreement have undergone intensive study.[90] Before traveling to Toro himself, Johnston gave Bagge the option of setting up a tax collection system either through chiefs appointed by Bagge directly or through Kasagama's chiefs, allowing them a 10 percent rebate. Bagge chose to rely on Kasagama and his chiefs, thus supporting decisively their authority. This decision more than any other procured for Kasagama and the Batoro chiefs the Toro Agreement of 24 June 1900, which formalized the system of royal collaboration.[91]

Discussion

In a little more than a year from Bagge's arrival to Johnston's mission in June 1900, Toro had undergone a profound transformation. The development of a system of hierarchically arranged authority centering on the new

[88] Bagge to Commissioner, 4 September 1899, *ESA* A4/21; Grant to Commissioner, 11 September 1899, *ESA* A4/20.

[89] Bagge to Johnston, 29 March 1900, *ESA* A4/27, and Johnston to Bagge, 14 April 1900, *ESA* A5/9.

[90] D. A. Low and R. C. Pratt, *Buganda and British Overrule* (London: Oxford University Press, 1960). Cf. Low, "Uganda: The Establishment," pp. 77–82.

[91] Johnston to Bagge, 14 April 1900, *ESA* A5/9. Cf. Low, "British," p. 560.

Mukama and based on the Buganda model of government
was the result of gradual incremental changes started as early
as 1891. However, the swift granting of real responsibility to
the system by the British overlords was the culmination of a
revolutionary change. From a band of refugees and outcasts,
Kasagama had welded together a viable political system of
subordinate chiefs capable of supporting the weight of imperial overrule.

The political transformation of Toro was initiated by a period of disruption and crisis. The disruption of Toro was
wrought by war and disease, as in Ankole and Bunyoro, the
depredations of the Sudanese guardians of Toro's "independence," and the prestations of an impoverished Company and
colonial overrule. The crises, climaxed by Kasagama's flight
to Kampala in 1895, were the product of persistent centrifugal
pressures from the outlying counties combined with
Kasagama's disillusionment and distrust of his British patrons
for their early failures to protect and support him as he required. His restoration by the Protectorate Government with
the assistance of the Anglican Church hierarchy ended the period of crises, but as elsewhere, opened wide the doors for increasing dependence on alien power. The crises at court provided the entering wedge for the forces of collaboration
within Toro.

The clash with the European officer in 1895 resulted in a
period of heavier reliance on Kasagama's church and Ganda
allies. By 1898, however, he was ready to resume allegiance
to the British and accept again their patronage. Although he
had secured the religious conformity of a large number of his
chiefs, Kasagama had faced both pressure for incorporation in
Buganda and the threat of latent secessionist tendencies in the
border counties. These pressures compelled Kasagama's reliance on the British authorities, who, in the wake of their
own crisis in 1897, found it necessary to depend on their royal
client and permit increases in his own powers. Moreover,
over the years it had become evident that of Kasagama's two
patrons, the British were best able to protect the Toro kingdom while requiring less in homage and service as overlords

than the Ganda chiefs. Mwanga's unsuccessful rebellion in Buganda in 1897 had proven to Kasagama that the risk of resistance was too high. Loyal clientage to British patrons could, on the other hand, pay handsome dividends. Acceptance of British authority and patronage, signalized by Bagge's policy of consistent support of royal prerogative, enabled Toro to throw off its dependence on Ganda patrons and tutors in favor of the looser-fitting colonial yoke, soon formalized in the Toro Agreement.

Toro's uniqueness lies in the conjunction of royal authority and active collaboration. Unlike Ankole, where royal prerogatives were diminished by the onset of imperial intervention, the origins of Kasagama's reign in an act of usurpation and succession to royal office had made his authority itself heavily dependent on his position vis-à-vis Anglo-Ganda imperialism. It is this relationship that we have characterized as royal clientage.

Indeed, the nature of Toro's response to British imperialism hinged on this notion of clientage. Two aspects of the notion are relevant for understanding Kasagama's resistance. First is the question of the compatibility of multiple clientage contracts. Thus, whereas Kasagama and his regime could owe fealty to both British and Ganda patrons simultaneously, he could not in the British view be a colonial dependent of more than one external power. Numerous acts of "insubordination" and conflict were generated by the misunderstanding of the dual allegiance possible in clientage when the expectations of one patron conflicted with the obligations owed by the client to other patrons.

The second relevant aspect of clientage is the question of its compatibility with ideas of royal and state sovereignty. Although we have argued that in Kasagama's view, the obligations of clientage did not impair his status as a ruling monarch of a sovereign kingdom, it was this view that led him into serious conflict with his overlords. Conflict over tribute, raiding, and demonstrations of insubordination were the primary form that resistance took in Toro, both for Kasagama and for his supporters and chiefs in Mwenge and the other counties.

Pressure on Kasagama to accept subordinate status as a colonial dependent was the root cause of the Ashburnham affair. Only when dependence was sweetened with consistent support for Kasagama's royal authority within Toro did conflict abate and a firm collaboration between the British and Batoro become possible.

Kasagama's intransigence and the resistance of Byakweyamba and other county chiefs were not the only form that anticolonial resistance took in Toro. The resistance to Kasagama and his British backers by the previous hierarchy of Nyoro chiefs until they were driven from the country by superior force must not be omitted. Furthermore, the forms of resistance to incorporation within the expansionist Toro state on the part of the semiautonomous chieftaincies of Busongora and Kitagwenda and the achephelous areas of Bukonjo and Bwamba represent important examples of anticolonial resistance to Toro subimperialism. Nonetheless, the main resistance to imperial domination in Toro during the 1890s came in the muted form of the struggles of Kasagama's regime to assert its sovereignty and independence of action within the framework of political relations that we have called clientage. The regime of collaboration and dependence that had emerged under Kasagama's rule would continue the traditions of muted conflict into the colonial era.

CHAPTER V

Mbaguta and Ankole Collaboration

In July 1895, the cry went out from the royal enclosure amidst wailing and ululations of grief, "The milk is spilt." The word and the grief spread that Mugabe Ntare V had died. Household fires were extinguished in the kraals. The royal drum, Bagyendanwa, was overturned, and the nation—or at least the pastoral and political section of the nation—was thrown into deep mourning. The wives of Ntare were ordered put to death and his royal sister, Magwende, committed suicide, as did many of the king's close relatives and companions. The Hima chiefs, taking their herds, fled the country, as without a monarch all was chaos in Ankole.[1] Even had Ntare left an undisputed heir, which he did not, the country was in for a profound crisis. Coming after years of hardship and difficulty, Ntare's death and the disputed succession was to prove the double crisis that would pave the way for the loss of sovereignty to the expanding British Protectorate of Uganda, established the year before.

Disease and Dislocation: 1891–1895

Ntare's death from pneumonia was sudden and unexpected, but the crisis it brought must have been anticipated by many of the Hinda princes and courtiers who would ensure continued chaos for two more years. It is hard to say how much of the chaos was the product of the king's death or of his heirless state. Nkore tradition makes much of the death of the Mugabe as a time of trouble, grief, and dislocation.[2] But

[1] Cf. J. Roscoe, *The Banyankole* (Cambridge: Cambridge University Press, 1923), pp. 51ff; S. R. Karugire, *A History of the Kingdom of Nkore* (Oxford: Clarendon Press, 1971), pp. 246–247; A. G. Katate and L. Kamugungunu, *Abagabe B'Ankole*, 2 vols. (Kampala: East African Literature Bureau, 1967), 1:154–156.

[2] S. R. Karugire, "Succession Wars in the Pre-Colonial Kingdom of Nkore," in *War and Society in Africa*, B. A. Ogot, ed. (London: Cass, 1972), pp. 9–34.

trouble and dislocation had become endemic in Ankole in the last years of Ntare's reign, and the condition of the kingdom on the eve of crisis must be understood before we can estimate the impact of succession war and British intervention.

When Lugard left Ankole in June 1891, he left the kingdom already in the throes of the worst natural disaster it had ever experienced. It is doubtful if the protection Lugard offered, even if implemented, could have saved the kingdom from the ravages of rinderpest and smallpox that were descending upon it. By the end of 1892, when the diseases had run their course, Ankole was in a political crisis. It is impossible to make accurate estimates of the extent of devastation caused by the loss of cattle to rinderpest, which spread across Ankole from Bwera in the east to Igara in the west. This same epidemic was not restricted to Ankole but continued to devastate pastoral society across the eastern African landscape and as far south as Cape Colony.[3] In Ankole, memories generated by the rinderpest onslaught among the pastoralists are the only index we have of the impact. The actual economic loss in head of cattle must be multiplied by the crucial place that cattle held in pastoral ideology and social organization. Without their large herds of cattle to bind together the Hima clans, to lubricate the system of clientage, and to support the authority of chiefs and king, the very fabric of traditional society must have been rent. Certainly if the decimation of herds reported by Lugard in mid-1891 continued through the following year, the memories of the traditionalists are not far wrong in estimating the havoc of the epidemic.[4]

But cattle disease was just the beginning of the troubles. In 1892, a smallpox epidemic also struck the Banyankole. Although the terrors of smallpox among a population lacking any natural immunity must certainly have been extreme, the Ankole social order once again appears to have had a multi-

[3] Cf. C. van Onselen, "Reactions to Rinderpest in Southern Africa, 1896–1897," *Journal of African History* 13, 3(1972):473–488.

[4] F. Lugard, *The Diaries of Lord Lugard*, 4 vols., M. Perham, ed. (Evanston, Ill.: Northwestern University Press, 1959), 2:220. Cf. Katate, *Abagabe*, 1:142–143, and several interviews in A series, expecially A/11, Buningwire, 5 August 1968.

plier effect on the disease's impact. It appears that the disease struck first at the royal capital at Muti and spread from there to outlying areas. The result of this was that the Hima chiefs and courtiers, especially the Hinda princes and the handful of Iru *emitwe* leaders, were to suffer disproportionately from the onslaught. Traditional historians list no fewer than 13 major chiefs who succumbed to the disease. They included the same Prince Birere who had signed Lugard's treaty the previous year as well as five other Hinda princes and five Bairu war leaders and courtiers. The loss of such prominent political figures was, to say the least, a severe shock to the kingdom.[5]

Perhaps the most significant victim of smallpox for the future of Ankole was Kabumbire, Ntare's only surviving son and the most likely successor to his powers.[6] His death not only left Ntare without an heir apparent, it also intensified the atmosphere of insecurity and suspicion at the court that the dual epidemics had created. It was not long before suspicion and fear were claiming their own victims to add to those who fell to more natural causes. In 1893, Ntare's suspicions fell on Nkuranga, his uncle and the most popular of the Hinda princes. With Kabumbire dead, a fit of jealousy led Ntare to plot against Nkuranga, whom it was said would succeed in placing his line on the throne instead of Ntare's. Ntare manufactured a dispute and dispatched a company of Ganda soldiers called *abangonya* under the command of the young Shambo chief, Mbaguta, to execute Prince Nkuranga. The abangonya were a military unit of fusiliers created by Ntare from among the Ganda Christian refugees who had settled in eastern Ankole in 1888. Mbaguta had been named their captain and became chief of the border region in which they resided. Nkuranga was killed along with two of his sons in battle with the abangonya. A third son, Rwakatogoro, who was too young to have taken part in the fighting, was spared and entrusted to an aged Muhinda to be brought up.[7]

[5] Katate, *Abagabe*, 1:143–144, and Interview A/11 Buningwire, 5 August 1968.

[6] Ibid.

[7] Katate, *Abagabe*, 1:147–149. Interviews A/5 Murumba, 27 July 1968, and A/47 Gasyonga, 12 September 1968.

It was at about this time that Prince Igumira, Ntare's half-brother, gave his own son to Ntare for adoption, as it was customary that no important man should be childless.[8] Igumira's son thus became the legal heir of Ntare and ultimately would succeed to his throne as Mugabe Kahaya II. Meanwhile, the insecurity and apprehension over a succession crisis were not allayed. Fears of interregnum chaos and succession war were to be justified in due time.

The end of the epidemics did not lead to a return to normal. On the contrary, the political crisis generated by the decimation of Ankole's herds only deepened. In order to replenish the herds so vital to the life of the kingdom, it was necessary and considered proper to carry out raids against neighboring societies. The first expedition was reported against the Ntungamo region of western Rwampara. This raid was relatively successful and spurred the Ankole warriors to greater efforts. In 1893, after a mission of espionage had established the reputation of Ruhara, an Iru retainer of the Hinda dynasty, a major expedition was launched against Rujumbura and Rwanda to the west and south. The expedition was under the command of Prince Igumira, who emerged as a leading military figure. The success of this raid was literally fabulous, and the herd that was brought back to Nkore was remembered as numbering in the thousands. The names of Igumira and Ruhara were praised, but nemesis was not far from the fields of rejoicing.[9]

In 1894, Rwandan armies seeking cattle and revenge invaded Ankole. They drove on the capital at Katete, forcing Ntare to abandon it and fall back to rally his defenses. Government was further disorganized as the chiefs and emitwe were called together to counterattack and defend the monarchy. Four major war leaders were killed in the defense, and large herds of cattle were driven away by the victorious

[8] Interview A/1 Katate, 24 July 1968. Katate, *Abagabe*, 1:161. Karugire, *Kingdom of Nkore*, p. 238.

[9] Katate, *Abagabe*, 1:144–147; Interviews A/1 Katate, 24 July 1968; A/18 Kagaga and Nyabayangire, 20 August 1968, and A/41 Mbata, 9 September 1968.

Rwandan invaders. Before the Rwandan armies had completely withdrawn, Ntare's illness and death added a new
element of crisis to Ankole's deepening troubles.[10]

Ntare may well have asked in these troubled days about the
friendship and protection that Captain Lugard had promised
him in the name of the British Company on the eve of his nation's adversity. Indeed, these Rwandan armies had crossed
into Uganda from German territory over an internationally
recognized boundary and were far more of a threat to Ankole
than the perambulations of Emin Pasha that had prompted
Lugard's fears and promises. Ntare had upheld his part of the
agreement, attacking an Arab caravan from the south shortly
after Lugard's departure. But the bankrupt Company had
transferred its responsibilities in 1893 to the newly established
British Protectorate. Did Ntare have a right to expect protection from the new British authorities in Uganda? Lest there
be any doubt of British responsibility for protecting Ankole,
Major Cunningham of the Protectorate administration had
been dispatched to enter into fresh negotiations with Ntare in
June 1894. This was in response to the threat posed to British
interests by the passage of a column from German East Africa
under the command of Major Langheld through Ankole in
1893. Cunningham had explicit instructions to enter into a
treaty that saw the need for defense against Rwanda as a threat
to Ankole and the British sphere.[11]

Negotiations were opened by Ntare with Cunningham
through the offices of an envoy. No benefits had accrued to
Ankole from the previous arrangements, and Ntare may well
have been loath to enter into new agreements. He once again

[10] Katate, *Abagabe*, 1:149–154, for major events of Nkore's defense. Cf.
Karugire, *Kingdom of Nkore*, pp. 229–230.

[11] D. A. Low, "The British and Uganda, 1862–1900," D. Phil. diss., Ox-
ford, 1957, pp. 274–277. Colvile to Ntare, 18 June 1894, E[ntebbe] S[ecretariat]
A[rchives] A3/2; Cunningham to Commissioner, 21 August 1894, ESA A2/1.
Katate, *Abagabe*, 2:66–73; F. L. Williams, "Early Explorers in Ankole,"
Uganda Journal 2, 3(1935):201–205; D. Weekes, "The Journey of Cunningham
Through Ankole in 1894," *Uganda Journal* 37(1973):55–62.

refused to meet with the European emissary personally. Instead, Mbaguta, the captain of the abangonya, was deputed to
treat with Cunningham as the king's representative. It was
during these meetings that Mbaguta appears to have assumed
the title of Enganzi, literally a star near the moon, indicating
the Mugabe's favorite. Cunningham assumed that this indicated that he was Ntare's "prime minister." On 29 August, a
new treaty was signed that repeated the 1891 agreement, substituting Her Majesty's Government for the British East Africa Company as "sovereign."[12] Once again the promises of
protection would prove a hollow reed, as Cunningham proceeded to lead his column out of Ankole. The next European
would not arrive until 1898 after four more years of adversity.

A closer look at Mbaguta and his role may enable us to understand the workings of Ankole's chiefly politics. He was a
Mushambo whose ancestors were from the western area of
Ankole that had formerly been the kingdom of Mpororo.
Mbaguta's grandfather had migrated to the Nkore kingdom,
and his father had become a warrior for the Mugabe.
Mbaguta himself was born in Nshara county in eastern Ankole in about 1868 and as a boy served at the royal court. It
was in the late 1880s that he got his first important chiefly appointment. Baganda Christian refugees had been allowed by
Ntare to settle in the Kabula region on Ankole's eastern margins. Mbaguta was sent there to lead them, and he succeeded
in organizing these armed men, who might have proven
dangerous, into a disciplined body of fusiliers in the service of
the Mugabe. This force—the abangonya—was used effectively in cattle raids against Rujumbura (part of Mbaguta's
former homeland) and against Rwanda. It was the abangonya
under Mbaguta's personal command who were charged with
the execution of Prince Nkuranga in 1893, an incident that
seems to have earned Mbaguta the lasting condemnation of
the royal clansmen. In 1894 he was still leading the abangonya

[12] Cunningham to Commissioner, 24 September 1894, *ESA* A2/2, includes a diary account of the negotiations. A copy of the treaty is also found
in H. F. Morris, *A History of Ankole* (Kampala: East African Literature
Bureau, 1962), pp. 47–48.

and was an important chief in eastern Ankole, but it is doubtful if he was indeed the Enganzi, Ntare's favorite.[13]

The title Enganzi had previously belonged to a Mwiru chief
named Muhigi, who had been Ntare's favorite from the first
years of his reign. The title did not mean "prime minister" in
the parliamentary sense as it later came to be used, but rather
indicated the Mugabe's favorite at court, a close companion
and friend rather than an important political or administrative
figure.[14] When Muhigi died in 1894, the title was abandoned
during the remaining months of Ntare's regime. If there was
a replacement as Ntare's favorite, it would appear to have
been either Rugumayo, the veteran war leader, or Bitsa, a
judge under Ntare.[15] Cunningham's report contains the only
mention of Mbaguta being Enganzi under Ntare and it was
repeated years later by Mbaguta's eulogist.[16] However, we
should probably regard Mbaguta's assumption of the title as
an indication of his aspirations rather than as fact. His familiarity with the Ganda situation, where the "prime minister"
or Katikiro had become a leading political figure, may also
have influenced him. There is no doubt that his special posi-

[13] S. R. Karugire, *Nuwa Mbaguta* (Kampala: East African Literature
Bureau, 1973), pp. 9–23. Cf. F. L. Williams, "Nuwa Mbaguta, Nganzi of
Ankole," *Uganda Journal* 10, 2(1946):126–127; Katate, *Abagabe*, 1:145–146.

[14] Karugire, *Kingdom of Nkore*, pp. 110–111, and personal communication,
14 August 1969. Contrast K. Oberg, "The Kingdom of Ankole in Uganda,"
in *African Political Systems*, M. Fortes and E. E. Evans-Pritchard, eds. (London: Oxford University Press, 1940), pp. 145–150.

[15] On Muhigi, Interviews A/38 Kantayomba, 5 September 1968, and A/6
Rwabushongo, 30 July 1968. On Rugumayo, Interviews A/38 Kantayomba,
5 September 1968; A/30 Mbanga, 29 August 1968; A/11 Buningwire, 5 August 1968, and A/8 Mugoha, 31 July 1968. Also G. Wilson to Commissioner,
20 December 1895, *ESA* A4/3, records the names of "Visa [Bitsa?], Katikiro
to Ntali, Gumaya [Rugumayo?], a second Katikiro"; Mbaguta is mentioned
in the letter without a title of office. Katikiro is the Luganda term generally
rendered as "prime minister."

[16] Cunningham to Commissioner, 24 September 1894, *ESA* A2/2; Wil-
liams, "Nuwa Mbaguta," pp. 127–129. Contrast E. Kamuntu, F. Kamurari,
S. Mbojana, E. Turyagyenda, and D. Rulewira, "Mbaguta and the Adminis-
tration of Ankole," joint research paper, Ntare V Senior Secondary School
(Mbarara, 1967). Note also that Cunningham's reference to "Magota"
(Mbaguta) is as "Katikiro" not Enganzi.

tion as leader of an army of Baganda had made him fluent in Luganda and conversant with Ganda custom and political developments.[17] And it would seem his aspirations for political leadership were in this direction, for in a short while, aided by the succession crisis and by the British, his ambitions were to be achieved.

Succession Crisis: 1895–1899

The death of Ntare V was followed by a period of mourning symbolized by the suicide of his wives and several followers and the scattering of the leading princes and chiefs of the country. In diaspora they would either sit and wait for the pretenders to the throne to put forward their claims or begin selecting their champions to support in the struggle for power that followed the death of a childless monarch.

At the death of Ntare, Prince Kahitsi seized the royal drum, Bagyendanwa, the royal herds, and the other symbols of kingship. It is conceivable that he had aspirations of his own for the throne, but equally possible that he hoped simply to gain an advantage in the coming struggle and thereby to become kingmaker rather than king.[18]

[17] Interviews A/5 Murumba, 27 July 1918, and A/48 Mugyerwa, 18 September 1968. Cf. Karugire, *Mbaguta*, pp. 21–22.

[18] Kahitsi's position in the royal lineage can be seen in this partial genealogy adapted from Morris, *History of Ankole*, p. viii.

MUTAMBUKA   (d. circa 1867)

Mukwenda	Rukongye	Makumbi	Nkuranga	Bacwa	(Ntare V)
		Kahitsi	Rwakatogoro		
			Igumira NTARE V (1867–		
			1895)		
			KAHAYA II (1897–		
			1944)		
		GASYONGA II			
		(1945–)			

Key: Bagabe are italicized. Pretenders are partially underlined. Morris takes Ntare to be the son of Mutambuka, whereas Karugire (*Kingdom of Nkore*, p. 238) has him as the son of Bacwa and grandson of Mutambuka. I have preferred Karugire's genealogy on this point.

The popular choice for Ankole's leader appears to have been Igumira. As a military figure he was unparalleled by any of the Bahinda and seems to have had great popularity with the Bairu of Shema and the western areas, perhaps due to his connection with the Iru hero, Ruhara. Ruhara was a member of the Yangwe clan, which has been described as the Iru branch of the ruling Hinda lineage. His own popularity with the Bairu seems to derive from his high position at court, albeit in humble service, and from his success as an espionage agent during Ntare's war on Rujumbura in 1893, which was directed by Igumira. By virtue of his household position, he had further developed close personal ties to Igumira and acted as foster father to Prince Kahaya. Thus, popular support was guaranteed to Igumira should dispute lead to warfare.[19]

Competition among the Hinda princes for accession to the throne arose quickly after Ntare's demise. Prince Mazinio emerged as a pretender very early, but was driven into exile in German territory by the threat of Igumira's forces. Another Muhinda, Manyatsi, made a more serious bid for power. He put forward as his protégé the boy Rwakatogoro. Rwakatogoro, as the son of Nkuranga, Ntare's uncle and the victim of Ntare's jealousy, had a strong claim to succession, based on the strength of his genealogical proximity to the deceased monarch and the popularity of the dead Prince Nkuranga in the memories of the pastoral classes.[20]

To meet the challenge of Rwakatogoro's claims, Kahitsi and Igumira found it necessary to unite behind their own protégé, Ntare's adopted son, Kahaya. Kahaya, who was about 16 years old at the time, was in fact Igumira's biological son. It may be supposed that his enthronement would have made Igumira the real power in the country.

It should seem odd that Kahitsi and Igumira did not press their own claims to royal office. They were both princes of the blood and genealogically and politically well placed. However, it appears that each was disqualified from reigning

[19] Katate, *Abagabe*, 1:155; Interviews A/1 Katate, 24 July 1968, and A/28 Kamujanduzi and Katundu, 28 August 1968.

[20] Interview A/47 Gasyonga, 12 September 1968, and G. Wilson to Commissioner, 20 December 1895, *ESA* A4/3.

as Mugabe by traditional rules of physical disability. Prince
Kahitsi was naturally left-handed, while Igumira was wall-
eyed in one eye. These "imperfections" were enough to dis-
qualify them from taking office themselves, but not from ruling through a protégé if they could find and control one.[21]

Having agreed on Kahaya as their candidate, it was necessary for the princes to muster support from the leading men
of the kingdom and, as was customary, from whatever
neighboring powers were willing to intervene in the hope
that support in kingmaking would create a debt of gratitude
in the new regime. It was by this avenue that British influence
would once again assert itself, the agency being the connection running from British to Baganda to Mbaguta, the ambitious and spurious Enganzi.

Mbaguta was one of those leaders who watched and waited
for the Hinda princes to settle their affairs and find a new
monarch. But he did not wait long before choosing his side.
By mid-1895 he had put his unique services at the disposal of
Igumira's faction. His role in the death of Nkuranga must certainly have predisposed him to favor the candidacy of Kahaya
rather than that of Nkuranga's only surviving son,
Rwakatogoro.[22]

Mbaguta's services consisted in being the man best prepared to seek the support and protection of certain external
powers. His experience as leader of the abangonya war band,
composed as it was of Christian Baganda, had made him the
likely emissary in any dealing with Buganda's Christian leaders. And in as much as Buganda was the center of the growing British Uganda Protectorate, Mbaguta was the best emissary to the British government. Perhaps this is why he had
been selected to negotiate with Major Cunningham in 1894.
In 1895, he would play an important role in securing the recognition and support of the British and Ganda authorities for
the candidacy of Kahaya.

[21] I owe this point to D. A. Low, personal communication, 3 January
1968, from his own researches on the succession dispute. Cf. Karugire, *Kingdom of Nkore*, pp. 247–248.
[22] Cf. Kamuntu et al., "Mbaguta," p. 3.

The following letter from George Wilson, subcommissioner for Buganda, explains the situation at the end of 1895:

On July 31, Kampala messengers to Ankole returned
with definite news of the death of Mtali [Ntare] about
the middle of that month. Ankole was in a disturbed
condition. Further messengers were sent to the borders
to gather information. These returned early in October,
reporting that several claimants had endeavored to take
advantage of the state of anarchy brought about by
Mtali's death: but these had been reduced to two boys:
one produced by Kaish [Kahitsi] and Gomira [Igumira],
two of the strongest brothers of Mtali and alleged to be
the true son of Mtali; the other produced by Manyasi
[Manyatsi] another brother of Mtali, reported by him to
be the son of an older brother of Mtali. Mwanga and the
Uganda chiefs were strongly inclined towards Manyasi's
protege, from the fact that he had always held cordial relations with Uganda: particularly since he induced Mtali
to shelter the Christians at the time of their expulsion
from Uganda by the Mohammedans.

Kaish on the other hand, had the reputation of being a
turbulent character, strongly opposed to Uganda and—
so the Uganda chiefs said—European influence in Ankole
affairs. Manyasi was reported to have been driven out of
Ankole and to have taken refuge with the Pokino in
Buddu, carrying with him a large herd of cattle.

On the 17th October, a Muhima named Amani appeared at Kampala with envoys from Kaish and Gomira.
The envoys begged for the support of H. M. Government and the King of Uganda [Kabaka of Buganda] for
the son of Mtali. Whilst the matter was under discussion
Manyasi himself appeared. When questioned, he denied
the existence of the reputed son of Mtali. I asked Amani
and the envoys if they were prepared to remain in Kampala whilst messengers were sent from the Government
and the King. Amani and the envoys at once agreed. As
representing the Government Mohamed Daud was sent.

The King sent a Mkungu named Gidson and a chief of lower grade to assist him.

The messengers have now returned and individually and collectively report as follows:

"At Lunga we met Kaish and Gomira together. The other chiefs had principally gone to fight Marinia [Mazinio], a pretender to the throne without any acknowledged claims, who fled into German territory. We then met Kaish and Gomira again, who desired us to wait for the return of the war party, as they would be able to represent the whole of the present Ankole territory. We waited nine days for this party to return. At the conference then held, there were present: Kaish and Gomira; Visa [Bitsa], Katikiro of Mtali; Gumaya [Rugumayo], a second Katikiro; Gurakimitti, uncle of Mtali; Liamgwizi [Rwamagwizi], and Kazungu, brothers of Mtali, and others. The conference was unanimous in declaring that Mtali had given birth to a son by a woman who had died soon after childbirth. This woman, becoming pregnant, had been sent by Mtali to Gomira's wife to be delivered. There were witnesses to the negotiations between Mtali and the parents of the woman on the occasion of her becoming Mtali's wife. The chiefs in conference desired Mohamed Daud and Gidson, who had both seen Mtali, to identify Mtali's son by his likeness to Mtali out of a number of youths to be gathered together for the purpose. We waited two days. On the third day two bodies of people gathered near to us, and the chiefs appeared and asked us to carry out the wish of the conference. We had no difficulty in doing so; the son—for we now have no doubt he is such—being particularly recognisible from the projecting teeth and thick limbs peculiar to Mtali, besides of course a general likeness in features and expression. Kaish said he was sorry that Manyasi was absent as he was sure he would have waived his claims under these circumstances. The Ankole chiefs accuse Manyasi of having bolted with Mtali's cattle on the day of Mtali's death and they will only agree to his residing again in Ankole on condition that he gives up the cattle to Mtali's heirs. Another conference was held and the chiefs have sent Dwakisaya and Kales, two of Mtali's known official messengers, with a large tusk of ivory weighing about 2½ frasilas to H. M. Government; and a small tusk and five head of cattle to Mwanga, besides minor presents to chiefs, as an earnest of their sincerity in begging support and protection in placing Mtali's son on the throne and in governing Ankole. Kaish and Gomira to be appointed guardians or regents. Kaish during these negotiations has been most cordial, and together with Gomira, has expressed the most earnest solicitude for the friendly assistance of the Government."

Manyasi is still in Mengo, but the King and Uganda chiefs now consider that his part is played out and they support the claims of Mtali's son, being quite convinced from the evidence acquired by the messengers of the legitimate claims of Kaish's and Gomira's protege.[23]

It is clear from the first paragraph of this letter that the succession dispute was perceived as offering the Anglo-Ganda alliance a promising opportunity to gain "influence in Ankole affairs." The conference at Lunga not only confirmed Kahaya as the legitimate heir to Ntare in British eyes, but confirmed the utility of Anglo-Ganda support to Igumira's faction. British willingness to concern themselves with Ankole's domestic affairs, and their ignorance of Ankole succession rules in removing the opposition from the field of conflict (as evidenced by the fate of Manyatsi's claims), were not lost on the Ankole politicians as they prepared themselves for future power struggles.

Igumira and Kahitsi thus became joint regents for the young Mugabe Kahaya, having won a bloodless victory over Manyatsi thanks to the Anglo-Ganda intervention. Kahaya's camp for a short time included all the major factions in the country. Mbaguta, not as yet a power in his own right, at-

[23] Wilson to Commissioner, 20 December 1895, *ESA* A4/3.

tached himself firmly to Kahaya's retinue. It was probably around this time that Mbaguta actively assumed the title of Enganzi and a position of proximity and trust in the royal establishment of Kahaya. His confirmation in that post by the British *"Balozi"* or Commissioner came several years later when no one else could be found to escort the visiting Commissioner to Kahaya's capital.[24]

From early 1896, the threads of the succession dispute become extremely difficult to disentangle. It appears that Prince Kahitsi was soon angling for personal advantage. He invited Kahuzi, a chief from Koki—an area to the east of Ankole—to take control of Bukanga on the eastern edge of Ankole's Isingiro county. Kahuzi would owe personal allegiance to Kahitsi. Furthermore, Kahitsi continued to keep possession of Ntare's regalia and cattle, which he had seized at the time of the late Mugabe's death. He also requested that the British set up a station in Ankole, no doubt hoping to attach them to his own following, which was quite large. Igumira appears to have been unable to prevent Kahitsi's independence. Mbaguta, having stayed in Kabula, was beginning to be troubled by Ganda dissidents who had settled in that area.[25]

In 1897, Mbaguta joined forces with Igumira and, with a Ganda army to back them up, proclaimed Kahaya's succession and built a new capital (royal kraal). This appears to have led to a major transfer of allegiance by Kahitsi's followers to the new monarch. But Kahitsi's power was not at an end. He remained a "regent," enriched by Ntare's wealth.[26] Mbaguta's intervention into royal politics seems merely to have separated the main contestants and coincidently to have placed Mbaguta at the center of Ankole's dynastic struggle.

In mid-1897 the situation was further complicated by the rebellion of Kabaka Mwanga of Buganda and his flight to

---

[24] Kamuntu et al., "Mbaguta," pp. 4–5, date his recognition as 1896, but Katate, *Abagabe*, 2:11–12, and Karugire, *Mbaguta*, pp. 38–39, place it in 1900. Regardless of formal British confirmation of the title, Mbaguta was closely attached to Kahaya's faction from its inception, and both owed their positions to British support and eventual confirmation.

[25] Low, "British," p. 479 and Katate, *Abagabe*, 2:1.   [26] Ibid.

German East Africa. His return through Ankole precipitated the crisis that led directly to the establishment of a British presence in Ankole. But before this, sides shifted several times. The early stages of hostility found Igumira and Mbaguta favoring Mwanga and the rebels against the imperial authority while Kahitsi continued to invite a British victory. Mbaguta actually led an army against British forces in August 1897. The defeat of Mwanga's army in these early engagements led to a quick reversal of allegiance by the Ankole court. When the rebels began to disturb Ankole's domestic tranquility by raiding, Kahaya responded to British pressure for an outpost in Ankole by declaring that he and his chiefs were ready to cooperate. This shift left Kahitsi holding a losing hand, as Kahaya's personal following, along with Mbaguta's and Igumira's support and British recognition, clearly would leave him diplomatically outmaneuvered and militarily outclassed.[27]

When in December 1898, after several delays, R. J. D. Macallister, the first Collector for the Protectorate, arrived, he came at the behest of the young monarch and his Enganzi, Mbaguta. Kahitsi was even mentioned as being likely to give trouble as early as January 1899, and British suspicion of Igumira was also aroused.[28] A crisis was not long in coming.

Macallister wrote: "The three parties in Ankole, the King's, Igumira's and Kahitsi's are all outwardly friendly but I fear that Igumira would cause trouble if he saw the slightest chance of success."[29] Macallister also feared that Kahitsi's party might engage in raiding if the station were withdrawn. Mbaguta, who as Enganzi was part of the King's party, was not suspect in any way. He clearly was in a good position, acting as interpreter and envoy to the British, to influence the situation in his own and Kahaya's behalf.

When in February Macallister asserted British authority by successfully demanding that Kahitsi turn over Ntare's cattle

[27] Low, "British," pp. 479–484, for a lucid account of this complex of diplomatic shifts.
[28] Macallister to Commissioner, 1 January 1899, *ESA* A4/15.
[29] Macallister to Commissioner, 19 June 1899, *ESA* A4/18.

to Kahaya, Kahitsi's power was clearly waning. Later that year, Macallister permitted a test of armed strength between Kahaya's forces, led by the young Muhinda, Rwamugwizi, and Kahitsi's few remaining adherents. Kahitsi had been ordered from place to place in Ankole, removed from authority, relieved of his cattle, and denied access to the royal court. His defeat in battle by Rwamugwizi led to Kahitsi's retirement to pastoral obscurity and put the final seal on the succession of Kahaya, opening the way for a new alignment of forces within the kingdom of Ankole.[30]

Setting in the Keystone: 1899–1901

With the elimination of Kahitsi as a political force and the end of the dynastic dispute, the rivalry for power within the Hinda ruling lineage was replaced by a new tension. The succession crisis and the inability of the Bahinda to unite behind a single leader and to consolidate the various Hima pastoral clans under Hinda leadership had allowed a dangerous growth in the power of the British protectors and those most willing to work with them. Despite Britain's preoccupation elsewhere and consequent slowness in entering the Ankole arena, the apparent failure of Ankole's traditional rulers to recognize the threat from the Anglo-Ganda alliance proved disastrous to Ankole's independence. Whether recognition of the threat would have proved sufficient to provide the means for meeting that threat is uncertain and, indeed, unlikely. We might with strong reason contend that nothing Ankole's leaders could do would seriously inhibit the tide of imperial advance sweeping Uganda in the 1890s. Nonetheless, the failure of men such as Igumira and Kahitsi to perceive the threat to Hinda sovereignty and to act accordingly early in the struggle paved the way for the emergence of Mbaguta and those who perceived the "threat" in terms of comparative political advantage and not sovereignty or independence.

In 1895 there were no British residents in Ankole, and the

[30] Macallister to Commissioner, 27 February 1899, *ESA* A4/16; 10 and 20 July 1899, *ESA* A4/19; 10 and 20 August 1899, *ESA* A4/20; Katate, *Abagabe*, 2:1–11; Interviews A/2 Macwa, 25 July 1968, and A/7 Mugoha, 26 July 1968.

Baganda were settled in a border region with little or no
power at court or in state affairs. By 1899, a British civil
officer was established at the new headquarters at Mbarara
and was accompanied by Ganda functionaries and a company
of police. The royal court was established near Mbarara at
Kamukuzi, and Mbaguta became the constant agent of each
party in its dealings with the other. His position as liaison
gave him power beyond that of any previous court official
and led to conflict with other political leaders who still retained independent power in the kingdom.

Igumira retained his power as acknowledged leader of the
Hinda party. These pastoral clansmen who for centuries had
determined the political life of the kingdom were unprepared
to reckon with the new forces unleashed by the colonial penetration. Their notions of government were in conflict with
the needs of a colonial superstructure, and they failed to
change their pastoral lifestyles to meet the new demands. The
problems created by systematic administration and regular
taxation, such as the need to settle in one place, acquire literacy and a new regard for punctuality and "modern" values
were difficult even for the younger men. An alliance between
the old guard and the alien forces was quite impossible.

It was Mbaguta, and to a lesser extent the youth, Kahaya,
who were best suited to their new roles as colonial collaborators. Kahaya's suitability lay primarily in his youth and
his weakness. In 1899, he was 19 years old, and although he
had been Mugabe for at least two years, he had been under the
tutelage of his regents, Igumira, and Kahitsi, until "quite recently."[31] One British visitor described him as "an overfed
and fat youth with a dull unintelligent face." All agree that he
was under the domination of his counselors and that "his
Katikiro [Mbaguta] is the real ruler of the country."[32] At
least, it is clear that Mbaguta was the real ruler of the king.
The country was another matter.

Mbaguta's suitability as collaborator was far more impres-

[31] Macallister to Commissioner, 10 July 1899, *ESA* A4/19.
[32] A. Cook, Journal letter of 3 December 1899, *C[hurch] M[issionary]
S[ociety]* G3/A7/02. Cf. A. Tucker, "A Missionary Journey Through Nkole,"
in *CMS* G3/A7/02.

sive than Kahaya's passive qualifications. A man of keen mind
and powerful personality, he has become legendary as a be-
nevolent tyrant, a man who treated even the Hinda princes
like Iru servants and freely caned those whom he felt most
needed disciplining. His youth and attendant social flexibility
also must have allowed him some latitude denied older men
of strength such as Igumira and Kahitsi. He was only 31 in
1899.[33]

But Mbaguta's major asset was his early experience with
the Baganda. His fluency in Luganda and his familiarity with
Ganda custom had made him a thoroughgoing Ganda-phile.
According to the Anglican bishop, he had:

> discarded to a large extent the dress or rather the undress
> of the Bahuma and generally appears clad like a
> Muganda. His household is arranged after the fashion of
> the Baganda and so far as instruction in Christianity
> would improve his standing in the world he would I be-
> lieve accept it.[34]

He showed the way in these matters and brought the Mugabe
to the acceptance of Christianity. He was baptized as an Anglican with the Mugabe in December 1902, and confirmed by
the Bishop of Uganda the following October.[35]

Mbaguta's ability to deal with the British and Baganda had
led to his establishment as a major court official. In 1899,
however, he controlled only the small area of Ngarama in
Isingiro county and could not use control of cattle or territory
to build up a personal following. Only his title as Enganzi to
Kahaya and his role as liaison to the newly established British
resident made him the likely leader of the royal party of collaboration. In place of a traditional following, Mbaguta made

[33] Interviews A/1 Katate, 24 July 1968; A/5 Muramba, 27 July 1968; A/4
Kirindi, 30 July 1968; and A/9 Kamugungunu, 2 August 1968.

[34] Tucker, "Missionary Journey," p. 23, *CMS* G3/A7/02.

[35] M.M.L. Pirouet, "The Expansion of the Church of Uganda," doctoral
diss., University of East Africa, 1968, pp. 229–230, and A. Tucker, *Eighteen
Years in Uganda and East Africa*, 2 vols. (London: Edward Arnold, 1908),
2:230–232.

every effort to ingratiate himself with the European officials and missionaries in an attempt to attach them as supporters to his party.[36]

Still, Mbaguta was in an excellent position to make himself the "arch-collaborator" of the Ankole regime, the keystone of the local colonial rule. He became the nexus between the traditional political system and the external influences that were pressing in upon it. As Enganzi, Mbaguta emerged as the chief intermediary between the royal court and the resident British and Ganda officials in Ankole. From this position he assumed leadership in the creation and direction of those policies such as taxation and road building that were the conditions of Ankole's growing subordination to imperial overrule. This, of course, exposed him to grave risks of unpopularity. Yet, as Kahaya's closest commoner official, he could act as colonial innovator while retaining the vital semblance of legitimacy that the cloak of traditional royal authority lent him.

Moreover, Mbaguta's commoner status enabled him to exercise the real rulership of the country without threatening to assume royal prerogative and jeopardize Kahaya's titular sovereignty. As a Mushambo, he could never be a candidate for royal honors. Instead, he became Ankole's "great commoner," and from that position he dominated the political stage for over four decades. But, first, he had to parlay his position of leverage into a position of power by means of an alliance and collaboration with the Anglo-Ganda overlords. He had to use this alliance to undermine and eliminate his rivals, establish and extend his independent power base. At this game of politics, Mbaguta proved extremely adept.

Mbaguta's chief rival for political leadership of Ankole was the powerful Hinda prince, Igumira. Initially, Igumira, as a county chief and member of the royal family, commanded far more respect and authority than the upstart Enganzi. But he proved incapable of coping with the new forces created by collaboration. First, he tried to remove Mbaguta from his

[36] Katate, *Abagabe*, 2:5; Interview A/1 Katate, 24 July 1968; Pirouet, "Expansion of the Church," pp. 223–224; Karugire, *Mbaguta*, pp. 33–40.

crucial position as liaison by ordering all the chiefs to leave the capital at Kamukuzi and return to their home districts, an order that sent Mbaguta back to the remote Ngarama area. In his place, Igumira had appointed the Muhinda, Kijoma, as Enganzi and now insisted that his own followers carry Kahaya's messages to the Europeans. This ploy failed when the proposed visit to Ankole by the British Commissioner forced Kahaya to recall Mbaguta in order to escort the Commissioner to the capital from the Toro border. It appears that no one else could be prevailed upon to assume the awesome responsibility of dealing with so high an official of the Protectorate. The inflexibility of Igumira's position created by his own inability to command cooperation with the British without undermining his own authority proved decisive. Mbaguta was officially recognized as Enganzi by the visiting Commissioner, confirming Igumira's worst fears.[37]

With this defeat, the initiative passed from Igumira to Mbaguta. Igumira moved away from court and resumed his pastoral habits. Mbaguta quickly set out to use his influence to inflame the European officer, Macallister, against Igumira. Igumira in turn may have encouraged Kijoma, his closest supporter, to try to assassinate the Enganzi. The European point of view quickly came to reflect that of Mbaguta's faction. By March 1900 Macallister's suspicions of Igumira's party had reached the point at which he was considering the deportation of three prominent chiefs as a warning to the "reactionaries." This idea was generated by a rise in anti-European feeling among the Banyankole that followed the imposition of new taxes. Mbaguta was clearly identified with those taxes, and the resentment against them cannot be separated from fear of his growing power. Particular grievances, as elsewhere, operated to bring to consciousness the general discontent with changes in the political situation.[38]

In August 1900, Igumira made claim to an area belonging to Musinga, the independent ruler of Igara to the west of

[37] Katate, *Abagabe*, 2:5–12.
[38] Interviews A/1 Katate, 24 July 1968, and A/5 Murumba, 27 July 1968. Macallister to Special Commissioner, 26 March 1900, *ESA* A4/29.

Igumira's Shema county. Mbaguta took this occasion to support the claim of Musinga before R. R. Racey, the new Collector. With the new European official Mbaguta seems to have formed an alliance immediately. Racey at once planned to arrest and deport Igumira for his offense against Musinga. Igumira was arrested on 20 September and exiled to Kisumu, Kenya, ending all hope for the creation of an Ankole resistance movement under his leadership.[39]

Racey's request for permission for Igumira's deportation described him as the "ringleader of the party in opposition to Her Majesty's Government."[40] The Hinda party, once the only party in the Ankole state, had become a party in opposition, and through opposition to Mbaguta's party of collaboration had come to oppose Her Majesty's Government. It was a dangerous course.

Igumira's cattle and goods were seized and divided among his heirs, subchiefs, the government, Kahaya, and Mbaguta. Most important, his chieftaincy in Shema and parts of Kashari was given to Mbaguta as a reward for cooperation with the British authorities. Overnight Mbaguta became not only the leading member of the royal household, but the most powerful territorial chief in Ankole. The profits of collaboration for the collaborators and the loss to those who resisted the change of rule were amply demonstrated. The power of the new government was boldly asserted and the position of the new collaborationist regime consolidated in the Ankole heartland.[41]

Following Igumira's arrest, Kijoma, Igumira's kinsman and political associate, decided to flee British territory, whether for fear of reprisals by Mbaguta or simply out of distaste for the turn of events we do not know. In November 1900, Kijoma drove his cattle toward Karagwe in German East Africa. A party of police under Surur Effendi was sent to arrest him. A battle followed in which Surur Effendi was speared and 14 Banyankole were killed. Kijoma made good

[39] Racey to Special Commissioner, 1 September 1900, *ESA* A15/1.

[40] Racey to Deputy Commissioner, 28 September 1900, *ESA* A15/1.

[41] Racey to Special Commissioner, 2 October 1900, *ESA* A15/1.

his escape with his herds into German territory. Other supporters of Igumira had their cattle confiscated, and still others
went into voluntary exile. With Igumira and his followers in
exile or otherwise out of power, the path was clear to for-
malize the new system of rule.[42]

Discussion

Between 1899 and 1901 the British officers representing the
Uganda Protectorate and a handful of Baganda and Banyankole collaborators, led by the Enganzi Mbaguta, had achieved
a revolution in Ankole politics. The claim of the royal clan to
rule the country had been challenged by upstarts. The Hinda
leadership had been divested of much of their authority and
even exiled from their kingdom. A "great commoner" had
used his connections to assume vast governmental powers
never before possessed by a nonroyal official. This seizure of
power would be followed by the creation of a new regime.
By August 1901, a new Ankole kingdom under the titular
sovereignty of Mugabe Kahaya, the protection of the British
government, and the effective rule of Mbaguta and a new
class of collaborating chiefs was established.

This revolution in Ankole politics was the climax of a
decade-long crisis. Beginning with a series of natural and
political calamities that shook the foundations of the old regime, the succession crisis created a situation of sustained instability. It was this situation that permitted the peaceful, but
profound, penetration of new external influences, carried by
British and Ganda administrators and missionaries. The same
situation of sustained crisis allowed those members of Ankole
society who were willing and able to sacrifice traditional
habits and authority to restore stability and achieve new authority by means of collaboration.

The transformation of Ankole politics under the strain of
the crises of the 1890s resulted from, first, the failure of the

[42] Katate, *Abagabe*, 2:12–14 and 19–20; Racey to Special Commissioner, 14
and 16 November 1900, *ESA* A15/1; Interview A/36 Rutabindwa, 3 September 1968.

traditional leadership to mount a serious resistance in the face of the colonial impact, and second, the emergence of a second tier of leadership willing to make the necessary compromises. The failure of royal leadership—of the old ruling elite and especially the Bahinda—to recognize and cope with the new challenge to the sovereignty of their dynasty and the independence of their kingdom was an aspect of the structural weakness of the Ankole political system. The ruling elite's failure to respond forcefully to the challenge was evidenced by the tendency of individuals within that elite to compete with their fellows for the relative advantages of political prominence. Rather than submerge their differences in what might have become a "patriotic front" against external aggression and imperialism, in defense of sovereignty and independence, the Hinda leaders, especially Kahitsi and Igumira, became bogged down in local competition for the role of kingmaker or for the power behind the throne. Even in the showdown situation between Igumira and Mbaguta, the former was unable to compel the compliance of his supporters and allies and ultimately unwilling to put his cause to the test of arms, which would have required a call for the support of the Ankole masses. Rather than a trait of personality or an error of policy, these weaknesses were an endemic feature of Ankole's socially stratified and politically repressive society. The failure to perceive the challenge as a challenge to sovereignty and to respond to it by the creation of a mass resistance movement can best be understood as concommitants of the structure of Ankole politics and of Ankole's political elite in the 1890s.

The political career of Mbaguta, the "great commoner," can be understood in structural as opposed to personal psychological terms. His peculiar position as liaison or power broker between the traditional Ankole hierarchy and the imposed colonial system was crucial. The role of "interpreter" was monopolized by an individual who alone managed the political transactions between the two systems. This key role in the transitional political system I have labeled "arch-collaborator," emphasizing the singular nature of the position of power broker and intermediary. Not only was Mbaguta's previous experience unique due to his exposure to external influences prior to the onset of colonial contact, but his position within the social and political hierarchy singled him out as the best candidate for the position of arch-collaborator. His status as a high-ranking commoner, outside both the royal line and the Hinda clan, presented no threat to the sovereignty of the dynasty. As a Shambo pastoralist of chiefly rank, he was still able to command the allegiance of a considerable following within the tradtional system of status and clanship. Furthermore, whereas men of royalty had their sovereignty to lose, a commoner chief had only power to gain through collaboration with the imperial agents. Thus, the commoner origins and international connections of the arch-collaborator were central to the political structure of collaboration in Ankole.

CHAPTER VI

The Establishment of Collaboration

WELL before Kabarega was captured and Bunyoro resistance was ended, a new regime of collaboration was emerging behind the lines of battle. This regime was based on the creation of a body of chiefs who were able to command some popular respect and, at the same time, were willing to work with the invaders of Bunyoro in governing it as a conquered territory. In Toro, a regime headed by Kasagama emerged from the ambiguous clientage relationships of the 1890s into full-blown collaboration with British authority. In 1900, the signing of an agreement modeled on the Buganda Agreement of the same year formalized this collaboration. Similarly in Ankole, the establishment of a new regime of collaboration was recognized by the British, and the members of a new ruling group were rewarded and confirmed in power by formal agreement in 1901. The key to these agreements and to the nature of the new regimes was the emergence of a body of chiefs who established the new regimes and who became by that very process the new "Establishment" of their respective kingdoms.

Submission of the Nyoro Chiefs: 1895–1899

The defeat of Kabarega's forces in April 1895 by an enormous invasion army of Sudanese and Ganda troops under British command produced large-scale defections of Nyoro chiefs and their subchiefs.[1] The defections made possible the establishment of a new regime of collaborating Nyoro chiefs under British control. As men of chiefly rank and experience, the defecting chiefs retained an aura of legitimacy that would prove of great utility in the pacification of the country. Be-

[1] Cunningham to Commissioner, 17 July 1895, E[ntebbe] S[ecretariat] A[rchives], A4/2.

yond pacification, chiefs and important men of the old regime became the necessary local manpower for operating a "native state" in Bunyoro. The British quickly recognized the utility of submission of the chiefs for military pacification, but were relatively slow to erect a new edifice of collaboration based on the chiefs. However, various Nyoro chiefs who came forward to submit played an active part in producing conditions favorable to effective collaboration.

The first important chief to defect was Kabarega's general, the commander of the King's barusura, Rwabudongo. His surrender in Toro in 1895 and his willingness to "use his best offices with the various chiefs who remain[ed] hostile"[2] was the first step in establishing Nyoro collaboration. But Commissioner Berkeley was slow to perceive the value of Rwabudongo's offer to collaborate in pacification. Instead of returning him at once to Bunyoro, attempts were made to settle him and his followers under Kasagama in Toro. For a short while, Rwabudongo was appointed to the title of Mukwenda, an important county chieftaincy in Toro.[3] Following this he was called to Kampala, where he requested to be settled in Kyaka, Toro. Confusion regarding his status in Kyaka led to hostilities against Rwabudongo's followers, and by the end of 1895 the situation in Toro had made Rwabudongo's peaceful settlement there quite impossible.[4]

By October 1895, the value of Rwabudongo's cooperation in the settlement of Bunyoro had revealed itself to the British authorities. They briefly believed that Rwabudongo's previous position in Bunyoro was that of prime minister or Katikiro, but it was later understood that such a post did not exist in Bunyoro. Nonetheless, the exaggeration of his previous eminence was only slight, and the British did well in

[2] Berkeley to Ternan, 27 September 1895, *ESA* A5/1.

[3] J. P. Wilson to Jackson, 10 June 1895 (2), *ESA* A4/1. Cf. Interview B/14 Kamese, 27 October 1968.

[4] Berkeley to Ternan, 27 September 1895, *ESA* A5/1; Ashburnham to Commissioner, 15 and 29 December 1895, *ESA* A4/3. Virtually from his arrival, Rwabudongo was at odds with Kasagama over the confiscation of Rwabudongo's goods and women by the Toro monarch (e.g., J. Wilson to Commissioner, 10 June 1895, *ESA* A4/1; Berkeley to Ashburnham, 10 December 1895, *ESA* A5/1).

trying to employ so important a figure in their pacification efforts. Although still under instructions to settle in Kyaka, Rwabudongo was only to be settled there "subsequent to his carrying out certain instructions under the direction of the O[fficer]. C[ommanding]. Unyoro."[5] These instructions sent Rwabudongo to Masindi in order to use his influence with other Nyoro chiefs to get them to submit. The political potential of such cooperation was still not fully appreciated by the military mind of Protectorate officialdom. It was merely hoped that such cooperation might facilitate military occupation of the territory.[6]

The second breakthrough in the creation of a regime of collaboration came in July 1895. The major factor in producing the breakthrough and the enlarged opportunities for collaboration was Kabarega's attempt to establish a fifth column within the government of occupation. To do this, Byabacwezi, the county chief of Bugahya, was ordered by Kabarega to return to Bunyoro and work with the British with a mind to the king's eventual restoration.[7] It was a policy destined to backfire and create conditions for Kabarega's permanent exclusion from power.

Byabacwezi's submission in July was only the most important in a large number of capitulations by Nyoro chiefs at Hoima. Even Kabarega's stalwarts, Ireta and Kikukule, expressed interest in the possibility of submission at the time, and Kabarega himself sent to inquire the terms for his own surrender.[8] Nothing positive came of these other inquiries, but Byabacwezi seems to have found the terms offered him quite agreeable. From the time of his submission, Byabacwezi gradually became the most significant figure in the British-controlled regime.[9] He became the keystone of colonial administration, Bunyoro's arch-collaborator.

---

[5] G. Wilson to O. C. Toro, 2 October 1895, *ESA* A4/3.

[6] Berkeley to Ternan, 27 September 1895, *ESA* A5/1.

[7] J. Nyakatura, *Abakama Ba Bunyoro-Kitara* (St. Justin, P.Q., Canada: 1947), translated as *Anatomy of an African Kingdom*, G. N. Uzoigwe, ed. (New York: Anchor, 1973), p. 204.

[8] Cunningham to Commissioner, 17 and 30 July 1895, *ESA* A4/2.

[9] Interview B/1 Muganwa, 3 October 1968.

With two key men available for service under British direction, the elaboration of a regular native administration under
Nyoro chiefs awaited only the surrender of an adequate
number of subchiefs. After Kikukule and Muhenda were captured in January 1896, and released two months later, they
were settled as subchiefs under Rwabudongo in southern
Bunyoro in March 1896. Along with three others, Kikukule
and Muhenda were briefly recognized by the British as the
local authorities in Bugangaiza and Buyaga counties under
Rwabudongo's paramountcy.[10]

This chieftaincy hierarchy in southern Bunyoro was the
first instance of the creation of a semblance of "traditional"
political authority under British overrule in Bunyoro. As
such, it deserves some attention despite its short duration.
The hierarchy centered on the position of Rwabudongo as the
top territorial chief. This was curious because Rwabudongo,
as general of the barusura, had not held territorial authority
under Kabarega. He was outside the administrative hierarchy,
responsible for military affairs, and probably the leader of a
"military" faction at court. This faction, if it can be called
that, represented the interests of those captains of barusura
companies who were directly appointed by Kabarega and
provided a counterweight to the authority of the administrative or territorial chiefs during the period of Kabarega's consolidation of power.[11] We should not imagine that the lines
between military and territorial chiefs were completely distinct. On the contrary, various territorial chiefs, including
Byabacwezi, were also captains of their own barusura units.
Moreover, the appointment of a military figure to an administrative post over territory was not without precedent.
For instance, both Kikukule and Ireta had parlayed their military appointments into chiefly titles under Kabarega.
Nonetheless, the creation of a major territorial chieftaincy
under Rwabudongo as superior to several subchiefs was a
major gain for the military interest vis-à-vis the territorial

[10] Pulteney to Commissioner, 23 March 1896, *ESA* A4/4.
[11] Cf. G. Uzoigwe, "Kabarega and the Making of a New Kitara," *Tarikh*
3, 2(1970): 9–11.

chiefs. More important, if the old factional rivalry between military and administrative chiefs could be transposed from Kabarega's regime to a new regime under British control, it would add an important advantage to future collaboration. There was little time to see if such a competition would aid collaboration, as the situation in southern Bunyoro was soon to be radically altered.

In April 1896, the Ganda Catholics and the Toro Kingdom were confirmed in possession of the southern portions of Bunyoro by the Protectorate government. All of the former Kitara Empire that lay south of the Kafu and Ngusi rivers, including the cradleland of the kingdom, the Mubende region, were annexed to either the Toro Kingdom or opened for occupation and administration by Ganda chiefs of the Catholic faith and party. The creation of these "lost counties" rooted up the first experiment in collaboration. Rwabudongo was told to remove his followers from Kyaka and the south[12] and was settled at Kitanwa, where he was to administer the northwesternmost province of Bugungu, including Bugoma and Kibero along the eastern shore of Lake Albert.[13]

The settlement of Byabacwezi at Hoima and Rwabudongo at Kitanwa mark the beginnings of a chiefly administration of northern Bunyoro under British sponsorship. These two men provided the basic ingredient of legitimacy for a new regime and enabled other chiefs to emerge as co-collaborators. At this time, an old and infirm subchief named Bikamba was elevated to the chieftaincy at Masindi. He had been a minor chief under Kabarega and hence could claim the loyalties of the Banyoro of this region, but he himself was suspected from the outset of divided loyalties.[14] It might be remarked that these first three chiefs were all from the agricultural class. They were neither members of the royal clan nor of the Huma pastoral group, who had dominated the chiefly hierarchy before Kabarega's reign.

[12] Ashburnham to Commissioner, 4 April 1896; Pulteney to Commissioner, 19 May 1896; Sitwell to Commissioner, 27 May 1896, *ESA* A4/5.

[13] Pulteney to Commissioner, 25 June 1896, *ESA* A4/5.

[14] See Pulteney to Commissioner, 1 July 1896, *ESA* A4/5; Interview B/6 Nyakatura, 18 October 1968.

In September 1896, the first Mubito was appointed to a major chieftaincy. Rejumba was the son of Prince Rionga, who had opposed Kabarega's succession as Mukama of Bunyoro and had remained in exile and opposition during Kabarega's long reign. So although Rejumba was of Kabarega's Bito clan, he inherited a tradition of opposition to the monarch and of collaboration with alien opponents of Bunyoro dating back to the days of Sir Samuel Baker and the "Egyptian menace."[15] Rejumba was settled at Fowiera in Chope (Kibanda) district and was publicly proclaimed as chief there under protection of the British authorities in October 1896.[16]

At the same time as Rejumba's appointment, a chief called "Mugemma" was proclaimed over the territory between Rejumba's Fowiera district and the fort at Pajao near Murchison Falls. Mugema was a title of office, and no mention has been found of the titleholder's identity in the colonial records or among the oral testimony collected. The appointment of "Mugemma" completed the partition of Bunyoro on paper. It permitted a rough sketch map of the new province of Bunyoro to include the boundaries of five numbered counties and a list of the respective county chiefs as follows:[17]

County #1 (Kibanda) under Rejumba
County #2 (Kihukya) under "Mugemma"
County #3 (Bugungu) under Rwabudongo
County #4 (Bugahya) under Byabacwezi
County #5 (Busindi) under Bikamba

By naming five equal partners in the government of the kingdom, directly under a European official, the British sowed the seed of strenuous competition among the chiefs for primacy. Rivalry surfaced in February 1897. At that time, the

[15] A. R. Dunbar, *A History of Bunyoro-Kitara* (Nairobi: East African Institute of Social Research, 1965), pp. 38–49, 53–62, 70–71, and 92; Interview B/17 Labwoni, 22 October 1968.

[16] Pulteney to Ternan, 7 September 1896, and Ternan to Berkeley, 27 November 1896, *ESA* A4/6.

[17] Ternan to Berkeley, 27 November 1896, *ESA* A4/6.

British removed Rwabudongo from Bugungu and sent him to Kampala. Accusations against his loyalty to the new overlords were raised by Byabacwezi, Rejumba, and a subchief named Amara. Whatever the substance behind the accusations, competition, especially between Rwabudongo and Byabacwezi, had surfaced for the first time. The rivalry would persist until Rwabudongo's death in 1900. The actual charge against Rwabudongo was his "failure to administer" the distant western district over which he was placed. In fact, he had refused to settle in his own county and had instead remained in the area of the capital.[18] The importance of being close to the capital, where competition for office, honors, and power was keenest, was the cause of Rwabudongo's "failure to administer" remote Bugungu. As if to confirm this, his accuser, Amara, was named to replace him as chief of Bugungu. Amara remained only until May 1897, when he died of poisoning, the victim of Kabarega's "magic."

When Major Thruston returned to Bunyoro from his leave in June 1897, he was able to analyze the imperfections of the Bunyoro regime from an informed yet fresh perspective. In a letter to the Commissioner in Kampala, employing a style imitative of Machiavelli's The Prince, Thruston summed up why he considered that the Bunyoro administration was "leading to exercise of authority to the detriment of life and property."[19] The first reason for this was that government was by force alone, the population being "at heart hostile to the Administration." This is a considerable change from Thruston's earlier view that the chiefs were the main obstacle to pacification while the peasantry were anxious for peace.[20] It is to Thruston's credit that he was able to view the situation afresh and abandon his earlier theory, which accounted for resistance solely in conspiratorial terms and saw the peasantry as passive and compliant. Although the peasantry were by no means up in arms against the occupation, his view of them as hostile "at heart" seems justified by later events. The problem

[18] Pulteney to Commissioner, 1 February 1897, ESA A4/7.
[19] Thruston to Commissioner, 30 June 1897, ESA A4/8.
[20] Thruston to Commissioner, 17 March 1894, ESA A2/4.

to alien administration presented by popular hostility was
further aggravated by the fact that Kabarega remained at large
and hostile, and although in exile, he was actively "stirring
the people to sedition."[21]

According to Thruston's analysis, the second reason for
governmental failure was the nature of the chiefly administration itself. Of the five chiefs who governed under Thruston's
guidance, "one only is of the number of the original Great
Chiefs; two are parvenues, two are descendants of hereditary
enemies of Kabarega. These last four have little or no influence in the provinces, and one of them is probably in active
league with Kabarega."[22] The collaboration was failing because the collaborators were without credibility among the
people in the face of Kabarega's continuing royal resistance.
So although military force was sufficient to prevent invasion
and reduce rebellious actions, it was insufficient to provide effective government. Moreover, Thruston went on:[23]

> The collapse of the original primitive but strong feudal
> form of government led to the absence of any system of
> administration that can provide for law and order and
> civil and criminal jurisdiction.

The chiefly administration set up during the previous year
had not filled the breach made by the collapse of Kabarega's
regime. Thus, Thruston concluded, "The country at present
can hardly be said to be under a government at all; it is rather
under a military occupation or at most a weak military government."[24] And time alone was no solution to the problem
of weak government.

The solution, however, Thruston believed, was not difficult. In a brief essay on the principles of ruling native states
under protection, Thruston outlined his plan. Kabarega was
not to be reinstated, but rather his son should be placed on the
throne under a regency. Loyalty, Thruston argued, was not
to a person but to the throne's occupant of royal blood, and if
there was to be development in Bunyoro and not just security

---

[21] Thruston to Commissioner, 30 June 1897, *ESA* A4/8.
[22] Ibid.   [23] Ibid.   [24] Ibid.

for Buganda's frontiers, such loyalty must be promoted. The development of a collaborating regime, he continued, required the creation of a royal figurehead to ensure the allegiance of the commoner class.[25]

The idea of a regency was not new in Uganda, but its application to Bunyoro was different and precedent-setting. The Ankole succession crisis of 1895–1897 had led to a regency of sorts. But in reality that regency was a product of the temporary balance of power between traditional authorities and owed little or nothing to British designs for successful overrule. In Bunyoro, the notion of regency was invoked by the British with the distinct purpose of using the regents during the Mukama's minority as pliable tools. It would be applied during the minority of kings and chiefs in various areas for some time to come.

Thruston's idea was not put into effect in Bunyoro until March 1898. Fresh rumors that Kabarega had died reached Kampala, where George Wilson, the acting Commissioner, took them "to be more authentic than those previously received." With this in mind and considering the "steadying influence" that the presence of a Bito occupant of the Nyoro throne would have, Wilson decided to place Kabarega's ten-year-old son, Kitahimbwa, on the throne.[26] Kitahimbwa had been captured several years earlier and sent to Kampala to be educated. His brief Christian education and his youth no doubt led the colonial officials to promote his cause as a potentially pliable instrument. He arrived in Masindi on 23 March and was installed as Mukama on 3 April 1898, in a ceremony "as impressive as the circumstances" would permit.[27]

At the same time, a general amnesty for those who had followed Kabarega was issued. The amnesty and the appointment of a successor to Kabarega (the British still believing the

[25] Ibid.

[26] G. Wilson to Salisbury, 16 March 1898, P[arliamentary] P[apers], C8941, and Interview B/39 Bikundi, 16 November 1968.

[27] Fowler to Commissioner, 16 March 1898, and Bagnall to Commissioner, 23 March and 3 April 1898, *ESA* A4/10.

rumors of his demise) was expected to effect a complete change "in the political aspect of affairs in Unyoro."[28] To assist in this change, Wilson issued instructions for the creation of a chiefly regime. The proclamation of the juvenile Kitahimbwa as sovereign necessitated the establishment of a three-man council of regency, which was to be appointed by Her Majesty's Government. This council of regency, acting for the monarch, would then appoint a Katikiro or prime minister and the first ranking chiefs of the country. The Katakiro and great chiefs, acting as a governing council, would be responsible for the appointment of lesser grades of chiefs to fill out the chiefly hierarchy and administer the territory. Wilson's instructions began the transplanting to Bunyoro of the ideas of chiefly hierarchy and executive authority which the British understood and which drew its outlines, terminology, and inspiration from a Ganda model of government.

A governing council of six men was selected, five of whom were the county chiefs of Bunyoro's five counties. Rejumba was temporarily appointed as Katakiro in addition to his post as chief of Fowiera (Kibanda). This must have been a disappointment to Byabacwezi, whom the British administration thought "would be equally good if not better," were it not for a feud into which he had entered with the heirs of Amara, the Bugungu chief.[29] But this council and Katikiro never fully operated and soon collapsed in the face of the problems that remained unsolved.

The first problem, of course, was that Kabarega would not so conveniently remove himself by dying and, what was

---

[28] G. Wilson to Fowler, 5 March 1898, ESA A5/4.

[29] G. Wilson to Fowler, 5 March 1898, ESA A5/4, and Dugmore, Report, n.d. #228, Port Alice, ESA A4/10. The council included the following chiefs: Rejumba (Kibanda county); Byabacwezi (Bugahya county); Mgenji (Kihukya county), a Teman appointment with no hereditary claim; Msoga (Bugungu county), a nephew of Amara, ruling under the regency of Kiiza, a subchief; Kavalli (Busindi county), a son of Bikamba ruling under the regency of Katalikawe, a subchief (per Interview B/21 Munubi, 31 October 1968); and Katarega (? county), a refugee from Ganda-occupied Bunyoro living in Rejumba's district.

worse, he continued his resistance.[30] Second, Rejumba apparently failed to inspire the support required to run the council. The whole apparatus was dependent on a strong and capable manager as Katikiro. Attempts to secure a Katikiro who could run a regime of collaboration and the conflicting attempts of political rivals to secure the position became the main domestic obstacle to the functioning of the new regime. When Kitahimbwa's installation was first proposed, it was suggested that "a trustworthy Muganda chief might be sent . . . to look after him, and act as 'Katikiro.' "[31] This suggestion was repeated despite growing hostility to Ganda influence in Bunyoro. Such an expedient might well have settled the rivalry engendered by conflict over the important post, but it was another three years before a similar plan was adopted. In the interim, the position of Katikiro and with it the role of "great commoner" remained a bone of contention among the leading chiefs.

After his installation, Kitahimbwa was sent back to Kampala for further education and was reinstalled later in 1898.[32] The regents had not appointed a new Katikiro, and control of the council of regency became the focus of competition. In March 1899, Rwabudongo had returned to the political arena in Bunyoro, and the Regency council was composed of himself, Byabacwezi, and an old man approaching senility named Matabere.[33] The stage was thus set for the working out of the rivalry between the only two leaders whose power dated from the old regime.

Byabacwezi had emerged as the leader of the "progressive" party. He was chief of the largest and most populous county and had the largest personal following. In November 1895, Byabacwezi invited the first Protestant missionaries to establish a mission in Bunyoro, and by 1899 he was the undisputed

[30] The first doubts as to his death appear in the British sources in June 1898. Cf. Berkeley to Salisbury, 13 June 1898, *PP* C9123.

[31] Bagnall to Commissioner, 23 March 1898, *ESA* A4/10, and Evatt to Commissioner, 21 November and 2 December 1899, *ESA* A4/22.

[32] Berkeley to Price, 4 September 1898, *ESA* A5/4.

[33] Enclosure in Evatt to Acting Commissioner, 17 March 1899, *ESA* A4/16, and Evatt to Acting Commissioner, 21 May 1899, *ESA* A4/17.

"pillar" of the Anglican Church in Bunyoro.[34] This assured him of Church Missionary Society support and the aid of the Ganda Christians who came to Bunyoro in the wake of the Anglo-Ganda invasions. Such men as Mika Fataki, a Musoga, educated and baptized in Buganda, and Daudi Mbabi, a baptized Mubito from Busongora, were men who settled in Bunyoro and began contributing to the ascendancy of Ganda-style government. They became the rising stars of Byabacwezi's faction.[35] However, because of a certain irresoluteness of character and failings of Christian virtue with regard to drink and women, Byabacwezi himself was viewed as weak and ineffectual by the colonial administrators, who were loathe to honor him with the title of Katikiro.[36]

Byabacwezi's rival, Rwabudongo, was an older man and was more attached to Nyoro tradition than the chief of Bugahya. This attachment showed up in his hostility to the missionary influence, which, of course, was compounded by the CMS support for his rival. Rwabudongo received some recognition for being one of the first chiefs to move into active collaboration with the British, but was considered "an exceedingly cunning and clever man."[37] This reputation for cunning was enhanced by his earlier lackluster performance as chief of Bugungu, which led to suspicion of his playing a double game. His supposed hostility to the Protestant mission also counted against him. Nonetheless, the British decided to name him as provisional Katikiro in June 1899.[38]

What were the roots of the rivalry between these two chiefs? The antagonism between Byabacwezi and Rwabudongo probably "dated from the time when Kabarega had quarreled with the traditional chiefs and given precedence to the wishes of the *barusura*."[39] The factional antipathy was in-

[34] M.M.L. Pirouet, "The Expansion of the Church of Uganda," doctoral diss., University of East Africa, 1968, pp. 133–145.

[35] Interviews B/30 Rukayi and Fataki, 11 November 1968, and B/45 Mbabi-Katana, 25 April 1969. Also, S. Mbabi-Katana, "Uganda's Grand Old Man," *Uganda Herald*, 25 July 1953, p. 5.

[36] G. Wilson to Johnston, 6 September 1900, *ESA* A12/1.

[37] Ibid.

[38] Evatt to Commissioner, 14 June 1899, *ESA* A4/18.

[39] Pirouet, "Expansion of the Church," p. 141.

tensified by the presence of both leaders at the district capital of Masindi, where they resorted to mutual recriminations in an effort to curry favor with the British officers.[40] Opposition to Rwabudongo's candidacy was led by the Protestant mission, who championed Byabacwezi as the early convert and pillar of the Church. The British officer, Colonel Evatt, correctly interpreted Rwabudongo's resistance to mission activity in terms of the mission's unguarded support for his rival. Evatt also blamed his "failure" to realize "that the CMS is a religious body devoid, in principle or desire, of political or administrative influence."[41] Evatt's conception of the role of the CMS is far more remarkable than Rwabudongo's, considering the part played by the mission in promoting the political careers of its adherents throughout western Uganda.[42]

With Rwabudongo's appointment the rivalry came to a head. Byabacwezi, rancourous at losing the high post and always somewhat hostile to the child-king, Kitahimbwa, began to show his disdain for the new arrangements by the symbolic usurpation of royal prerogatives. For instance, he began insisting on being greeted by the term formerly reserved for the reigning Mukama. This act of disrespect to royal privilege seems to have poisoned the relations between the Bito dynasty and Byabacwezi's progeny down to the present.[43] Rwabudongo, of course, opposed Byabacwezi's arrogation of royal prerogative, and hostility remained the dominant theme in their relations. To check usurpation of authority by either leader, the British appointed a Regency Council including both of them as co-regents, first with the Bito chief, Re-

[40] Evatt to Commissioner, 21 May 1899, ESA A4/17. Cf. A. B. Fisher, "Diaries," entries for May–June 1899 (microfilm, Makerere University Library, Kampala).

[41] Evatt to Commissioner, 14 June 1899, ESA A4/18.

[42] Dr. Pirouet's thesis is replete with evidence of the intimate connections between the missionary effort and political and administrative life. "Expansion of the Church," pp. 59–62, 86, 150–153, and 254.

[43] Ibid., pp. 140–141; My own interview with Byabacwezi's son (B/36 Jawe, 14 November 1968) seems to have failed because of Mr. Jawe's suspicions regarding historians' hostilities to his family. He was persuaded to talk at all only by my insistence that I was studying the chiefs particularly rather than dynastic history. Cf. Interview B/11 Kakooko, 22 October 1968.

jumba, and later with Matabere as the third partner. These arrangements and the rivalry that necessitated them ended abruptly with Rwabudongo's death in December 1900.[44] Byabacwezi became the arch-collaborator without rival by default.

During this time Kitahimbwa had retained a tenuous hold on his title of Mukama, being in constant trouble with the administration and the missions. His youth was certainly an obstacle to his enjoying the respect of either his own people or the alien kingmakers. Moreover, his attachments to what were seen as traditional Huma laxity—drinking and dancing—and his association with a "conservative" group of young Huma men devoted to such "laxity" set the forces of both church and administration against him. Kitahimbwa was finally removed in 1902 and succeeded by his older brother, Andereya Bisereko Duhaga II, who by temperament and deep Christian faith was more acceptable to the mission, Byabacwezi, and the colonial authorities.[45]

Bit by bit a framework for administration had been built up. Starting from a sketchmap and five chiefs, a regime with a titular monarch, a "great commoner," and a hierarchy of chiefs had been developed through the collaboration of those chiefs with their imperial overlords. In 1901, the arrangements were extended and regularized by further efforts to enhance the attractiveness of collaboration and indirect rule.

The Bunyoro Arrangement of 1901

In July 1901, the post of Katikiro was still vacant and the system of chieftaincy remained unsettled. The British administration, guided by George Wilson, finally had recourse to a

[44] G. Wilson to Johnston, 6 September 1900, *ESA* A12/1. Cf. Interview B/14 Kamese, 27 October 1968, and *Bunyoro Church Magazine, 1931–1941*, cyclostated selections, Father A.B.T. Byaruhanga-Akiiki, trans., p. 3.

[45] Spires to Johnston, 28 March 1900, *ESA* A4/27; Johnston to Spires, 13 April 1900, *ESA* A5/9; Pirouet, "Expansion of the Church," p. 158; Interviews B/39 Bikundi, 16 November 1968, and B/34 Princess Alexandria, 11 November 1968. Cf. Tomkins to Commissioner, 16 October 1902, *ESA* A12/2.

plan originally suggested in 1898. It was decided to bring in Jemusi (James) Miti, a Muganda of chiefly rank, to organize the government of Bunyoro on the Ganda model. Miti had previously served in Bunyoro as an interpreter and returned to Bunyoro only under pressure from the Protectorate Government and at the express request of Kitahimbwa and his chiefs.[46]

By this time, the kingdoms of Buganda and Toro had signed agreements that fixed the rights and responsibilities of the chiefs. Ankole would follow suit in August 1901. Bunyoro, however, was a different case. First of all, it was a conquered province. The Mukama ruled "by courtesy" of the Protectorate government, and the chiefs were apprised of "the essential points of difference between themselves as Chiefs of [B]Unyoro and the Chiefs of [B]Uganda,"[47] who ruled by agreement. Second, Bunyoro was far behind its southern neighbors in matters of literacy and religion, which were the prerequisites to efficiency "from an administrative point of view."[48] Thus, the decisions to introduce Miti as a tutor in governmental practice and to establish a new system of chieftaincy on the Ganda model were not tied to an agreement but rested on administrative fiat and the petition of the Bunyoro regime of collaboration for assistance. Within a month of Miti's arrival, he and the Nyoro chiefs, assisted by the CMS missionary, A. B. Lloyd, were able to submit a "Proposed System of Chieftaincy in [B]Unyoro." The proposal included a chart showing ten independent county chiefs with subchiefs for each of them. Both chiefs and subchiefs bore Ganda titles of office. No Katikiro was named and, according to Miti's biographer, 13 Baganda were appointed at various levels.[49]

[46] P. M. K. Lwanga, *Obulemu Bw'Omutaka J. K. Miti Kabazzi* (Kampala: Friends Press, n.d.), pp. 1–11. Cf. G. Wilson to Jackson, 14 August 1901, *ESA* A12/1.

[47] G. Wilson to Johnston, 6 September 1900, *ESA* A12/1.

[48] G. Wilson, Report on Unyoro to Sir Harry Johnston, 1901, pp. 15–16, *ESA* A12/1.

[49] G. Wilson to Jackson, 14 August 1901, and Enclosure in same, *ESA* A12/1. CF. Lwanga, *Miti*, pp. 12–13, who omits two county chiefs from his list.

It is extremely difficult to expose the inner workings of the decision-making process in selecting the chiefs. Interviews and Nyoro traditional histories are either silent or credit only the Mukama according to the formula that all decisions flow from the monarch. It appears that the new arrangements were jointly initiated by the leading Nyoro chiefs, who had asked for Miti's guidance. They seem to have been anxious to secure recognition of the Mukama and of their own titles from the Commissioner and had devised a "practical delimitation" of their territories quite "spontaneously." At the same time, although it appears that the chiefs were largely self-selected, the role of Miti in "giving a definite shape to the new system" and the role of Lloyd in translating and tabulating may well have had an impact on the selection in favor of Ganda and Christian chiefs. Certainly, the knowledge that the proposal would go to Wilson, acting for the administration, was guaranteed to ensure some level of education and efficiency as criteria that the leading chiefs, especially Byabacwezi, would require of their peers.

Of the ten county chiefs named in the proposals of 1901 (see Table 6-1) only one, Paulo Byabacwezi, ruled under both

Table 6-1
Proposed County Chiefs, Bunyoro, 1901

Name	Title	County	Background
Paulo Byabacwezi	Mukwenda	Bugahya	A hereditary county chief and captain of barusura. Submitted 1895. Baptized Protestant.
Antoni Kirube	Kangao	Kibanda	A thatcher from Buganda, possibly brought by Miti. By his name a Roman Catholic. Little known.
Komwiswa	Mugema	Chope (?)	A Mubito; son of Rionga and brother to Rejumba. A pagan with five Protestant sub-

Name	Title	County	Background
			chiefs. Omitted by Lwanga, as he probably never took office.
Mika Fataki	Sekibobo	Kihukya	A Musoga captive educated in Buganda and then sold to Bunyoro, where he became a murusura under Rwabudongo. Baptized Protestant.
Basigala	Kimbugwe	Buruli (?)	A pagan Munyoro, little known and illiterate.
Katalikawe	Kitunzi	Busindi	A murusura and sub-chief under Bikamba, whom he succeeded in 1897–1898, de facto.
Jemusi Miti	Kaigo	Bujenje	A Protestant Muganda of chiefly rank. Worked as an interpreter in Bunyoro and was sent to organize administration.
Daudi Mbabi	Katambala	Buruli	A Musongora captured by Nyoro army and sold to Buganda. Educated and baptized Protestant in 1893. Treasurer to Kitahimbwa in 1893 and leading Ganda-phile.
Tibansamba	Kaima	Bugungu	A Musora murusura under Kabarega; settled in Bugungu prior to his appointment.
Kiiza	Pokino	Bugungu	Little known; probably the Mugungu regent to Msoga, Amara's nephew and heir. Omitted by Lwanga and probably never confirmed.

Kabarega and the new regime. In fact, only three others were, properly speaking, Banyoro (Basigala, Komwiswa, and Katalikawe),[50] and only one of the three had served Kabarega—Katalikawe was a minor chief and murusura. At the risk of falsely emphasizing generational differences, it would seem necessary to account for Byabacwezi's successful accomodation to the new regime in terms of his relative youth and brief tenure as Kabarega's chief. Byabacwezi's father had ruled Bugahya until the first years of the 1890s, and Byabacwezi had inherited his title only shortly before the invasions of Bunyoro began. So although he had some experience and the legitimacy of inherited titles, Byabacwezi was not a long-time companion and supporter of the ousted monarch, as was Rwabudongo, for instance.

Byabacwezi's "aristocratic" legitimacy was complemented by his status as a "munyoro." Here we use the word in its original meaning: a free man not born to a pastoral clan. Byabacwezi's father was not a Muhuma, although his mother was, and he was raised in something of a pastoral tradition. He was thus able to "represent" both important classes of Nyoro society, being simultaneously an aristocrat and "commoner" chief. Add to his status his vast wealth in land and followers inherited from his father and Byabacwezi stands out as ideal candidate for "great commoner." His ready acceptance of Christianity and Protestant denomination, whether the result of temperament, political ambition, or divine grace, completed the catalogue of his qualifications for the role of arch-collaborator.[51]

Perhaps the most notable discontinuity in chieftaincies was the disappearance of Rejumba's name from the charts of office holders. Rejumba had been a member of the Regency Council and chief of Chope district. He was a Mubito who had volun-

---

[50] Excluding Kiiza, who was a native of the semiautonomous and culturally divergent district of Bugungu.

[51] He is invariably described by Nyoro informants as the most powerful and important chief under Duhaga II. Cf. Interviews B/1, B/11, and B/36. Occasionally he is named as Katikiro (Interview B/7), but in fact he never held that title.

teered to collaborate against Kabarega. It appears that the difficulties in governing the ethnic minority area of Chope had proven quite unmanageable, and Rejumba had retired. He was replaced in the proposal by his brother, Komwiswa.[52] Komwiswa was the only Bito chief named in the proposal, and it appears that he was never confirmed in office.[53] The claim to office that the Babito held by right of their kinship to the monarch ceased being a factor in chiefly recruitment. Replacing Komwiswa in Chope was Daudi Mbabi, a Musongora named as chief of Foweira in the proposal, who found governing the Bachope fraught with danger. Conflict and armed resistance in Chope led to Mbabi's removal and almost cost him his life.[54]

In addition to the absence of Bito chiefs, the proposal contained no chiefs of the Banyonza clan. The Banyonza, as Kabarega's maternal uncles, had vested interest in the support of his reign. Either as reward for this support or as insurance against insubordination, several chieftaincies, particularly in southern Bunyoro, had become the possession of Myonza relations of Kabarega. These chiefs, as brothers of Kabarega's official Queen Mother (Ninyamukama), steadfastly supported Kabarega's resistance.[55] The loss of the former southern counties of Kyaka, Mwenge, and Toro to the new Toro kingdom under Kasagama and the consequent expropriation and expulsion of the Nyonza chiefs may have added to their determination to resist. Their resistance meant that no Munyonza would be named chief under British overrule for several decades.

Who, then, became the county chiefs—the political elite— of the new regime? It is clearly difficult to make firm gen-

[52] Interview B/17 Labwoni, 28 October 1968.

[53] It appears that neither Komwiswa nor Kiiza of Bugungu were confirmed by Wilson. Bagge to Commissioner, 16 May 1902, ESA A12/2, and Interview B/6 Nyakatura, 18 October 1968.

[54] Interviews B/6 Nyakatura, 18 October 1968; B/45 Mbabi-Katana, 25 April 1969. Cf. Bagge, Report on Unyoro District, December 1901, ESA A12/1.

[55] Interviews C/22 Kabaziba et al., 27 January 1969; C/23 Bitamazire, 27 January 1969.

eralizations from the ten or so names of the 1901 chiefs. Nonetheless, two relatively clear and distinct sources for the recruitment of chiefs seem to emerge from an examination of chiefly careers. The first source was the barusura leaders who had served as appointed military officers under Mukama Kabarega. Four chiefs—Byabacwezi, Fataki, Katalikawe, and Tibansamba—had at one time led barusura companies. The second category included those men of alien origin who had some experience of both Nyoro and Ganda political culture. This group consisted of Jemusi Miti, Daudi Mbabi, Mika Fataki, and Antoni Kirube. It should be noted that Fataki was unique in having "qualified" for recruitment by both criteria. Fataki was a Musoga by birth and on that basis a neutral in the struggle for supremacy between Buganda and Bunyoro. After a brief career in Buganda where he learned the use of firearms and the rudiments of Christian religion in the service of Apolo Kagwa, he moved to Bunyoro where he made his talents as a marksman available to the barusura unit of Rwabudongo.[56] Three chiefs are left out in this accounting—Komwiswa, Kiiza, and Basigala. However, this may be excused, as the first two appear never to have been confirmed in office and the latter was very shortly removed.

Of the chiefs with military credentials, Byabacwezi, the captain of the *ekibali* regiment, was also a territorial chief under Kabarega, whereas Katalikawe, after leaving his military duties, had become *mumyuka* (the title of the top-ranking subchief) under Bikamba in Busindi.[57] But it is their military experience and responsibilities that appear to have enabled these men to command both the respect of their underlings and of the British administration.

Why was Kabarega's military system a fertile ground for the development of collaborating chiefs? It appears that the attainment of status on the basis of personal achievement rather than ascription was good preparation for the achievement of appointive chiefly office under colonial overrule. Although

[56] Interview B/30 Rukayi and Fataki, 11 November 1968.
[57] Interview B/21 Munubi, 31 October 1968.

the criteria for appointment to leadership in Kabarega's barusura was different from those abilities required of colonial chiefs, both systems recognized and rewarded personal abilities and loyalty to a superordinate authority. This suggests why prior barusura leadership was linked to the achievement of chiefly office after 1901.

The second attribute of colonial chiefs, alien origin and cross-cultural experience, might equally have been put in terms of their experience of Christian religion, as all four of the "aliens" were baptized and educated Christians.[58] No doubt literacy, which could only be acquired through religious training, was an important criteria of recruitment to administrative posts. Still, the peculiar fact of a dual cultural background among the "alien" chiefs suited them especially well for the role of collaborators and political brokers between differing political traditions. The achievements of Jemusi Miti, Daudi Mbabi, and Mika Fataki during the first decade of the twentieth century as "Nyoro" chiefs attest to both their personal qualities of flexibility and leadership as well as to the importance of the role of cultural and political brokerage in the smooth functioning of the collaborating regime in Bunyoro.

Royal Collaboration in Toro

Until 1900, Toro had appeared to the British as a cockpit of chiefly rivalries and competition. Starting with a meager claim on one county of the old Kitara Empire, Kasagama had used British support and the chaos following in the wake of the war against Bunyoro to extend his claims. Mwenge, which had long threatened to establish complete independence, was reduced to subordination. The southern chieftaincies in Busongora and Kitagwenda were incorporated after repeated incidents of resistance. Claims to Bwamba in the far west and Kyaka and Nyakabimba in the east were success-

[58] Pirouet notes a tendency for ex-barusura to become Christian catechists, again linking the categories. Cf. "Expansion of the Church," pp. 132–133 and 152.

fully pressed by the Toro monarch. Kasagama became the ruler of a large and populous "confederacy" recognized as such by the British overlords as Bunyoro's power was forced out of the region. This sudden growth of the Toro regime produced a situation in which the exact "constitutional" relations between the confederated counties and the monarch of Toro were vague and anomalous. With British recognition of the chiefly hierarchy under Kasagama, the monarch emerged as both arch-collaborator and monarch of Toro, a difficult dual role. The terms of his sovereignty were unclear, and his power vis-à-vis his subordinates was undefined. The failure to clarify the relations between the Toro government and the British Protectorate and with it the internal relations of the kingdom would trouble the kingdom into the twentieth century.

The signing of the Toro Agreement in June 1900 was intended as more than the formalization of protectorate status. It was meant to be both fundamental law for the kingdom and the guarantee of certain powers to the Toro collaborators. As such it is remarkable how little attention the document received at the time. Sir Harry Johnston, who negotiated the Agreement for Her Majesty's Government, barely mentions it in his two-volume opus, *The Uganda Protectorate*.[59] And Kasagama dismisses the actual signing with one sentence in his "diary."[60] The negotiations were effortless, perhaps even careless, compared to those preceding the signing of the Buganda Agreement earlier in 1900.

The Agreement itself[61] began by setting out the names and approximate boundaries of six "administrative districts." A short clause then noted that the areas bordering the Congo Free State not included in the enumerated districts were to

[59] H. Johnston, *The Uganda Protectorate*, 2 vols. (London: Hutchinson, 1904), 1:251.

[60] O. W. Furley, "The Reign of Kasagama in Toro," *Uganda Journal* 31, 2(1967):188.

[61] The following account is based on "The Toro Agreement, 1900," as published in Uganda Protectorate, *Laws of the Uganda Protectorate 1910* (London: H.M.S.O., 1910).

"be administered by the principal European official placed in civil charge of the Toro district." The third clause named the six "hereditary" rulers of the districts and specified their relationship to the protecting power in questions of succession and violation of the Agreement. The four remaining clauses dealt with "waste" lands, forest and mineral resources; hut tax and gun tax; administration of justice; and the distribution of tax revenue of official estates to the collaborating chiefs and royal officials. The signatures of Sir Harry Johnston, Daudi Kasagama, and five other divisional chiefs and four witnesses completed the document as originally filed. However, a memorandum signed by Johnston and first printed in 1905 was added. This note, dated 29 June 1900, dealt with exemptions and exceptions to the Agreement as published in 1900. It throws light on the various anomalies contained in the document and provides a clue to the working of local political pressures on the formulation of the constitutional arrangement.

The first part of the note refers to exemptions from hut and gun taxes for certain personages. These include the Kabaka or King of Toro, the Katikiro (Prime Minister), the Mujasi or head of the king's police force, the Namasole (Queen Mother), the Rubuga (Royal Sister), and the recognized chiefs of each of the five administrative subdivisions. Luganda titles of office are used throughout the Agreement. The second part states in addition to the persons listed above that tax exemptions and estates of "ten square miles each" would be granted to the following:

"The Kimbugwe, the Sekibobo, Kangawo, Mugema, Kaima, Mukwenda, Kasuju and Kago." These Luganda chiefly titles refer to chiefs of subdivisions or counties within the administrative district of Toro. This presents an administrative anomaly. The term Toro was used to refer to two distinct political entities. On the one hand, Toro was a single county that was itself subdivided into administrative units under "county" chiefs. It becomes necessary to speak of the *Toro kingdom* under the Mukama Kasagama as a confederacy of six hereditary chieftaincies listed in the Agreement, one of

180 CONFLICT AND COLLABORATION

which, *"Toro proper,"* was itself divided into eight counties under chiefs whose rank in relation to the other county chiefs is left undefined, a point for future contestation.

A second anomaly was a reflection of the first. The position of Kasagama was as both Mukama of the Toro kingdom and administrative chief of "Toro proper." Was Kasagama then merely *primus inter pares*, a paramount chief, or in fact a king with additional responsibilities in his home county? The Agreement left Kasagama's position and powers highly ambiguous.

In order to understand the anomalous structures of collaboration, it is necessary to place the constitutional arrangements in an historical perspective. We can begin by examining the list of chiefs ordained by the Agreement and Note of 1900 in Table 6-2.[62]

Table 6-2

The Agreement Chiefs in Toro, 1900

Counties Confederal:	Titles	Chief	Clan
Toro	Kabaka	Daudi Kasagama	Bito-boyo
Mwenge	Pokino	Nasanaeri Kagwahabi	Bito-itwara
Kyaka	Luwekula	Sirasi Kagoro	Bito-itwara
Kitagweta	Kitunzi	Samwiri Nyama	Bito-itwara
Kitagwenda	Katambara	Edwadi Bulemu	Bito-jawe
Nyakabimba	Chambalango	Samwiri Kato	Bopi
Dependent:			
Burahya	Kaima	Zakaliya Kibogo	Gweri
Bunyangabo	Mukwenda	Louis Tibagwa	Fumambogo
Nyagwaki	Mugema	Rukambuza	Sambu
Ibanda	Kangao	Korokoro	Cwamba
Busongora	Kimbugwe	Mikaeri Rusoke	Gumba
Butanuka	Kaigo	Tomasi Bamya	Cwezi
Kibale	Sekibobo	Samwiri Kwitakulimuki	Bito-boyo
Bwamba	Kasuju	Petero Tigwezire	Yaga

[62] Uganda Protectorate, *Laws 1911*. The data on chiefly personnel are drawn from the following interviews: C/7, C/8, C/12–16, C/18, C/19, C/21–23, C/26, C/29, C/32, C/35, and C/38.

The first category of counties, which we shall call the con-
federate counties (Mwenge, Kyaka, Kitagweta, Kitagwenda,
Nyakabimba, and Toro), represent a political settlement between the demands for hierarchy and centralization by
Kasagama of Toro and the centrifugal demands of the other
leaders. The demands by Babito Baitwara for autonomy that
emerged under Kasagama's "kinsman," Yafeti Byakweyamba, were accommodated within the colonial system by
giving hereditary chiefly title in three counties to Yafeti's Itwara clansmen. Kagwahabi was the direct inheritor of
Yafeti's titles and estates in Mwenge, whereas Kagoro and
Nyama divided the Itwara claims to the eastern regions by the
creation of two counties, Kyaka and Kitagweta, in which
they respectively laid claim to hereditary chieftaincies.[63]

The separatist tendencies of Kitagwenda, ruled by a regent
for the hereditary Bito ruler, Edward Bulemu, were similarly
contained by the confederal formula. Bulemu was recognized
as the hereditary chief by the Agreement. His uncle and regent, Kakyentule, was removed and replaced by Kasagama's
trusted supporter, Nikodemu Kakurora, who acted as royal
intendant. Traditional evidence places this arrangement at
around 1898, well before the Agreement, but there is some
confusion regarding the date in archival sources. Certainly by
June 1900, this system of formal recognition of Bulemu's
claims under direct royal supervision or intendancy was in
operation.[64]

The last confederal county, Nyakabimba, like Kitagwenda,
was on the margins of Toro's effective power. Originally part
of Kabarega's realm, it was detached from Bunyoro by the
Ganda occupation of the "lost counties" and became a borderland between Ganda and Toro territories. Samwiri Kato, who
had been a minor chief under Kabarega, apparently favored
union with Toro rather than Buganda. The western portion
of the Nyakabimba area was federated with Toro in 1900

[63] Cf. Sitwell to Commissioner, 29 November 1896, *ESA* A4/6.

[64] Interviews C/21 Bamuroho, 23 January 1969; C/12 Mujasi, 17 January
1969; C/40 Binyomo, 12 February 1969, and C/8 Basigara, 15 January 1969.
Cf. J. Wilson to Commissioner, 31 December 1902, *ESA* A12/2.

under Kato as the hereditary chief.[65] The name Mugema is a Luganda title, which appears to have been joined to the Chambalango title and substituted for Kato's actual name on the document.

Confederal status was developed in practice to resolve the problems of centrifugal tendencies. These tendencies resulted from both the geographical factor of distance from the center and sociological factors of the previous autonomy of the outlying chieftaincies and the fissiparous forces within the Babito clan (Baboyo versus Baitwara). They were temporarily accommodated by the confederal elements of the constitution established by the Agreement.

What, then, was the history of the eight counties listed in the Note that were not confederal but were directly controlled by Kasagama as Kabaka? In these counties the chiefs were appointed by the King and had no hereditary standing in law. We shall refer to them as *dependent chiefs* and *dependent counties*. The two most senior men among the dependent chiefs were the pagans, Rukambuza and Korokoro. Despite Kasagama's forceful political advocacy of Protestant over Catholic chiefs, these men managed to remain clear of religious "parties" and retain office. Both men had served Kasagama's father, Nyaika, and had been refugees from Toro under Kabarega. They joined Kasagama on his return to Toro with Lugard in 1891. They were rewarded with the first chieftaincies created in 1892, Rukambuza becoming Mugema of Kyaka while Korokoro became Kangao of Nyagwaki. Rukambuza was later removed to Nyagwaki as Mugema, and Korokoro retained the Kangao title as ruler of the Ibanda district. These areas are located in the present Busongora and Bunyangabo counties. The loyalty to Kasagama of these refugee chiefs was demonstrated and assured by long service to the Baboyo dynasty, even in its time of trouble.[66]

---

[65] Interviews C/26 Katemba, 28 January 1969; C/7 Balya, 13 January 1969, and C/8 Basigara, 15 January 1969.

[66] Interviews C/29 and C/38 Rwakiboijogoro, 29 January and 11 February 1969. Pirouet, "Expansion of the Church," pp. 80–86. Sir George Kamurasi Rukidi III, "The Kings of Toro," Joseph R. Muchope, trans., Department of History, Makerere University, Kampala, 1969, pp. 30 and 39.

Next in seniority were the Protestants, Zakaliya Kibogo and Mikaeri Rusoke. Both these men were resident in what became Toro when Kasagama returned, and both were quick to rally to his support. In 1892, Kibogo became Mujasi, the King's military commander, and led Toro's forces against Kabarega's invading armies. In addition to his military services, Kibogo's loyalty was assured by the Christian marriage of Damali to Kasagama in 1896. Damar was a Mugweri kinswoman to Kibogo, and the marital linking of the royal clan to Kibogo's clan created a political bond as well. When Kasagama's first county chief of Burahya, Danieri Kakete, a Roman Catholic who had been converted in Buganda, ran afoul of the British administration, Kibogo was recommended to replace him as Kaima. Kibogo also retained his position as Mujasi.[67]

Mikaeri Rusoke was one of Kasagama's most effective chiefs. Having joined Kasagama in 1891 as a very young man, he quickly worked his way to high office by royal appointment. In 1898, he was appointed county chief in Busongora. Along with this office, Rusoke became Muhanika, or treasurer, probably due to the important revenue-producing salt lakes located in his Busongora territory. He was also a founding member of the first independent Anglican Church Council in Toro, formed that same year. Rusoke's brother, Nikodemu Kakurora, was Kasagama's agent in Kitagwenda. Rusoke went on to become Katikiro to Kasagama after serving as county chief for almost two decades. Kakurora's daughter, Kezia Byanjeru, was wedded to George Rukidi III and became the Nyinamukama (Queen Mother) to the last Toro King.[68] These close personal ties between the royal family and the Gumba clan of Rusoke and Kakurora were forged on the basis of the loyalty and service of these brothers to the Toro throne during this first decade of the restoration.

[67] C/24 Mpaka, 28 January 1969; C/25 Kalyegera, 28 January 1969; C/35 Kyamulesire, 31 January 1969. Contrast Interviews C/36 Kakete, 10 February 1969 and C/40 Binyomo, 12 February 1969.

[68] Interviews C/16 Kibooga, 20 January 1969; C/21 Bamuroho, 23 January 1969, and C/8 Basigara, 15 January 1969. Cf. Pirouet, "Expansion of the Church," p. 84.

The chief political virtue of both Petero Tigwezire and Samwiri Kwitakulimuki was their loyalty to Kasagama, expressed in a religious idiom. Both were early Protestant converts and members of the first independent Church Council in Toro. Petero Tigwezire was the son of a minor chief under Nyaika. When Kasagama returned, Tigwezire was appointed to a minor chieftaincy, and in 1896 he became the ninth Mutoro to be baptized. He married a Christian woman in 1897 and six months later was promoted to the Kasuju title in Bwamba, replacing the Bito chief, Kasami, who had refused to establish himself in Bwamba county, remote and secluded as it was behind the northern tip of Ruwenzori. The Bwamba chieftaincy was a particularly difficult assignment, as the Bwamba were ethnically and politically distinct from the Batoro and attempts to establish regular administration and taxes were met with armed hostilities. Tigwezire was eventually removed as a result of Baamba hostility, but after several years as an evangelist, again rose to high chiefly authority.[69]

Kwitakulimuki was the only Bito chief appointed by Kasagama. Although he was of Toro's royal lineage, he was not in the line of succession. He was appointed by Kasagama as a subchief in Burahya and was raised to Sekibobo of Kibale in about 1897. He appears also to have been an early Protestant convert, with the Christian name of Samwiri, and was a leading churchman in December 1898, when he too was named to the Toro Church Council, the governing body of the independent Anglican Church in Toro.[70] The close ties between the Protestant church and Toro kingdom government have been stressed many times. Perhaps the single most important indication of loyalty and support of Kasagama's rule was adherence to the king's religion. In this Samwiri Kwitakulimuki provides a useful if somewhat ambiguous test.

[69] Interviews C/18 Mukidi, 21 January 1969, and C/19 Tigwezire, 22 January 1969. Interviews C/37 Karamagi, 11 February 1969, and C/34 Basigara, 31 January 1969. Ormsby to Tomkins, 12 June 1902, *ESA* A12/2, and Minute on Toro, 7 January 1908, *ESA SMP* C46/08.
[70] Interview C/35 Kyamulesire, 31 January 1969.

In November 1903, Kwitakulimuki, motivated by the desire to expand his household to include another wife, changed his religion. He became a Muslim, taking the name Aramazani. The British officer reported his motive as sexual and not political. In May 1905, Kasagama brought charges of misappropriation against Kwitakulimuki for a second time, and he was removed from office. It is difficult to judge how great a role Kwitakulimuki's "conversion" played in his removal, but it is impossible to discount it entirely. Five years after the Agreement, religious partisanship was still very much a part of Toro politics.[71]

If, as we have suggested, adherence to the Protestant faith was the key loyalty test of Kasagama's administration, how can we account for the presence of two Roman Catholics among the "dependent chiefs" on the list of 1900 Agreement title holders? Tomasi Bamya and Leo Tibagwa were both able administrators, but they lacked the main qualification for appointment by Kasagama, i.e., loyalty to his "political party." Bamya came from a chiefly family and had been a captive in Buganda, where he was converted. He appears from later evidence to have been a useful administrator. When his county of Butanuka was merged into Bunyangabo in 1904, he accepted the demotion and continued to serve as a subchief and later as a regent in Kitagweta. He was eventually appointed county chief in Kyaka in 1907, succeeding to the post of the Catholic chief, Sirasi Kagoro.[72]

Louis Tibagwa's career is even more checkered than Bamya's. Tibagwa's father had served the Mukama Nyaika, and Tibagwa himself was a prosperous pastoralist when Kasagama returned to Toro in 1891. He was appointed chief first in Burahya and then made Mukwenda in Bunyangabo after Rwabudongo's fleeting appointment there in 1895. Tibagwa appears to have been at the center of the agitation for

[71] Report, November 1903, ESA A12/4, Cubitt to Sub-Commissioner, 16 February 1904, ESA A14/1, and Galt to Commissioner, 12 May 1905, ESA A14/2.
[72] Interviews C/27 Kanihire, 29 January 1969, and C/8 Basigara, 15 January 1969. Minutes on Toro Chieftainships, ESA SMP 850/07.

Roman Catholic participation in government. Tibagwa had the advantage of being one of the few Catholics who were also Huma pastoralists, and his appointment was therefore more acceptable to Kasagama.[73]

However, the official appointment of Nasanaeri Mugurusi, a staunch Protestant supporter, as Katikiro opened a new phase in the religious controversy in 1899. The Catholic mission vehemently protested the appointment of this "fanatic" to high office, which put him in a seat of judgment over Catholics. According to Pere Achte, "Entre les mains, les Catholiques sont comme les souris entre les griffes du chat."[74] Achte recommended separate channels of adjudication for Catholics and removal of sole responsibility in interdenominational disputes from Kasagama's administration. Tibagwa, as recognized leader of the Roman Catholic chiefs, appears to have been pushed toward usurping independent authority as head of a Catholic state-within-a-state. Protestant informants suspected him of trying to set himself up as a king under pressure from the Catholic mission. He was summoned to court and appears to have explained his dilemma as leader of the Catholics and subject of the Protestant king to the satisfaction of the British officer. Kasagama is credited with Solomonic wisdom in allowing him to remain in office, but it appears that the palaver in question merely secured a statement of satisfaction with Kasagama's justice from all the Catholic chiefs and recognized the right of appeal from Kasagama's courts to the British administrator.[75]

Tibagwa remained as Mukwenda through the signing of the Agreement in June 1900, but was removed shortly after. He was accused by Mugurusi of bringing a knife to a royal reception and intending to assassinate Kasagama or his Euro-

[73] Interview C/32 Kutambaki, 30 January 1969, and M. Nyakazingo, "Kasagama of Toro, A Despotic and Missionary King," seminar paper, Department of History, Makerere University, Kampala, 1968, pp. 24–26.

[74] Achte to Ternan, 20 July 1899, ESA A6/6. Cf. Interview C/7 Balya, 13 January 1969, who makes him Katikiro in 1897.

[75] Nyakazingo, "Kasagama," pp. 23–24; Interview C/40 Binyomo, 12 February 1969, and Bagge to Ternan, 20 August 1899, ESA A4/20.

pean guest. Despite eventually being cleared of these charges, he was removed from office and spent a short period in exile in Bunyoro. He remained under a cloud of suspicion and so was replaced as Mukwenda by another Catholic chief, Mariko Rwakaikara.[76]

What can we conclude about the nature of chieftaincy within Toro proper and its significance for the constitutional arrangement of the confederacy? First, it is clear that the chiefs of the eight counties of Toro proper were much more the king's men than those of the confederal counties. Their appointments were his prerogative, and by and large he selected men who were loyal and long-time supporters of his rule. Loyalty was largely equated with membership in a religious party, but there was a political accomodation with the opposition Catholic party that allowed for two of the eight chieftaincies to be held by them. This accomodation was largely the product of the strength of the Catholic mission in preserving an area for their own influence to operate within Kasagama's realm. The chiefs directly under Kasagama in Toro, whether Catholic or Protestant, were far less apt or able to be independent than those of the confederal counties.

What does this mean for relations with the other five counties? Despite the existence of two distinct kinds of units, the Toro Lukiiko (Rukurato), the governing council of the confederacy, recognized only one kind of county chief, all equally subject to the Mukama. Kasagama pressured to increase the size of the Rukurato by the recognition and seating of his dependent chiefs. He tried to have the eight dependent chiefs recognized and granted full chiefly privileges at the time of the signing of the Agreement. Their inclusion in the appended Note manifested this pressure.[77]

The second anomaly of the 1900 Agreement mentioned earlier pertained to the status of Kasagama as Kabaka (King) and

[76] Interviews C/40 Binyomo, 12 February 1969, and C/32 Kutambaki, 30 January 1969; Baile to Johnston, 11 October 1900, *ESA* A14/1. Cf. C/34 Basigara, 31 January 1969.

[77] Maddox to G. Wilson, 3 September 1904, *ESA* A22/1, and Knowles to Commissioner, 19 April 1904, *ESA* A14/3.

county chief of Toro simultaneously. This situation stemmed from the ten-year history of the Toro secession and shares its roots with the constitutional ambiguity of the counties. Although the agreement names and delineates six administrative subdivisions including Toro, it names administrative chiefs in only five, naming "Chief Kasagama . . . as the Kabaka or supreme chief" over all of the subdivisions.[78] This was primarily the result of the same historic situation that had given Toro a confederal constitution. From the beginning, efforts to bring outlying areas to recognize Kasagama as sovereign had led to friction.[79] Lugard, Cunningham, and finally Johnston, in recognition of these centrifugal forces, had adopted a confederal expedient.

Kasagama's own attempts to recreate a centralized monarchy like his father Nyaika's political system embodied countervailing centripetal forces. He had succeeded in reducing secessionist tendencies in Mwenge and Kitagwenda by application of armed force on several occasions. He used his own loyal supporters, especially the Katikiro, Nasanaeri Mugurusi, to lead soldiers against dissident subordinates.[80] And perhaps most significantly, he had asserted his authority at the capital to assure that all "foreign relations" with the Baganda, the British, and the missions were in his hands. Ultimately, it was Kasagama's control over access to the British and their police that meant that the centripetal forces of royal government would triumph.

Access to the British was preserved as a monopoly of the court at Kabarole by its proximity to Fort Portal, the government station in Toro since Owen's time. Proximity, plus the recognition of Kasagama as a royal figure by the British, enabled him to funnel all the inputs of British power through Kabarole. It also made it possible for Kasagama to play an active role in the political life of Toro, which centered on his

---

[78] "Toro Agreement, 1900" in Uganda Protectorate, *Laws 1911*, pp. 993–995.

[79] Cf. M. Bovill and G. R. Askwith, comps., *"Roddy" Owen* (London: John Murray, 1897), pp. 61–62.

[80] Interviews C/44 Winyi, 19 February 1969, and Sitwell to Commissioner, 9 October 1898, *ESA* A4/13.

court. This active role in itself helps to illuminate some of the "constitutional" anomalies that existed in 1900.

In both Ankole and Bunyoro, the leading political actor collaborating in the establishment of British overrule was a commoner. Only in Toro was the role of monarch and arch-collaborator fused in one person. By his royal blood, Kasagama came to be recognized as "Kabaka" over all of Toro. But British recognition of royal rank, as we can see in Ankole and Bunyoro (and Buganda), did not lead to royal power necessarily. By his active collaboration, Kasagama was simultaneously recognized as "supreme chief" and the head of government, the actual ruler of Toro. It was by his guardianship and vigorous exercise of royal power that Kasagama became a "royal collaborator."

In support of the contention that the situation of "royal collaboration" led to the anomaly of the dual role of Kasagama, we might examine the situation of Kasagama's leading commoner, the Katikiro. By 1900, Nasanaeri Mugurusi, who witnessed the signing of the Agreement with his mark, had effectively replaced Yoswa Rusoke as Katikiro of Toro. Rusoke, a Musita from Butanuka, was a prominent, wealthy, but older man. He retired from his office as Katikiro in about 1897 without blame and remained an important political figure, being appointed as a regent to a county chief as late as 1907.[81] Mugurusi was a younger and particularly dynamic man. He was a staunch, even "fanatic" Protestant and an important military leader.[82] However, he is not listed as a county chief in the Agreement and had no assured revenue or land grant. He was entirely dependent on Kasagama for the support of his office and title. Whatever rewards Mugurusi received were from Kasagama's royal coffers and estates. Only many years later was the position of Katikiro in Toro given official standing and remuneration.[83]

[81] Interviews C/10 Rusoke, 16 January 1969; C/6 Nkojo, 11 January 1969; and C/7 Balya, 13 January 1969. Cf. Interview C/8 Basigara, 15 January 1969.

[82] Interviews C/13 Mugurusi, 17 January 1969; C/6 Nkojo, 11 January 1969 and C/15 Okwiri, 20 January 1969. Cf. Achte to Ternan, 20 July 1899, *ESA* A6/6, for his military record prior to 1900.

[83] Galt to Commissioner, 1 May 1905, *ESA* A14/2, and G. Wilson to Elgin, 21 April 1906, *ESA* SMP 518/06.

What did this mean for the functioning of the Katikiro under the Agreement? Without an independent economic or political base, Mugurusi served as a minister in the oldest sense: he ministered to the needs and desires of his monarch. In foreign policy Kasagama appears to have used Mugurusi merely to arrange for negotiations which were conducted by the monarch himself. This stands in sharp contrast to the latitude given to the leading commoner chiefs of Ankole and Bunyoro. In military policy, Mugurusi seems to have been equally subordinate to his civilian and royal master. We have no indication that he ever raided on his own account, whereas there is strong reason to believe that he was the chief instrument of Kasagama's military efforts to secure the subordination of resisting chiefs. Only in religious matters does Mugurusi appear to have had personal interests as a "fanatic" of the king's Protestant party. Even here the evidence is such that his fanaticism may well have accorded with Kasagama's own early policy of religious monopoly. Lastly, in the Katikiro's functions as judge and messenger for the court, it would appear that Mugurusi acted throughout as a faithful minister to his king without the self-assertion that are the earmarks of the "great commoner" in the neighboring kingdoms.

Eventually Mugurusi was appointed as a county chief in addition to his title as Katikiro. Upon his removal as Katikiro in 1914, he remained a county chief until his complete retirement from politics in 1919.[84] Despite this additional authority and despite Mugurusi's acknowledged strong personality, he remained in the shadow of Kasagama throughout his 20 years and more of service to the Toro kingdom. In 1900 the Katikiro's post was potentially the most powerful commoner post in the kingdom. Its occupant was a man of ability and strength. Yet the post was so dependent on the Mukama's support that even the capable figure who filled it was no threat to the king's autonomy. The Mukama Kasagama both reigned and ruled in Toro.

[84] Minute by G. Wilson, 6 July 1907, *ESA* SMP 850/07; "Toro Chiefs," *ESA* SMP C72, and Interview C/13 Mugurusi, 17 January 1969.

The New Regime in Ankole: 1899–1901

The enthronement of the young Mugabe Kahaya and the emergence of his Enganzi, Mbaguta, as arch-collaborator were the first steps in establishing a collaborating regime in Ankole. However, the creation of a collaborating court is not the same as the creation of a new regime. The keystone was ready, but without the stones of the arch to support it the colonial edifice would crumble. The stones, in this case as elsewhere in Uganda, were the county chiefs whose willingness and ability to administer territory as subordinates to the Ankole court and the British authorities formed the pillars of collaboration.

Subordinate chiefs had existed in Ankole under Ntare V, but these *bakungu* were Hima pastoralists who, incidental to herding their cattle, collected taxes and attended Ntare's court. At best a very rough territorial division and political hierarchy existed, and even this was largely shattered by a decade of disease, destruction, and crisis. A new structure of subordination to the authority of the court and its commoner leader, Mbaguta, had to be erected. This would be achieved by Mbaguta's cunning and often brilliant use of his alliance with the British agents, Macallister and Racey. Collaboration at the center would be made to yield collaboration throughout the Ankole district by mid-1901 and would set in motion the political processes of colonial government. Although the most powerful kingdom in the region, Ankole was surrounded by petty monarchs and semidependencies, which upset the symmetry and hierarchy of administration in the area. Before an agreement modeled on the Buganda Agreement of 1900 could be signed, this hodge-podge would have to be reduced to a compact and regular hierarchy of chiefly authorities centered on the court of Kahaya.[85]

On the eastern frontier the problem was solved quickest. Here, where Ganda influence was strong, a simple solution lay at hand. The Kabula area had been under Mbaguta's effective rule since Ntare's death, but its disturbed state in 1897,

[85] G. Wilson to Commissioner, 3 August 1901, *ESA* A12/1.

combined with Mwanga's rebellion, had brought on limited hostilities between Ankole and the Protectorate government. To restore stability, Kabula was simply detached from Ankole and annexed to Buganda in 1899. Although this briefly threatened to have a disturbing effect on Ankole, the loss in this area was soon compensated by expansion westward. A tribute imposed by the British but payable to Buganda was a further source of irritation to Ankole. It was rescinded in favor of regular hut tax and gun tax levies after only one payment.[86]

Bukanga, in Ankole's southeast corner, almost suffered the same fate as Kabula. A Muslim chief named Kahuzi from Koki (an independent area absorbed by Buganda) had been brought into Bukanga by Kahitsi. He remained after Kahitsi's decline and appears to have been the British choice as chief. However, a Munyankole chief named Kanyabuzana was unwilling to acknowledge Kahuzi's authority. Macallister, the first district officer, credited this to religious differences between the Muslim Kahuzi and the pagan Kanyabuzana. The conflict was climaxed by an argument over access to water resources reflecting the dispute over territorial jurisdiction in Bukanga. Kahuzi pushed the issue to the point of war and finally attacked Kanyabuzana's kraal. In the fight that followed, Kahuzi was killed by Kanyabuzana's son and his men were routed. The following day Kanyabuzana raided Kahuzi's herds and fled into Karagwe in German territory. A Muslim chief from Bukanga was brought in to rule Bukanga, and by August 1901 it appeared that Bukanga too might very well be annexed to Buganda.[87]

[86] Macallister to Commissioner, 16 October 1899 (#879 and #881) *ESA* A4/22. Macallister to Special Commissioner, 11 December 1899 *ESA* A4/23 and 26 March 1900 *ESA* A4/27.

[87] Macallister to Special Commissioner, 9 July 1900, *ESA* A15/1; A. G. Katate and L. Kumugungunu, *Abagabe B'Ankole*, 2 vols. (Kampala: East African Literature Bureau, 1967), 2:14–15; Interview A/40 Kabuhaya, 7 September 1968. The informant said that his father, Kanyanbuzana, informed Kahaya of Kahuzi's death and was advised by Kahaya to flee to German territory in Karagwe to escape prosecution by the Protectorate authorities. See also "The Administrative Divisions of the District of Ankole," *ESA* A15/1.

To the north and west there were several tributary kingdoms that were absorbed into the Ankole kingdom. During
the period before the agreement, these kingdoms suffered a
reduction in status and experienced occasional military interventions in order to accommodate them to the new order.
The first to undergo pressure from the new regime was the
Shambo kingdom of Igara.

Igara was ruled by Mukama Musinga, a member of the Benemafundo house of the Shambo clan. He had already come
into conflict with the Ankole administration first in 1899 over
an attack on some Nyamwezi porters and again over a land
dispute with Igumira in 1900. In January 1901, he was ordered to travel to Mbarara to recognize Kahaya's primacy as
the paramount chief of Ankole. He was to be met by
Mbaguta and Racey, the district officer, at the swamp that
marked the Igara border with Ankole's Shema county. Just
before he crossed over from Igara, he drew his own knife
and disemboweled himself. Several reasons are given for
this suicide. First, as a Mukama, Musinga was theoretically
Kahaya's equal and was forbidden by tradition to look upon a
fellow ruler. Fear of meeting a European (Racey was at the
border) is also mentioned. But most likely, he feared that he
was to be arrested and deported just as Igumira had been. It
was widely believed at the time that Igumira had been killed
by the Europeans after being tortured.[88]

With Musinga out of the way, the Ankole authorities
placed his ten-year-old son, Mkotani, on the throne and made
Bakora, his paternal uncle, sole regent during his minority.
Mkotani was the oldest son of the previous Mukama, but was
only about ten years of age in 1901. Bakora exercised the
powers of both a county chief and Mukama of Igara. He alone

---

[88] Macallister to Commissioner, 16 October 1899 (#883), *ESA* A4/22, and
Racey to Special Commissioner, 1 September 1900, *ESA* A15/1; M. T.
Mahoney, "The Suicide of Musinga," *Uganda Journal* 22, 1(1958):85–86; H.
F. Morris, *A History of Ankole* (Kampala: East African Literature Bureau,
1962), p. 36; Katate, *Abagabe*, 2:16–20; Interviews A/21 Biyindo, 23 August
1968, A/3 Katukura and Kafwisagye, 25 July 1968, and A/25 Rukunyu, 26
August 1968.

picked Igara leaders to be subchiefs under himself and his nephew. Mkotani thus was recognized by the British authorities as a hereditary county chief to the people of Igara. In their eyes he became their Mukama.[89]

Beyond Igara lay the area of what became the county of Bunyaruguru. Originally divided into several petty chieftaincies, the area included the highland of the Bunyaruguru escarpment and the rift valley lowland over to the Kazinga channel. Beyond Kazinga, the authority of Toro began. In addition to its remote and difficult position, Bunyaruguru's people, the Bakunta, were notorious among the Banyankole for their practice of witchcraft.[90]

In January and February 1900, Macallister conducted an expedition against a recalcitrant chief named Dari. This involved him in action against some 11 chiefs and the burning of several villages. In March he had reduced the profusion of recognized chiefs by naming one man, Kuriafire, chief over all Bunyaruguru, except the Kazinga area. There he appointed a local Mubito chief, Kaihura. Other chiefs were recognized for the regions of Kamsusa and Ndusi. By November, Kuriafire's supposed subordinates had rebelled, and he was removed and the entire region unified under Kaihura and his son Kasigano and centered at Kichwamba on the escarpment. Kaihura, a Mubito with some claim to authority, proved able and willing to rule the area under Kahaya's sovereignty until his death in 1902. So this complex of competing chiefs in Ankole's smallest and remotest county was reduced to a standard hierarchy on the model of Buganda: an appointed county chief and several subchiefs responsible to him. This was achieved in less than one year by raising one man to authority and reducing others to subordination.[91]

[89] Interviews A/25 Rukunyu, 26 August 1968, and A/3 Katukura and Kagwisagye, 25 July 1968.

[90] Interviews A/16 Kafureeka, 13 August 1968, and A/32 Katate, 1 September 1968.

[91] Macallister to Special Commissioner, 10 February 1900, *ESA* A4/25; Macallister to Special Commissioner, 21 March 1900, *ESA* A4/27; "The Administrative Decisions" and Racey to Special Commissioner, 12

On Ankole's northern border with Toro lay the small tributary kingdom of Buzimba ruled by Nduru of the Balisa clan. The Balisa had established several petty dynasties on the fringes of Ankole and Bunyoro power. Nduru was able to rule by maintaining a precarious balance between the influence of either kingdom. Having been tributary before to one or another, Nduru was willing in late 1900 to proclaim his allegiance to Kahaya's rising fortunes and accept him as paramount.[92] This remained true only so long as no active interference from Mbarara was attempted. In 1901 Nduru became county chief of Buzimba with hereditary rights. By 1902 he found his new status incompatible with his previous independence of action and removed himself from office, fleeing with his cattle to Toro. He was replaced by the Muhinda, Henry Rwamugwizi, who had been sent as a royal intendant by Kahaya and Mbaguta.[93]

To the west, Ankole's expansion was confounded by an undefined boundary between British, Belgian, and German spheres. In western Rwampara, well within the British zone, the recalcitrant chief, Gwembuzi (of the Benerukari house of the Bashambo), was defeated and forced to submit to Kahaya's sovereignty. In May 1901, he attempted to flee to German territory, but was captured, his cattle confiscated, and his district, Ndaija, put under the authority of Ruhara, then county chief of Rwampara.[94]

More difficult to resolve were relations with Rugarama, the Mwenekihondwa Mushambo chief of Kajara, and Makobore of the Benekirenzi Bashambo of Rujumbura. Both chiefs used

November 1900, *ESA* A15/1. Ankole Monthly Report, July 1902, *ESA* A15/2; Interview A/5 Murumba, 27 July 1968, and Low, "The British and Uganda, 1862–1900," doctoral diss., Oxford University, 1957, pp. 557ff.

[92] Interview A/44 Mukindo, 10 September 1968. Nduru's name fails to appear in the September 1900 chief list in "Administrative Divisions," *ESA* A15/1, but he is listed among seven newly created *bamasaza* (county chiefs) in Ankole Monthly Report, December 1900, *ESA* A15/1.

[93] Interview A/44 Mukindo, 10 September 1968, and J. P. Wilson to Commissioner, 2 and 3 December 1902 (#80 and #82), *ESA* A12/2. Cf. Interview A/7 Mugoha, 26 July 1968.

[94] Ankole Monthly Report, May 1901, *ESA* A15/1.

the border to evade incorporation into any colonial regime for as long as possible, and Makobore was able to keep Rujumbura out of Ankole District permanently. (Eventually Rujumbura became part of Kigezi District.) From 1899 to at least 1902, both chiefs successfully defied the imperial forces. Rugarama threatened sharp fighting, and both chiefs skipped up and back across the supposed international boundary and steadfastly refused to acknowledge the sovereignty of Kahaya and the Ankole monarchy.[95] In April 1901, a revised chief list was sent to the central administration at Entebbe by Racey. Rujumbura was listed as being part of the district but not part of Ankole proper. After Makobore's name there is the note: "Requires special attention." Kajara is also listed with Rujumbura as being outside the kingdom. The more hopeful note after Rugarama's name read: "May come to terms in time and recognize Kahaya as P[aramount] Chief."[96] It took almost a decade to bring Rugarama to terms, and still it was not accomplished without bloodshed.

Buhweju is a hilly and difficult country that lies to the north and west of central Ankole. Like Buzimba, Buhweju had a Lisa royal line that survived in the no-man's land between Bunyoro and Ankole by paying tribute to one or the other and sometimes both powers. When Ntare came to Ankole's throne, he was aided by Ndagara, the Mukama of Buhweju, and relations between the kingdoms remained cordial until the new regime was established. By then Ndagara was an old man and not conducive to the changes of habit that were required of him. Macallister attempted to get Ndagara to come into Mbarara as early as May 1899. Ndagara was hesitant to come in at the time, perhaps due to his fears of the several Baganda employed in Ankole, who were reportedly anxious for war and loot and were pressuring Macallister to adopt a

[95] Macallister to Commissioner, 14 May 1899, *ESA* A4/16. Ankole Monthly Reports, April and May 1902, *ESA* A15/2, and Interview A/26 Rwakanaigisa, 27 August 1968.

[96] Enclosure in Racey to Cunningham, 24 April 1901, *ESA* A15/1. Cf. Minute by Eden, 26 July 1910, *ESA* SMP/931; Interviews A/15 Katungi, 10 August 1968, and A/26 Rwakanaigisa, 27 August 1968.

forward policy.[97] Macallister appears to have acted with restraint, and the crisis with Buhweju came when the more impetuous Racey adopted a forward policy.

In January 1901, Ndagara refused to come to Mbarara, although he willingly sent the tax and tribute levied on him. Moreover, his kinsman (described as his son), a youth named Igana, was sent to Racey with assurances of Ndagara's friendship, and a compact of blood brotherhood was made between them. In April, Racey felt obliged to lead a column into Buhweju. The column, swelled by uninvited Banyankole anxious for action, was enough to send Ndagara fleeing into the bush to avoid confronting his visitors, who were forced to return to Mbarara empty handed.[98]

Despite his own advice against it, Racey led a second expedition into Buhweju in July 1901.[99] On this occasion Ndagara was surprised at a small village and retreated into the nearby gardens, where he and many of his kinsmen and followers were killed by rifle fire from Racey's detachment of 60 constables. Later that day some of his chiefs submitted to Racey. A young son of Ndagara, Ndibarema, was brought forward as heir to his father's kingdom.[100] Ndibarema was about 17 years old in 1901. In the aftermath of the raid, which saw some 68 people killed and the suicide of many of the women at court, candidates for the honors of following Ndagara were difficult to find. Despite the existence of older brothers, who were loath to come forward, Ndibarema was advanced by the Buhweju kingmakers as the son of Ndagara's favorite wife, later Ann Kinyanda. An older brother, known as Ishe (the father of) Mujumba, became regent. Although several Balisa remained as chiefs under the regency, Mbaguta

[97] Interview A/14 Khunyirano, 9 August 1968. Macallister to Commissioner, 14 May 1899, *ESA* A4/16, Macallister to Commissioner, 2 June 1899, *ESA* A4/17.

[98] Racey to Johnston, 21 January 1901 (C11), *ESA* A15/1. Ankole Monthly Report, April 1901, *ESA* A15/1.

[99] Ankole Monthly Report, June 1901, *ESA* A15/1.

[100] Ankole Monthly Report, July 1901, *ESA* A15/2; Interviews A/14 Khunyirano, 9 August 1968, and A/24 Barah, 25 August 1968; Katate, *Abagabe*, 2:20–21.

managed to place some of his Baganda followers as sub-chiefs.[101] Again a regency and youthful "monarch" become the means of lending legitimacy to the *de facto* transfer of power to the collaborators. Buhweju was a smaller replica of the Ankole model. Effective power at the county level, as at the center, was exercised by a collaboration of outsiders and local political figures who were not previously sovereign and who could increase their own powers by cooperation with the new rulers of Ankole.

Two factors seem to lay behind Racey's impetuous policy in Buhweju. First, conflict with his police commander, Captain Mundy, seems to have edged him toward an energetic exercise of his dubious authority to order military actions. More important, it seems that Mbaguta played a role in aggravating the situation and provoking a clash. This was done both on behalf of his Ganda supporters, who favored a forward policy, and to strengthen his own hand in Ankole affairs. By provoking conflict with the neighboring principalities, Mbaguta encouraged the not unwilling British resident to reduce the outlying areas to subordination to the center. This in turn meant subordination to the administrative apparatus over which Mbaguta indisputably presided, as well as the increase in his ability to appoint his Ganda functionaries to the new posts created by the subimperial expansion.[102]

Whether from personal motivation or political pressure, Racey succeeded in reducing local opposition to the creation of a compact and uniform "greater" Ankole. His resort to military expedients earned for him and his police command-

[101] Interviews A/14 Khunyirano, 9 August 1968, and A/24 Barah, 25 August 1968. At the time of this investigation, Ndagara's son and successor, Ndibarema, was still living. His health, however, was very poor, and he was hospitalized twice during the months that field research was in progress. He was reputed to be extremely knowledgeable, but I was unable to see him despite the efforts of his son, Esau Khunyirano, to assist me. Mr. Khunyirano himself proved remarkably well informed and, like Mr. Barah, was an invaluable informant on Buhweju.

[102] Enclosures in Racey to Johnston, 21 January 1901 (C11), *ESA* A15/1. Ankole Monthly Report, April 1901, *ESA* A15/1, and Interview A/14 Khunyirano, 9 August 1968.

er, Captain Mundy, a fearsome regard by the Banyankole, which persists in the form of the Runyankole names given to these two Europeans. Mundy was known as *Kasigazi Rwitamanzi*, "The Killer of Great Men." His superior civil officer, Racey, is remembered as *Mpitsi Iribariya*, "The Hyena Who Eats You."[103] As a result of his impetuousity, Racey was removed as district officer in September 1901, one month after the signing of the Ankole Agreement, which his forward policy in extending the new regime had made possible.

The Emergence of a Hima Establishment

Simultaneous with the process of subordinating the outlying counties to the center, a second process of internal subordination was under way. The first stage in this process was the manner in which Mbaguta succeeded in displacing his rivals for personal dominance among the Hinda or traditional party. The exile of Igumira and Kijoma and the deposition of Kahitsi and Gwembuzi broke the back of the "conservatives" and ended any real threat of concerted resistance from the old ruling class of Ankole. But who could be found to operate the governmental machinery of the new regime of collaboration? The answer to this question can be found in a careful reading of the signatures on the Ankole Agreement. In addition to the signatures of the Mugabe Kahaya, his Enganzi, Mbaguta, and the four "Bakima," Nduru, Ndibarema, Kaihura, and Mkotani (with his regent, Bakora), there are the signatures of five other county chiefs named in the Agreement.[104] The emergence of these five counties and their chiefs provides a key to understanding the internal structure of collaboration in Ankole.

When Kahaya first ascended the throne in 1897, he presided over a motley collection of 22 "counties" shown in Table 6-3 together with their respective chiefs.[105]

[103] Interview A/46 Rwabushongo, 12 September 1968.
[104] "Ankole Agreement, 1901" in Uganda Protectorate, *Laws 1910*, p. 1005.
[105] Katate, *Abagabe*, 2:85–86.

Table 6-3
Kahaya's Chiefs, 1897

Subdivision	Chief
1. Nyabushozi	Matsiko
2. Kikyenkye	Kyoma (Kijoma)
3. Kabula	Karyebara (Kariebare)
4. Bwera-Mahogora	Mabangira
5. Shema	Igumira
6. Masheruka	Bagonera
7. Ruhorobero	Nyamajanja
8. Bukanga	Kakwekweto-Rujabuka
9. Isingiro	Rwamborjama
10. Kigarama	Isingoma Rwambagaza
11. Kakyera	Ibuza Rwambagira Mashega
12. Rwampara	Rukorea
13. Nyaihanga	Rwakaribi
14. Ndaija	Gwembuzi
15. Kajara (Bwishekatwa)	Rugarama
16. Ruguha	Kisiribombo
17. Nshenyi	Rubagumya
18. Igara	Rutondo
19. Bunyaruguru	Bampata and Rubata
20. Mitoma	Bucunku, Kijoma, and Kishokye
21. Buhweju	Ndagara
22. Kajara (Butaya)	Kataraiha

This list includes the "autonomous" areas that Ntare V had claimed as suzerain: Kajara, Buhweju, Igara, and Bunyaruguru, as well as Bwera-Mahogora and Kabula. These last regions were lost to Ganda occupation at around that time (1897), and officially ceded to Buganda in 1900. As far as we can tell, the remaining counties were ruled as in the past by the Bahinda and a few other, mostly Hima, chiefs. Only one chief, Isingoma Rwabagaza, can be identified as Mwiru, whereas five are certainly Bahinda.[106]

In 1900, a list of counties and their approximate number of huts was compiled by the newly arrived British adminis-

[106] Interview A/6 Rwabushongo, 30 July 1968.

trator, apparently for tax purposes.[107] An adaptation of
this list is shown in Table 6–4. The first thing to be
noted is the continued enumeration of 22 counties and the
inclusion of the "autonomous" areas of several Bakima
within the district. Bwera–Mahogora and Kabula are now
missing. Mbaguta still holds title only to Ngarama in
southern Isingiro. If we exclude the areas on the eastern
and western fringes, we are left with a list of 11 chiefs in
Ankole proper. Of these, Igumira is clearly the most important, controlling an estimated 10,000 huts and an addi-

Table 6–4

Kahaya's Chiefs in April 1900

Subdivision	Chief	Huts
1. Nyabushozi	Mayindo	300
2. Kabianda	Matsiko	100
3. Kikyenkye	Kijoma	2,000
4. Mizisi	Rwamugwizi	1,500
5. Nsongi	Bitsa	200
6. Nshara	Rutasharara	500
7. Kashari	Kahaya	2,500
8. Ngarama	Mbaguta	1,000
9. Rwampara	Ruhara	6,000
10. Buhihi (Ndaija)	Gwembuzi	500
11. Shema	Igumira	10,000
12. Bukanga N (Eastern)	Kanyabuzana	1,000
13. Bukanga S (Eastern)	Kahuzi	500
14. Ndusi (Western)	Katuramo	200
15. Buzimba (Western)	Nduru	500
16. Bunyaruguru (Western)	Kuriafirc	1,000
17. Kazinga (Western)	Kaihura	500
18. Kamsusa (Western)	Biasigwa	200
19. Buhweju (Western)	Ndagara	5,000
20. Igara (Western)	Musinga	5,000
21. Rujumbura (Western)	Makobore	20,000
22. Kajara (Western)	Rugarama	1,000

[107] "The Administrative Divisions of the District of Ankole," *ESA* A15/1.
The internal evidence indicates a date between March and July 1900.

tional 1,000 Hima pastoral kraals. He is followed by Ruhara of Rwampara with 6,000 huts. Kahaya himself is listed as chief of Kashari with 2,500 huts. Thus, the Mugabe held title over an area that was in fact controlled by Igumira, his regent, sponsor, and father. Kahaya's guardian and the former servant and supporter of Igumira, Ruhara, occupied the second most important chieftaincy.

The concentration of power in the hands of the Hinda party is further evidenced by the presence of three more Hinda chiefs on the list. Kijoma, with 2,000 huts, was extremely close to Igumira's faction, having been named as Enganzi to Kahaya by Igumira. In 1900, when Igumira was arrested, Kijoma rebelled and fled with his cattle to German territory, thereby losing his chieftaincy. Rwamugwizi, with 1,500 huts, had been Kahaya's general against Kahitsi in 1899. In 1901, he was sent to Buzimba as Kahaya's royal intendant, and in 1902 succeeded Nduru as county chief there.[108]

All of these Hinda-controlled chieftaincies were larger than Mbaguta's Ngarama. Another small territory of 500 huts in Nshara was controlled by the Muhinda, Rutasharara. He, along with Matsiko, who was chief over 100 huts in 1900, became signatories to the Ankole Agreement the following year. The remaining small chieftaincies of Bitsa (200 huts), Gwembuzi (500 huts), and Mayindo (300 huts) were also in the camp of the dominant Hinda party. Gwembuzi, a Mushambo, was chief in western Rwampara. He was removed from his post in 1900 when he refused to submit to the central authority and attempted to flee the country. Bitsa was a Musita (Hima), the same man who had served under Ntare as chief judge and was a prominent court figure. He died shortly before the signing of the Agreement.[109]

The chief Mayindo led a very checkered career. By clan a Mwishikatwe, Mayindo was one of three Iru chiefs in 1901. According to George Wilson, he was appointed by the first

[108] Interviews A/36 Rutabindwa, 3 September 1968, and A/7 Mugoha, 26 July 1968.
[109] Interviews A/1 Katate, 24 July 1968; A/23 Kanduhho, 24 August 1968, and A/8 Mugoha, 31 July 1968.

Collector, Macallister, "as a representative Whiro chief in order to give a helping hand to that race."[110] Again the claim for administrative initiative seems to be exaggerated. In fact, Mayindo was of a chiefly Iru family well before Macallister's arrival. His father, Kicubwa, had served Ntare as leader of the *Abarwani* regiment in Nyabushozi until Kicubwa's death from smallpox in 1892. Mayindo's older brother, Itiri, succeeded his father as military chief and died in combat against Rwanda in 1895. Mayindo succeeded to his family's estates and authority in Nyabushozi where the *Abarwani* tended their cattle. The appointment by Macallister would thus have been perfunctory.[111]

Mayindo was removed from office by the administration in 1901 when he refused to obey an order to transfer his chieftaincy. Thus, he was not a chief when the Agreement was signed, but was reappointed to the county chieftaincy of Nyabushozi in 1902. Mayindo, as an important Mwiru, who inherited his position as a "servant" to the dynasty, had his party affiliation assured by his succession to office.[112]

Thus, in 1900, Ankole itself was ruled by 11 chiefs, ten of whom were loyal to the potential opposition to colonial overrule. The predominance of the Hinda party was hardly a situation conducive to the establishment of regular administration by a collaborating elite. This situation was transformed by the end of the year. By that time, the hodge-podge of counties had been reduced to the point at which Ankole proper was governed by seven county chiefs all owing allegiance to Kahaya and his chief minister, Mbaguta.[113] The internal situation was then ripe for the solemnization that took place in August 1901. The first step was the removal of Igumira, the focal point of opposition to the new regime. He was replaced by Mbaguta as county chief of Shema and lead-

[110] G. Wilson to Commissioner, 8 August 1901, *ESA* A12/1.

[111] Interviews A/39 Zororwa, 5 September 1968, and A/6 Rwabushongo, 3 July 1968.

[112] G. Wilson to Commissioner, 8 August 1901, *ESA* A12/1, and Galt, Report for July 1902, *ESA* A15/2.

[113] Ankole Monthly Report, December 1900, *ESA* A15/1.

204   CONFLICT AND COLLABORATION

ing courtier. By this one change, the arch-collaborator, in addition to his county of Ngarama, gained control of Igumira's counties of Shema and Kahaya's Kashari. This effected a near complete reversal of the power relations between opposition and collaboration. Furthermore, while in April 1901, Rujumbura, Kajara, Buhweju, and Bukanga still required "special attention" or were effectively independent of Ankole control, the central kingdom had a new chiefly hierarchy as recorded in Table 6-5.[114]

Table 6-5

Kahaya's Chiefs, April 1901

County	Chief
Bunyaruguru	Kaihura
Igara	Bakora
Buzimba	Nduru
Shema/Ngarama	Mbaguta
Isingiro	Mazinio
Nyabushozi	Mayindo
Mitoma	Bucunku
Nshara	Rutasharara

A manageable number of chiefly officials and a compact grouping of counties had been drawn from the irregularities of Ankole's "traditional" constitution. And the management of the court and the chiefs had passed to Mbaguta and his British collaborators. All that remained was the signing of an agreement that would solemnize the new constitution and establish terms for future collaboration and the conditions of future conflict.

Discussion

By 1901, regimes of collaboration were established and operating over all three kingdoms of western Uganda. Re-

[114] Enclosure in Racey to Cunningham, 26 April 1901, *ESA* A15/1. G. Wilson to Commissioner, 3 August 1901, *ESA* A12/1.

gardless of the degree or type of resistance to imperial intrusion manifested by the people and rulers of the area, each independent and sovereign state had undergone a transition to dependence. In the course of this transition power passed not only out of the region to the alien conquerors, but to a new local ruling group within each kingdom. This local collaborating elite of chiefs and kings proved both willing and capable of managing the affairs of the imperial dependencies with a minimum of recourse to outside assistance or interference. Collaboration in many ways made imperialism economically possible while simultaneously allowing for some continuity in African political power and leadership. Far more than resistance, collaboration was an ambiguous and complex process requiring cautious and careful analysis.

The motives of collaborators, for instance, were ambivalent, wide-ranging, and inconstant. Mbaguta, Ankole's arch-collaborator in 1899, was in 1897 leading African troops against British-led armies. Naming him as a collaborator is not therefore to classify his character, rather only to characterize his behavior. To refrain from using this description in so clear cut a case would be a dereliction. Still, collaborators need not be forever stigmatized by their behavior. They may change their minds and their behaviors; they may at first resist, or decide only later on such a course. If we understand that collaboration was a policy subject to change, not a question of motive or of character, then the concept becomes more manageable.

Besides being changeable, collaboration with foreign regimes derives from a variety of motives: "The wish to keep a position of importance, or the hope of gaining such a position, the intention of working for an attractive regime or the habit of working for any regime, however unattractive."[115] Indeed, even patriotism and loyalty are motives found among collaborators as well as resisters: the desire to serve a monarch of the royal line despite his dependence on foreign kingmakers or the hope of preserving the best of the kingdom's values,

[115] Anil Seal, *The Emergence of Indian Nationalism* (Cambridge: Cambridge University Press, 1968), p. 9.

or the desire to regain the power to protect one's people from the ravages of war, defeat, and desolation. Loyalty, patriotism, avarice, and egotism are motives mixed and blended in varying degrees by the mind of the collaborator. "But in the physiology of colonialism it is results not motives that matter; and all those groups may be classed as collaborators whose actions fell into line with the purposes of the British."[116]

The policy of collaboration in western Uganda consisted in essence of accepting employment under British supervision as a "chief" as the African government officials came to be called. The duties of all the chiefs (and the "paramount chief" or king) were essentially those of local administration of law, taxes, and in the early period a minimum of social services, largely road building and repair and public works. In the organization of this administration a typical structure was evolved, derived from British modifications of Buganda's political structure, adapted to local conditions.[117] At the base of this hierarchy were village chiefs called *miruka* chiefs. These men were generally local men accepted by their fellow villagers as headmen, unpaid by the colonial authorities, but removable from above. Subcounty chiefs or *gombolola* chiefs were similarly unpaid, generally local men but with far more visibility and authority than the miruka chiefs under them. It was at the county chief level that real authority rested. The bakungu chiefs were the keys to effective administration. These men, from five to ten in each kingdom, were the leading beneficiaries and supports of colonial rule. They were *named* in agreements, composed the governing councils of the kingdoms, and collected rebates and later salaries from the administration. They were the top administrative officers of the state under only the king and the British resident.

Informally, the structure of the regime of collaboration was capped by the role of "arch-collaborator." In each kingdom, one individual assumed responsibility for carrying on the day-to-day operations of the regime. Central to those opera-

[116] Ibid.

[117] For example, A. Richards, ed., *East African Chiefs* (London: Faber & Faber, 1959).

tions was the continual contact with the representatives of alien authority and influence—"collectors," district officers, missionaries, European and Ganda functionaries, policemen and evangelists. In Ankole, this role was assumed by Mbaguta and confirmed by his being named Enganzi. He operated formally as prime minister and chairman of the ruling council, the Eishengyero. But it was his informal position as "foreign minister" that reinforced and underlay his formal position as the head of local government. Similarly, Byabacwezi assumed the function of "arch-collaborator" in Bunyoro. The chief formal differences here were the absence of a written agreement naming him as a bakungu chief and, second, the absence of an official title of "prime minister." Nonetheless, informally, he operated as the leading local chief, and was often thought of as "Katikiro."[118] Another variation was provided by the role of the alien Ganda chief, Jemusi Miti, who operated in many ways as co-head of local government. In Toro, the dual role of Kasagama as monarch and "arch-collaborator" has already been discussed. The novelty of a royal collaboration should not obfuscate the same basic structure of collaboration that sustained British rule elsewhere in western Uganda.

In examining the social origins of the bakungu chiefs, certain criteria appear to be relevant in understanding the basis of recruitment of this collaborating elite. First, the new ruling groups were not totally outside the old regimes. As D. A. Low has observed, these new rulers rose from the second rung of power to the top through a competitive process in which ability to secure alien support was crucial.[119] Nonetheless, none of the new elite were without some standing and backing in the old regime. Moreover, that standing was often on the basis of the achievement of high status rather than the ascription of status by high birth or breeding. Mbaguta's ambitious personality, the military abilities of the barusura captains-turned-chiefs, and the personal loyalty of Kasaga-

[118] Interviews B/1 Muganwa, 3 October 1968; B/7 Isoke, 19 October 1968; B/36 Jawe, 14 November 1968.

[119] D. A. Low, *Lion Rampart* (London: Cass, 1973), pp. 18–20, 89–90.

ma's followers have all been detailed. With few exceptions, the collaborating elite represented a group of men with something to gain by collaborating, namely, power. In addition, they had something of value to offer the foreign intruders, namely, a kind of legitimacy born of prior achieved status within precolonial society.

Second, the new elite appears to have been younger and more flexible than those who resisted.[120] The "old guard" was indeed an older and in many ways more conservative group. Youth and the concommitant lack of commitment to an older order combined with ambition and the ability to adapt to changing rules and conditions were important factors in the self-selection of the so-called "progressives." The ability to adapt, and specifically, the ability to operate between two cultural and political traditions was essential. Capability as a cultural and political broker between the demands of the British Protectorate and those of the African kingdoms was something no collaborator could be without. Whether expressed in terms of the bilingualism of Mbaguta and Kasagama or the foreign and Christian experiences of Mika Fataki or Yafeti Byakweyamba, the vital ability to cross back and forth between the local and the foreign appears again and again as central to the pattern of African collaboration with imperialism.

Collaboration provided for a considerable degree of continuity of lacustrine cultural and political traditions by allowing the preexisting social and political structures to adapt to incorporation in a world empire. In each of the three kingdoms that survived into the colonial era, similar regimes based on similar groups of collaborating African officials were established. These men were bearers of more than just the burdens of empire. They simultaneously carried with them the remnants of the African political culture in which they were raised. By making the compromises necessary for the effective collaboration between both the imperial and local African political systems, this African elite mediated between the past

[120] Ibid., p. 20.

epoch of independence and the transitional period of colonialism.

But the success of the collaborators in each kingdom should not mask the fact that they arrived at these common structures by very different routes. Eight years of war in Bunyoro was a far more rocky road to collaboration than the diplomatic high road taken by Mbaguta in Ankole. What determined the courses that were adopted? Although the personalities and characters of the leading protagonists of the contending policies of resistance and collaboration cannot be minimized, the social and political structures in which they operated were crucial to the determination of the responses to colonialism that they adopted. Bunyoro's militant national traditions, represented in the Bito dynasty's broad popular basis of support among herders and farmers, was far more conducive to resistance than the fragmented and class-ridden consciousness of Ankole's pastoral dominion. The class structure of lacustrine society and the political schisms and divisions within these three states are the keys to understanding how regimes of collaboration came to be established. As we shall see, these structures and schisms also determined the nature of African responses to colonialism during the difficult decade of adjustment that followed the establishment of collaboration.

CHAPTER VII

The Spirit of Unrest

IF the establishment of regimes of collaboration in the western kingdoms in 1900 and 1901 represented the climax of the imperialist upsurge of the previous decade, the years following that climax came to display the character of an anticlimax. The heroic figures of both the imperial and African casts seemed suddenly to vanish or diminish as the tasks that confronted them became the routinized and mundane concerns of legislation and day-to-day administration of an established system. The leaders of resistance had died or been exiled, whereas the collaborators had become subject to the constraints of their new bureaucratic roles. Even when the same towering figure of the 1890s crossed the divide into the twentieth-century colonial world, he seemed to lose stature or be pushed to the periphery of public life. Similarly, the pioneer missionaries, administrators, and soldiers of the *fin de siècle* gave way to a corps of educators, bureaucrats, and desk jockeys who lacked the calling, the fire, and the boldness of the first generation of Europeans in Uganda. The tasks required of both African and European colonial "leaders" were not those about which one wrote exciting memoirs or tales of personal adventure. For many of the participants in the earlier heroic age, life itself seemed to lose its zest.

Nonetheless, the first few years of colonial rule were to produce more than just a dull routinization of the regimes of collaboration. Before very long the collaborators themselves were to find that on taking stock of their achievements and examining their new roles, there was room for improvement. A period of counterclimax emerged during which, by agitation and civil resistance, Africans hoped that the balance struck with colonialism in 1900 could be readjusted in the direction of a larger area for indigenous participation. Sovereign independence was lost and was not to be regained

for over half a century. Nonetheless, with the realization of
that loss came the first attempts to find solutions to the problem of establishing an area of African autonomy and self-
respect. These efforts, which bore the stamp of a nascent anticolonial sentiment, marked the first emergence of indigenous
movements of social and political protest in the Uganda Protectorate. If they were not as dramatic as the armed rebellions
or insurrections in other colonial territories, these embryonic
anticolonial efforts were in many ways indicative of the direction and nature of the coming struggle for the restoration of
independence in the Uganda kingdoms.

Assassination in Ankole: 1905

On 19 May 1905, Harry St. George Galt, newly appointed
Subcommissioner for the western province of Uganda, entered Ankole en route from Fort Portal to Mbarara on tour. As
he settled for the night in the government rest house at
Ibanda, he must have contemplated his return to Ankole,
where he had served until 1903 as District Collector. Certainly he was aware of the capacity for intrigue and factionalism at the court of Kahaya. He could not have known
that his arrival was about to set off a desperate factional struggle, albeit a struggle by accusation and innuendo typical of
Hima politics. For as he sat on the verandah of the rest house
trying to read his Bible in the failing light, an African entered
the enclosure and speared the unsuspecting officer. The murder of Galt triggered not only a major political trial conducted
by the Protectorate government,[1] but opened for inspection
the political intrigue and partisanship of Ankole politics under

[1] Deputy Commissioner's Report, 30 July 1905, on Special Inquiry into
Circumstances of Assassination of H. St. George Galt, E[antebbe] S[ecretariat]
A[rchives] A12/6. This report, authored by George Wilson, comprises more
than 90 unnumbered pages of political information, disclosing more about
the imperial view of the collaborators than it does about the criminal aspects
of the case. Cf. H. F. Morris, "The Murder of H. St. George Galt," *Uganda
Journal* 24, 1(1960):1–15, for a discussion of the legal aspects of the case. Also,
Interviews A/1, A/4, A/5, A/7, A/9, A/43, and A/47 all offer differing views of
the Galt affair current among the Ankole factions at the time.

British overlordship. The inquiry into the assassination brought the underlying system of cleavages and hostilities to the surface, allowing an unobstructed view of the politics of collaboration.

The structure of politics in Ankole after 1901 modified the basic cleavages that had brought Mbaguta to power in the period just preceding the signing of the agreement. First, the conflict between the Shambo commoner, Mbaguta, and the Hinda Prince, Igumira, was transformed into a parliamentary rivalry between the "prime minister," Enganzi Mbaguta, and Igumira's close ally, the Iru courtier Ruhara. As a corollary to this central cleavage, a new kind of Hima/Iru schism emerged along with the formation of Christian denominational parties, which gave added fuel to the basically political differences.[2]

Ruhara's personal relations to the dynasty, his close ties to Igumira, and his avuncular relationship with the new Mukama Kahaya have already attracted our attention.[3] In the new situation Ruhara became not merely county chief of Rwampara, where he was clearly seen as a bailiff for the royal family, but he became the strongest and most unequivocal champion of the exiled Igumira and his policies. As such he fell into a position of continual friction with Mbaguta. This was expressed directly in debate and argument in the council of chiefs as well as less directly in the structural opposition that began to show itself.

By 1902, a Roman Catholic missionary, Pere Lesbros, entered Ankole, and the religious dichotomy that plagued Buganda and Toro was soon fully active there. That same year accusations against Pere Lesbros were made for promising "Ruhara that he would be 'as Mugwanya in Uganda' if he became a convert to Roman Catholicism."[4] Mugwanya, as

[2] Cf. Interviews A/1 Katate, 24 July 196; A/5 Murumba, 27 July 1968; A/13 Rugangura, 7 August 1968.

[3] See Chapter 6 supra.

[4] Commissioner to Collector, Ankole, 10 February 1902, *ESA* A15/1. See also *ESA* A15/1 C62 for correspondence between Lesbros and Racey. For Mbaguta-Ruhara friction, cf. Interviews A/1 Katate, 24 July 1968, A/13 Rugangura, 7 August 1968.

was well known in Ankole, was the most powerful Catholic
chief, with the title of Omuwanika or treasurer, and was second in power in Buganda only to the Protestant prime minister, Apolo Kagwa. This resulted in "defiant behavior" by
Ruhara in the eyes of the administration and began a long history of rivalry between the two Christian denominations.
Following Ruhara into his Catholic allegiance were the
Rwampara subchief, Bikwatsi, as well as two prominent
Bairu, Mayindo, who was a chief in Nyabushosi, and Nyemera, a chief in Isingiro.[5]

Already at this early stage the second social dichotomy was
becoming evident. Not only were these chiefs following "the
religion of Ruhara" rather than the religion of Kahaya, but
they were also coming to reflect the class division of Ankole
society into Hima and Iru groups. It is true that the Iru chiefs
were no mere cultivators. They were in many ways a part of
the ruling pastoral-dominated elite. Nonetheless, the class
system began to take on new coloration in the early days of
colonial rule as Bairu began to assert themselves as part of the
Catholic and royalist opposition to the Protestant establishment led by Mbaguta and the child king, Kahaya. This conflict came to an early climax in July 1902 when the strong-
headed Collector reported that he had found it necessary to
remove two Hima chiefs, Mazinio and Matsiko, from their
county chieftaincies and replace both of them with the Iru and
Catholic chiefs, Nyemera and Mayindo, respectively. The
grounds for dismissal were drunkenness and lack of influence
with their people. We can only guess at the reasons Kahaya
and the subchiefs nominated the replacements that they did.
In any case, in taking this drastic step the Collector must have
earned himself some debts of both gratitude and enmity. The
Collector was Harry St. George Galt.[6]

Besides the ouster of the Hima chiefs in Nyabushozi and
Isingiro, several other changes in chieftaincy deserve mention

[5] Interview A/49 Kaniola, 27 September 1968.
[6] Report for July 1902 and Galt to Commissioner, 24 July 1902, *ESA*
A15/2. Cf. Interviews A/12, A/29, A/33, A/34, and A/35 on Matsiko,
Mayindo, Mazinio, and Nyemera.

as background to the Galt assassination. In 1902, Kaihura, county chief of Bunyaruguru, died and was replaced by his son, Daudi Kasigano.[7] In the same year, Nduru, the traditional and recognized chief of Buzimba, unable to bear the restrictions of bureaucratic office, took his cattle and fled into Toro. He was replaced by the Hinda chief, Rwamugwizi, who became an important mediator between the royal and collaborating factions at court.[8] Most important, the death of Bucunku, the Hinda ruler of Mitoma who had made blood brotherhood with Henry M. Stanley in 1889, led to his replacement in 1903 by Gabrieli Rwakakaiga, another Muhinda, but one who lacked Bucunku's eminence and experience.[9] One minor appointment may claim some attention. Isaka Nyakayaga was a Protestant evangelist from Koki on Ankole's eastern fringe. He came to Ankole to preach, entered the chiefly hierarchy, and in 1904 ran afoul of Mbaguta. Nyakayaga lost some 60 goats, 12 cows, and his position as subchief to Rugarama in Kajara as a result of the Mbaguta's personal hostility.[10] Nonetheless, he had managed to gain reappointment as a subchief under Rwakakaiga in Mitoma by April 1905, in time to become deeply embroiled in the crime that shook the regime of collaboration in Ankole to its foundations.

One more character remains to be set in scene for the drama of crime and punishment: Prince Igumira. Having spent two years in exile from Ankole in Kisumu, although he had never

[7] Report for July 1902, *ESA* A15/2, reports the death and gives reason for skipping over the eldest son in favor of the youthful Kasigano for the succession. Kasigano was later removed during a dispute with his brother over boundaries, with power passing to one of Mbaguta's kinsmen. Knowles to Commissioner, 23 October and 21 December 1905, *ESA* A14/1, and Interviews A/5 Murumba, 27 July 1968, and A/16 Kafureeka, 13 August 1968.

[8] J. P. Wilson to Commissioner, 2 and 3 December 1902, *ESA* A12/2, and Interviews A/7 Muhoga, 26 July 1968, A/44 Mukindo, 10 September 1968, and A/13 Rugangura, 7 August 1968.

[9] Interviews A/43 Muhindi, 9 September 1968. Cf. Morris, "Murder," pp. 2–3.

[10] Statement by Isaka Nyakayaga, 4 May 1904, *ESA* A15/1, and Knowles to Commissioner, 26 May 1904, *ESA* A15/2.

been charged or convicted of any crime except that of being the most influential man in Ankole, Igumira returned to his residence in Kashari in September 1903.[11] It was felt that the new order was sufficiently stabilized to withstand the influences of the notable conservative and, moreover, it was likely believed that by returning him to pastoral life and excluding him from court life his influence might be further diminished. The example of Kahitsi, the once-powerful kingmaker who had retired to pastoral semiobscurity in Nshara, was not lost on the administration. However, Igumira, "the father of the country"[12] and the father of Kahaya as well, was to prove almost as powerful in "retirement" as he had proven in power.

News of the attack on Galt reached Mbarara on 20 May, and the district officer, Mr. Knowles, left for Ibanda with the local police commander on 26 May to begin inquiries into what was immediately perceived as an extraordinary and shocking crime. The murder of a European official of high rank under the conditions of administration that prevailed in Uganda in 1905 was far more than a simple felony. It was considered by British officialdom as having been politically motivated and hence a high crime against the state itself.[13] During Knowles' preliminary inquiry he examined all those present at Ibanda and called in the important chiefs of both Ankole and Toro. This failed to turn up any evidence beyond the murder weapon itself. The owner of the spear remained unknown. Suspicions turned to various suspects, especially the kinsmen of recent victims of Galt's harsh justice in Fort Portal. Briefly, at least, the Ankole chiefs were off the hook. But even Knowles reminded them of their responsibilities for apprehending the criminal and aiding the investigation, which he believed they were not doing to their utmost.[14]

[11] Commissioner to Sub-Commissioner, Western Province, 19 September 1903, *ESA* A13/1.

[12] For views on Igumira in retirement, see Interviews A/1, A/9, and A/41. On Kahitsi, see Interviews A/42 and A/34.

[13] Deputy Commissioner's Report, passim. *ESA* A12/6.

[14] Knowles to Commissioner, Ankole District Monthly Report, 30 June 1905, *ESA* A14/2. Cf. Morris, "Murder," pp. 3–4.

On 2 June, George Wilson, the Deputy Commissioner, arrived in Fort Portal from Entebbe with instructions to begin a special inquiry into the assassination. Wilson was probably the most experienced government official in the Protectorate and would prove a forceful investigator, stamping his personal judgments onto the facts of the case in no uncertain manner.[15] Wilson was convinced from the outset that the motive for the murder must have been political in the fullest sense: an attempt to disrupt and discredit European rule by Africans disaffected for racial reasons. Having brought Kasagama and his chiefs to Ibanda on 8 June and still finding no evidence against any Toro subject, Wilson began to investigate the possibility that Ankole subjects had committed the crime.

On 12 June, a break in the case came from an unsuspected source. A peasant from neighboring Buzimba county appeared before the tribunal and named another peasant, Rutaraka, as the murderer. Suddenly, the once sullen and uncooperative chiefs of Ankole came in with volumes of testimony as to Rutaraka's "extreme and habitual truculence which it was pointed out bordered on insanity."[16] Nonetheless, Wilson refused absolutely to believe that a mere "peasant would have undertaken to commit a crime of appalling magnitude. . . ." Indeed, Wilson steadfastly "refused to entertain the possibility of the absence of powerful instigators. . . ."[17]

A search was immediately begun for the accused culprit, which failed to turn him up until rumors of his suicide led to the discovery of the body of a man identified as the same Rutaraka. The body was hanged from a tree, a common method of suicide among the Banyankole. However, it soon was apparent that neither Wilson nor the Ankole chiefs believed the tale of fear or remorse and suicide. On the contrary, it was quickly accepted that Rutaraka himself had been the victim of a murder by hanging, but no plausible motive could

---

[15] See especially Deputy Commissioner's Report, prelude (paras. 1 and 8), conclusions (paras. 128ff), *ESA* A12/6, regarding native character and racial motivation of the offense.

[16] Ibid., para. 62.   [17] Ibid.

be uncovered by the investigators. Wilson clung to the conviction that the assassination was instigated by powerful figures for political motives even if the half-crazed Rutaraka had been their instrument. Rutaraka's "suicide" was interpreted by Wilson as a means of bringing the inquiry to a quick halt, thereby covering up the complicity of the real assassins.[18]

Suspicions regarding the instigators now were directed toward two Ankole chiefs, and Wilson soon came to believe that they were indeed the powerful figures behind the appalling crime. Rwakakaiga, the county chief of Mitoma, in which Ibanda was situated, had failed to appear promptly at the scene of the crime, had been dilatory in sending forward important witnesses, and had made positive attempts to obstruct the investigation in what may have been an attempt to protect Rutaraka's kin.[19] It was also learned that Kahaya had "surreptitiously agreed to install [Nyakayaga] in a sub-chieftaincy near Ibanda" despite the prohibition placed on his holding political office by the Collector. Evidence of Nyakayaga's uncooperativeness with the investigation was also tendered and led to the conclusion that he, along with Rwakakaiga, was implicated in a conspiracy to assassinate the Provincial Commissioner, Mr. Galt. According to Wilson, Nyakayaga's "complicity was never doubted from the moment of his impugnment."[20]

After these suspicions had formed in Wilson's mind, he called to Ibanda the one man in Ankole he considered capable of initiating such a crime, Prince Igumira. However, Igumira asserted that it was Rutaraka, a lone, crazed assassin, who was the guilty party, which struck Wilson "as prattle." Nonetheless, Igumira impressed Wilson as a man of character who "just missed being a most capable chief."[21] Indeed, after complimenting Igumira for being "as studiously polite as a mandarin and . . . brimming with common sense," Wilson directed that it would be advantageous to bring this knowledgeable and competent man in close contact with the admin-

[18] Ibid., para. 63.   [19] Ibid., para. 82. Cf. Morris, "Murder," p. 6.
[20] Ibid., para. 127.   [21] Ibid., para. 97.

istration.[22] Despite Igumira's cooperativeness and good sense, Wilson realized the he was confronted by a conspiracy of silence among the leading Hima chiefs and decided that if he was to press his investigation into the culpability of the Hima chiefs Rwakakaiga and Nyakayaga[23] he would have to change the venue of the inquiry to a more neutral ground. On 30 June, the trial was recessed to reconvene at Hoima in Bunyoro's "less repressive atmosphere."[24]

At Hoima, a strong case was made against Nyakayaga's involvement in instigating the murder, and confessions were obtained from Rutaraka's kinsmen that they had indeed strangled him on learning of his part in the crime. Rwakakaiga and Nyakayaga defended themselves on the grounds that the story of their instigation was fabricated and, moreover, there was no real motive that could be attributed to them. The suggestion that Rwakakaiga desired the death of a white man as revenge for the death the previous year of Prince Bucunku of smallpox, believed to be caused by witchcraft, was refuted on the grounds that both accused were Christians with long experience of Europeans. Furthermore, Rwakakaiga argued that he had no desire to kill Europeans, which he could have done at any time during his long acquaintance with them at court. Nonetheless, Wilson, preferring the testimony of Rutaraka's kinfolk against the Hima chiefs, delivered a verdict of guilty of conspiracy and recommended ten years of penal servitude and perpetual exile, death being considered an insufficient deterrent to crime among the Banyankole.[25]

Wilson's verdict was later supported by a formal trial in En-

[22] Ibid., para. 97ff.

[23] Wilson incorrectly identifies Nyakayaga as "a Muhima born in Uganda" (ibid., para. 64). He was in fact a Mukoki from the one-time independent kingdom of Koki on Ankole's eastern marches who came to Ankole as a Protestant evangelist with Rev. E. A. Clayton of the CMS. His Christian name, Isaka, is used throughout the Report. (Informal Interviews with Rev. Jeremy Bamunoba, 12 August 1968, and Mr. Ananyas Murumba, 13 August 1968.)

[24] Cited in Morris, "Murder," p. 7.

[25] Deputy Commissioner's Report, Conclusions, *ESA* A12/6.

THE SPIRIT OF UNREST

tebbe before the High Court, and a sentence of death was pronounced on the two chiefs by Judge G. F. M. Ennis. However, on appeal to the Court of Appeal for East Africa, the verdict was reversed on grounds of the contradictory and self-serving nature of the testimony of the main witnesses to alleged incriminating conversations between the accused and Rutaraka. Despite lingering suspicions of the guilt of the two chiefs, the three-man tribunal found that the lower court had convicted on insufficient evidence, and Rwakakaiga and Nyakayaga were acquitted in January 1906.[26]

By this time Wilson was Acting Commissioner, and he learned of the reversal with some astonishment. As chief administrative officer in the Protectorate, he felt that the return of either of the men to liberty in Ankole or for that matter the return of the acknowledged leader of the Hima chiefs, Igumira would be disruptive of the good order and administration of the Ankole kingdom. Rwakakaiga and Nyakayaga were therefore deported from Uganda to Kisimayu on the coast and Igumira was detained in Buganda, remaining in exile until his death almost 20 years later. Moreover, the Ankole Agreement was suspended and fines imposed on the entire population of Ankole. Inhabitants of Mitoma and Buzimba were singled out on the basis of their collective guilt for the act of racial murder, and each was assessed an extra fine and labor penalty.[27]

Although doubt lingered as to the guilt or innocence of the accused chiefs among the European observers and commentators, among Africans an even deeper doubt has persisted. Even the culpability of the man identified as Rutaraka has been impugned by some, who claim that the real murderer was alive and well in Ankole a generation after the crime was committed.[28] I do not propose to lay all the doubts to rest, as

[26] Morris, "Murder," pp. 10–15. Cf. J. Gray, "The Suspension of the Ankole Agreement," *Uganda Journal* 22, 1(1952):86–87.

[27] Elgin to Officer Administering Uganda Protectorate, 10 April 1905, *ESA* SMP 152/06, and "Igumira, Removal from Hoima to Kampala," *ESA* SMP 1680/09.

[28] Interview A/1 Katate, 24 July 1968.

I am unconvinced by any of the arguments. Instead, I propose to examine the accusations made then and more recently for evidence of the political motives and machinations that they reveal. The pattern of accusation and rebuttal during the inquiry will tell us far more about the character of Ankole politics in the first years of colonial overrule than they will about the guilt or innocence of any of the alleged criminals.

The first and most obvious target of accusations were outsiders: people who, if found responsible for the crime, would remove any stain of guilt from the accusers. For the Ankole chiefs and king, the logical target was Toro. And so by the time Knowles reached Ibanda in late May 1905, rumors were circulating that the murder had been committed by a Mutoro to revenge the execution of his father in Fort Portal on orders from Galt himself. Wilson found these allegations to be without substance and came to believe that the reactions of the Ankole chiefs were aimed at exonerating themselves rather than getting to the bottom of the case. It must be added that the Toro chiefs and Kasagama played a similar game, producing a list of five motives that would transfer suspicion to the Banyankole. Indeed, during the opening phase of the investigation under Knowles and Wilson, the chiefs of both kingdoms seem to have shared both a disposition to cast suspicions elsewhere and a somewhat lackadaisical attitude toward the crime itself. Even Mbaguta, who was the first Ankole chief to arrive in Ibanda to begin inquiries, asserted that it could not possibly have been a Munyankole or he, as Enganzi, would have known of it.[29]

One of the motives proposed by the Toro rulers seems indirectly to have brought results. Suspicion fell on a brother of Nduru, the chief of Buzimba county, who had fled to Toro territory. From the beginning of colonial rule, Nduru had found it difficult to work with the administration. When a young Hinda prince, Henry Rwamugwizi, was installed as his subchief to supervise his administration, he found it unbearable. Taking his cattle and close followers, he departed

[29] Deputy Commissioner's Report, paras. 1–59 passim, *ESA* A12/6. Cf. Morris, "Murder," p. 5.

Buzimba without notice and sought asylum in Toro. The Toro chiefs suggested that revenge for his flight and replacement as chief by Rwamugwizi might have moved Nduru's brother, Mucukura, to an act of violence against the administration. Although no further evidence was found against Mucukura, it was a peasant from Mucukura's estate who accused Rutaraka of the murder. The peasant was brought forward by a Toro chief on whom suspicion had fallen, and at the encouragement of Mucukura's wives he denounced Rutaraka and thus cleared both Mucukura and the Toro chief of any involvement.[30] The denunciation of Rutaraka opened up a new phase of the investigation and the second round of accusations.

The strategy of the Ankole chiefs after the accusation of Rutaraka shifted from blaming the Batoro to blaming the insane and violence-prone Rutaraka. But Wilson's incredulity of the lone assassin and his firm belief that "the crime [was] not personal, but racial and political in its bearings"[31] soon broke the Ankole chiefs into conflicting factions. Indeed, during the search for Rutaraka the attempts at obstruction and the "seal of silence" over the inhabitants of the vicinity of Ibanda indicated a consistent "Ankole policy throughout the whole inquiry" that gave "occasion for somewhat appalling suspicions."[32] The idea that the conspiracy in which Wilson instinctively believed might reach into the very topmost positions of authority in the kingdom was, to say the least, embarrassing. "After all, the 'suspects' are the hereditary rulers of the country: depose them and what better material can be substituted."[33]

Once suspicion fell on Rwakakaiga, a Hinda prince, the split became apparent. Mbaguta, the leading commoner chief, began not only to disassociate himself from the other

[30] J. P.Wilson to Commissioner, 2 and 3 December 1902, *ESA* A12/2. Interviews A/7 Mugoha, 26 July 1968, and A/44 Mukindo, 10 September 1968. Cf. Deputy Commissioner's Report, paras. 3–62 passim, and Morris, "Murder," pp. 5–6.
[31] Deputy Commissioner's Report, Conclusions, *ESA* A12/6.
[32] Ibid., para. 60.   [33] Ibid., Conclusions.

Ankole chiefs, but began to prejudice the European investigators against the Bahinda, alleging a conspiracy of which
he was innocent, but in which virtually the entire Hinda aristocracy was involved.

According to this version, a meeting took place at the kraal
of Igumira in Kashari, attended by various Bahinda including
Rwakakaiga, at which plans were made for the murder of a
European. Mbaguta learned of this and attempted in advance
to disassociate himself by telling the European officials of the
secret meeting.[34] The murder of Galt was the direct result of
this meeting, and Igumira himself, and possibly even Mugabe
Kahaya, were implicated. Nonetheless, when Igumira was
called to come to Ibanda, he was not placed under arrest and
his discussions with Wilson seem never to have touched on
any secret conclave.[35] What they did indicate to Wilson was
the truth of Mbaguta's "notorious unpopularity in his country." Wilson commented:[36]

> I began to learn the full effect of the exclusion of the An-
> kole Katakiro from disassociation with his fellows and
> discovered that his aid was rendered absolutely futile by
> the opposition with which any action from him was met.
> . . . I cannot but feel that the solid support that is offi-
> cially given to Mbaguta in Ankole, without any adequate
> effort to win over the rest of the chiefs, who after all, in
> actual fact, mean Ankole, is a great waste of well mean-
> ing effort. . . . Mbaguta has acquired no native follow-
> ing. I have myself witnessed his tendency to stand alone.
> . . .

In the case of Galt, Mbaguta chose again to stand alone.
The rest of the chiefs quickly countered the accusations against
Rwakakaiga by casting renewed suspicion on Mucukura,
which, failing for want of evidence, only heightened the
Deputy Commissioner's suspicions of a high-placed conspir-
acy. Indeed, Wilson soon learned that the chiefs, even when

[34] Interview A/5 Murumba, 27 July 1968. Cf. Interview A/1 Katate, 24 July
1968.

[35] Deputy Commissioner's Report, paras. 97–100, *ESA* A12/6.

[36] Ibid., paras. 89–96.

silent before him, had regularly reported developments to
Igumira.[37]

If the case for a Hinda conspiracy hinges on a secret meeting at Igumira's, it is on very shaky ground. Dynastic historians acknowledge that a gathering did take place at Igumira's
kraal at Kanyigiri, Kashari. But it is stated that the conclave
took place on the very day on which Galt was assassinated at
Ibanda. Rwakakaiga, Rwamugwizi, and Kahaya were present
at Kanyigiri, and although the meeting was not public, it was
certainly not a conspiratorial cabal planning a murder.[38]

> However, Mbaguta used the fact of this meeting at
> Igumira's to cast suspicion on the Bahinda. In fact,
> Rutaraka, the murderer, had planned to kill a Muhinda
> named Tariyabwiza. When he reached Tariyabwiza's
> place in Ibanda, he found him not in, so he killed Galt
> instead. He was not a drunkard, but a madman.

Regardless of the actuality of a conspiracy against Galt, the
conspiratorial atmosphere at Ibanda, with Mbaguta and
Igumira pitted against each other once again, led Wilson to
remove the inquiry to Hoima. Although highly critical of
Mbaguta's unpopularity and impressed by Igumira's character, Wilson felt it necessary to find a politically motivated
conspirator. Mbaguta was clearly blameless and without motive. Igumira and Kahaya were above suspicion because of
their popularity and standing among the chiefs. Rwakakaiga
and Nyakayaga were suitably placed to be held responsible
for obstruction and noncooperation and might even be tagged
with instigating the murder itself without bringing down the
entire kingdom government. At Hoima, and later at Entebbe,
that was to be the accusation and the verdict.

When additional witnesses against Rwakakaiga were
brought forward at Hoima who did not implicate any other

[37] Ibid., para. 100. Cf. Morris, "Murder," pp. 6–7.
[38] Interview A/47 Gasyonga, 12 September 1968. The quotation is translated from a statement by Samwiri Rwabushongo, an unofficial court historian, who assisted Omugabe Sir Charles Gasyonga during the interview. Cf.
Interviews A/7 Mugoha, 26 July 1968, and A/9 Kamugungunu, 2 August
1968.

Hinda chiefs, the chiefs apparently gave way. Wilson boast-fully reported:[39]

> Chiefs well known to be strong partisans of Gabrieli's have had to succumb to the weight of the evidence and the indisputable fairness observed in its acquirement, and so we have for instance Igumira, practically the ruler of Ankole, Ryamugwizi, an intimate friend, and Ruhara, a noted partisan in the preliminary Inquiry, acquiescing in the culpability of Gabrieli.

It is, of course, possible that Rwakakaiga and Nyakayaga did indeed conspire to instigate the murder, although it is hard to believe that any of the motives adduced for such a conspiracy were of much import.[40] What emerges as central to the case was not the question of guilt or innocence but of the existence of a polarization of the Ankole rulers into two antagonistic camps. On the one hand, we have Mbaguta and his British allies, who were "bound to support him through thick and thin. . . .";[41] on the other hand, we have Igumira and the leading chiefs drawn from the Hinda dynasty and its closest Hima and Iru supporters. This bipolarity, intensified by religious and ethnic differences, can be seen as a central fea-ture of Ankole politics during the colonial era. During that time, meaningful policy decisions were left to the imperial overlords, and the two groups of collaborating chiefs engaged in the shadow politics of intrigue that were ultimately condu-cive to unobstructed imperial rule. The ritual and ceremony that surrounded the kingdom government grew as the politi-cal content of kingship and chieftaincy shrank.[42]

Agitation in Toro: 1906

The crisis of collaboration in Toro that came in 1906 hardly deserves the name of crisis. Despite the fact that major

---

[39] Deputy Commissioner's Report, para. 127, *ESA* A12/6.

[40] Ibid., paras. 121–123; cf. Morris, "Murder," pp. 13–15.

[41] Ibid., para. 89.

[42] Martin Doornbos, *Regalia Galore* (Nairobi: East African Literature Bureau, 1976).

changes in the political structure of the Toro kingdom were
made as a result of protest and petition by the Batoro, the agitation was so slight as to cause no disturbances of normal relations of collaboration at the time and little or no memory
among the Batoro of the agitation *per se*. According to both
Toro and British historians, the Toro chiefs and their
Mukama merely petitioned the Protectorate authorities for
the redress of some formal grievances stemming from the
1900 Agreement and were met with sympathy and a quick,
effective response by the British. If it were only a question of
constitutional reform, that would be an adequate description.
In fact, however, the formal change in the Agreement made
in 1906 hid a far more significant change of the power relations in the Toro kingdom. More than the Agreement itself,
the reforms of 1906 stand as the confirmation of royal power
over an extensive new district and under the supervision of
the colonial authorities. It put an end to a decade-long history
of provincial secessionism and firmly centralized the kingdom
under the sway of Mukama Kasagama and his British supporters.

Before examining the "crisis" itself, we must delineate the
pattern of politics in which it took place. The main feature of
the collaborationist regime in Toro stemmed from the
anomalies in the 1900 Agreement discussed in the previous
chapter.[43] The dual role of Kasagama as both Mukama of the
Toro kingdom and county chief of "Toro proper" led directly
to the political division of his subordinate chiefs into two
groups. The county chiefs of Toro proper were in effect the
king's men, appointed with his approval, dismissed at his request, and in most ways completely loyal to the monarch. On
the other hand, the confederal counties were in the hands of
men with some independent claim to authority and who from
time to time might exercise that authority without reference
to their subordinate constitutional position as part of the
kingdom of Toro. The main point of contention within the
overall regime of collaboration was the question of subordinating the confederal counties to the center by gaining con-

[43] Supra, Chapter 6, pp. 177–190.

trol over the ruling council of chiefs, the Rukurato. The potential for conflict with the British overlords inherent in the competition for power between the Toro rulers became manifest in the years following the Agreement's enactment in 1900.

Political problems stemming from the constitutional anomaly began to surface shortly after the enactment of the Agreement. When the territory of Mboga to the west of Lake Albert was first attached to the Protectorate in November 1901, the traditional chiefs of Mboga voluntarily agreed to place themselves under Kasagama's suzerainty and accepted a Ganda-style county status and chiefly hierarchy. However, by December 1902, Mboga had been detached from Kasagama's control and placed directly under the supervision of the resident British officer. The authority cited for this change was that of the Toro Agreement itself, which did not make provision for the extension of Kasagama's authority over new counties, unnamed at the time of the Agreement.[44] As Mboga would eventually fall outside the area of British control, being ceded to the Congo Free State, the question became academic. Nonetheless, the problem of the limits of Kasagama's authority on the periphery of Toro proper had been raised and would appear again.

More pressing and more lasting problems were raised by Kasagama's attempts to exercise authority in Bwamba county, which lay around the northern slopes of Ruwenzori, even today a difficult journey from Fort Portal. In March 1902, an attempt was made by the county chief, Petero Tigwezire, to collect "hut tax" in Bwamba, which was still effectively ruled by its own local headmen. The attempt was met with armed resistance. Eleven men were killed, with Tigwezire returning to Fort Portal to call for a "punitive expedition" against the tax refusers in Bwamba. The resident refused to act, agreeing with the Baamba in seeing the alleged tax collection as an unjustified raid for women and ivory against a people who did not recognize Toro's right to rule.

---

[44] G. Wilson to F. Jackson, 21 November 1901, *ESA* A12/1, and G. Wilson to Commissioner, 29 December 1902, *ESA* A12/1.

Tigwezire was deposed by the Rukurato on charges brought by the British officer and orders minuted by the Commissioner. Moreover, the officer refused at first to countenance the appointment of another Mutoro chief in the region, preferring to allow the Baamba to select their own representative and to continue to live under their own headmen. Thus, although Bwamba was technically part of Toro proper, its peripheral location and its ethnic and political independence from Toro belied the constitution. Indeed, the Bwamba and Konjo districts of Toro remained an area of sedition and rebellion against the Toro kingdom government right through the colonial era.[45]

Despite the Bwamba case, between 1900 and early 1903 Kasagama had pretty much his own way with the Rukurato, ruling Toro in a highly despotic manner. From its inception the council consisted of all of the chiefs named in both the Agreement (five peripheral county chiefs and Toro proper) and the attached Note (eight chiefs from within Toro proper). This meant that including Kasagama's appointed Katikiro, the monarch controlled two-thirds of the council, 10 of 15 members. In addition, he had named Nikodemu Kakurora as regent for the adolescent prince of Kitagwenda. With Kakurora controlling one of the confederal county seats and himself backed by nine other appointees, Kasagama easily managed the debate and decisions within the council. He thereby controlled the flow of information to the British resident and the Protectorate regime. In 1900, Kasagama seemed assured of effective control of politics in colonial Toro.

The proof of this can be found in the successful attempts by Kasagama to place his own followers in chieftaincy positions and landed estates not only in Toro proper, where as county chief and sovereign he had the constitutional power, but in

[45] Wylde, Report for Toro, March 1902; Ormsby to Tomkins, 12 June 1902, and minute by Commissioner, 10 November 1902; G. Wilson to Commissioner, 20 December 1902, *ESA* A12/2. Cf. Interviews C/18 Mukidi, 21 January 1969, and C/19 Tigwezire, 22 January 1969. On rebellion among Baamba and Bakonjo, see M. Doornbos, "Kumanyana and Ruwenzururu," in *Protest and Power in Black Africa*, R. Rotberg and A. Mazrui, eds. (New York: Oxford University Press, 1970), pp. 1088–1136.

the confederal counties as well. Kasagama managed to place in power a long list of subordinates in both Mwenge and Kyaka counties without the consultation or permission of the county chiefs and to give away titles and estates in Kitagwenda.[46] The ability of a leader to place his men on the land and in office was the key indication of who exercised effective authority in the territory. With the by-passing of the county chiefs, Kasagama demonstrated that they were incapable of controlling their own counties. It was a situation that went counter to British practice elsewhere in the Protectorate and that would soon create stress in Toro as the confederal chiefs tried to reassert themselves.

The first attempt by a confederal chief to assert his authority came in the always troublesome county of Kitagwenda. The Mubito Prince Bulemu, who had succeeded his father in 1892 at the age of about 10 or 12, had not reached his majority by the time of the signing of the 1900 Agreement. Until 1898, he had reigned under the guidance of his uncle, Kakyentuli. In that year, Katikiro Mugurusi led a Toro army against the recalcitrant Batagwenda and Bulemu was forced under Mugurusi's tutelage. In 1900, Sir Harry Johnston had dispatched the young Prince to Entebbe to be educated to his chiefly responsibilities, leaving the new county of Kitagwenda under a regent appointed for Bulemu by Kasagama under terms of the Agreement. By November 1902, the British officer in charge of Toro recommended that Bulemu, having reached his majority, be returned to full power in his county. Bulemu was reinstated in March 1903, over the objections of Kasagama, who preferred to keep power in the hands of his trusted subordinate, Kakurora. Bulemu immediately proceeded to depose various Batoro who had been placed in chieftaincy positions and estates without his consent. He further began to assume his own place on the Rukurato. These acts appear to have precipitated the first showers of the coming storm.[47]

[46] Ormsby, Report for Toro, November 1902, ESA A12/2; Ormsby, Report for Toro, February 1903, and cover letter by J. P. Wilson, 10 March 1903, ESA A12/3.
[47] Interviews C/12 Mujasi, 17 January 1969, and C/40 Binyomo, 12 Feb-

The same month, J. P. Wilson,[48] the Collector for Toro, reported his first efforts to reconstitute the Toro Rukurato. Instead of allowing all the chiefs named in 1900 full voting rights on the council, Wilson gave seats to the five chiefs who had full county rank in the confederal counties, with only two seats going to Toro proper: one for Kasagama and one for his Katikiro. From having control of 11 seats as against four from the confederal counties, the tables were dramatically turned. Kasagama's powers of appointment in the confederal counties were being challenged successfully by Bulemu in Kitagwenda and the chiefs of Mwenge and Kyaka as well. Even control of his own ruling council seemed to be slipping from his grip. He countered by refusing to seat Bulemu's delegate to the council, citing as grounds his adherence to the Roman Catholic faith, which would have meant a change in the religious balance among the county chiefs.[49] The appointment of a second Katikiro to represent Roman Catholic interests in June 1903, despite Kasagama's vociferous opposition to such a course, marked a low point in Kasagama's power.[50]

The failure of repeated protests and loud refusals seems to have convinced Kasagama of the advisability of a course of action that would avoid confrontation with his British collaborators and supporters. Later in June, Kasagama politely petitioned the district officer to increase the representation of Toro proper on the Rukurato to give them six seats as opposed to five for the confederal counties. Approval was received from the Commissioner in Entebbe to increase Kasagama's representatives to parity at five seats each. It seems that Kasagama had discovered the key to victory in his struggle to regain control of the council and the kingdom. By polite petition and representations, he might achieve what his vociferous and uncompromising behavior could not. In August, Kasagama elected two of his subordinate county chiefs to the Rukurato, giving him parity on a council of ten. He

---

ruary 1969. Cf. Ormsby, Report for Toro, November 1902, especially enclosed statement by Bulemu.

[48] No relation to George Wilson.

[49] J. P. Wilson, Report for Toro, March 1903, *ESA* A12/3.

[50] J. P. Wilson to Commissioner, 4 and 20 June 1903, *ESA* A12/3.

wanted to elect three chiefs, which would have given him the deciding vote, but for the time being the British would not permit it. By November, the district officer noted the remarkable cooperativeness of the monarch, a "considerable change" over a three-month period.[51]

Early in 1904, Kasagama began to wage his campaign for control of all of Toro, using his new weapons of conciliatory language and petition. Having requested an interview with the Commissioner, Kasagama put to him various proposals regarding his ability to make appointments of subchiefs, distribute land, and have his subordinate chiefs in Toro proper upgraded to full county chiefs. Commissioner Sadler rejected this last request, but clearly heard Kasagama's presentation in an amicable mood.[52]

By July 1904, Kasagama had enlisted another ally in his quiet campaign. The CMS missionary in Toro, Henry Maddox, opened a correspondence with the administration in Entebbe through his Bishop, which brought the complaints of the Toro regime before the authorities in a most respectful and respectable manner. It was Maddox who had been responsible for translating the original Toro Agreement, which had been written in English, to the assembled chiefs in 1900. Little time was given for explanation of the terms, and Maddox, aware of the inconsistencies in the document, politely stated that "the natives quite fail to understand what the treaty means."[53] Indeed, it might be argued that even Maddox, the acknowledged expert on Toro affairs, was quite unaware of what the Toro regime was really complaining about.

But the heart of the issue was exposed in a letter from Maddox to George Wilson on 3 September 1904[54] in which four Toro complaints were enumerated. The first dealt with the anomalous position of Kasagama as his own subchief in Toro proper, but no indication was made as to why this was a

[51] Cubitt to Commissioner, 12 November 1903; also 10 August 1903, *ESA* A12/4.

[52] Minute by J. H. Sadler, Commissioner, 3 February 1904, *ESA* A12/4.

[53] Maddox to Commissioner, 30 July 1904, *ESA* A22/1.

[54] *ESA* A22/1.

cause of hardship rather than simple confusion. The following three complaints dealt with real grievances stemming from limitations placed on Kasagama and his chiefs by the ambiguous terms of the Agreement. Two of them had to do with the problem of land grants for the Toro rulers. The Buganda Agreement on which the Toro document was modeled by Sir Harry Johnston called for the distribution of both official estates and private freehold estates (later known as *mailo*) to all the county chiefs, the ministers, and the Kabaka himself.[55] The Toro Agreement had similar provisions, but the distinction between private and official estates was not being respected and no land had been granted to the subordinate county chiefs or the Katikiro. The failure to make the distinction between private estates held in perpetuity and official estates held only during tenure of office had already emerged as a source of friction in the confederal county of Kitagweta, and Maddox cites this as an example in his letter.[56] The related problem of the status and emoluments of subordinate chiefs probably rankled far more among Kasagama's closest supporters, but is not mentioned in the letter. The failure to reward subchiefs may well have been the first cause of the entire program of petition. Several of the younger, literate chiefs were beginning to bring pressure on the Mukama to push their case for landed estates before the British authorities in order that they might rank as equals to the older, "uneducated" chiefs.[57]

Complaints that Kasagama's own estates had been limited to holdings within Toro proper despite the explicit provision for his holding lands throughout the kingdom were mentioned third. Lastly, Maddox reported complaints that Kasagama's authority to hear cases was being circumvented by direct appeal to the European officer and that appointments of chiefs and members of the Rukurato were being made without the knowledge or consent of the Mukama,

[55] Cf. D. A. Low and R. C. Pratt, *Buganda and British Overrule* (London: Oxford University Press, 1960), especially chap. 5.

[56] Cf. Interview C/8 Basigara, 15 January 1969.

[57] Interview C/42 Mpisi, 17 February 1969.

who "felt that his recognized position as 'Supreme Chief' was undeservedly injured."[58] In sum, Maddox's letter suggested, and the Anglican Bishop concurred, that the Agreement be readjusted and its provisions consistently applied. The campaign to amend the Agreement was in high gear.

Nonetheless, no progress was made during the following year. Perhaps the impasse resulted from Kasagama's intransigence at the appointment of an independent-minded county chief, Kalyegera Rwakiomba, to replace the deposed Mubito Muitwara ruler of Kitagweta. Certainly, Kasagama's "unconciliatory manner" and "his childish and purposeless abuse of power towards his own petty ends"[59] did not encourage the new district officer, Mr. Haldane, to improve his political position within the kingdom. Nor did Kasagama's repeated demand to name subchiefs to the county chiefs without their consent improve matters.[60] In any case, the murder of Galt and the consequent absence of Kasagama and several of his leading chiefs at Ibanda and Hoima brought business in the Toro Rukurato to a standstill.[61]

Only in October 1905 did the campaign start up again, now in its decisive last phase. George Wilson received a draft of the complaints of the Toro chiefs. The District Officer, F. A. Knowles, and Nasanaeri Mugurusi, Kasagama's fiercely loyal Katikiro, then drew up a plan to put before the Rukurato followed by a petition to forward to the Protectorate authorities to readjust the Toro counties. Knowles commented that he looked forward "to being rid of this long vexatious question."[62] After all, it had been almost three years since Kasagama had lost effective control of the Rukurato and his ability to distribute titles and lands within the kingdom. It would take four more months to negotiate the new plan through the Rukurato and get the approval of Entebbe. But the end was at last in sight.

[58] Maddox to Wilson, 3 September 1904, *ESA* A22/1.

[59] Haldane, Report for Toro, January and February 1905, *ESA* A14/2.
[60] Ibid.

[61] Speke, Report for Toro, July 1905, *ESA* A14/2.

[62] G. Wilson to Commissioner, 17 October 1905, and enclosed draft, *ESA* A12/7, and Knowles to G. Wilson, 22 December 1905, *ESA* A14/2.

In April, Knowles filed an extensive report[63] on the proposed Agreement amendments that had passed the Rukurato and were being submitted to the Commissioner at Entebbe for his sanction. It was divided into two parts: the first included those changes that were in Knowles' view "obviously expedient" and on which he made supportive recommendations. Part Two was reserved for "controversial items" and dealt exclusively with the problems of land settlement, rents, and tenure.

Among the "obviously expedient" changes requested in the petition were, first, the removal of Kasagama's responsibilities as a county chief, and second, the immediate upgrading of four of his eight subordinate chiefs to full county chief rank and the eventual grant of that rank to the chief of Bwamba, which in 1906 remained ungovernable. There followed three further requests which were contingent upon the change in county chief status. First, the petition asked for the extension of the system of succession that operated in the other counties to the new county chiefs; i.e., the chiefs named their own successor, a practice that implied hereditary rather than appointive office. Only in cases of the removal of a county chief from office for cause would the selection of a successor revert to the Rukurato and Protectorate government for appointment. Second, the chiefs asked for the reopening of discussions of the grant of freehold estates (*mailo*). Last, the Mukama allowed his former share of taxation within Toro proper to be divided among the new county chiefs with a special provision for a rebate to go to the Katikiro, hitherto supported out of Kasagama's rebate as "Supreme Chief" of all of Toro Confederacy. A rider was added to provide support during their lifetimes for the three chiefs who were being demoted to subchief status and to renegotiate the allocation of revenue derived from the salt and iron resources of the kingdom. Knowles also suggested that the Toro Confederacy be restyled the Toro Kingdom in the amended agreement. This he affirmed would unify the country and make it "easier to govern."

[63] Knowles to Acting Commissioner, 19 April 1906, and enclosed petition, *ESA* A14/3.

Not surprisingly, it was the controversial matters of land settlement that went to the heart of the grievances of the Mukama and chiefs and was responsible for "the spirit of unrest" and "retarded progress" in Toro.[64] It was in terms of land and the revenue to be derived from control of land that the collaborating chiefs were to be remunerated for their services to the establishment and perpetuation of colonial rule. Although revenues from salt, iron, and ivory were important enough to remain a source of occasional friction for another decade,[65] the main source of support for the collaborating elite in an agricultural society was the land itself. And it was the land and its distribution that was the concern of the eight points of Part Two of the petition.

In brief, the Mukama, Katikiro, and queen mother were to receive extensive estates in each of the ten counties of the kingdom to be allotted from the so-called waste or uncultivated lands claimed by the crown in the 1900 Agreement. It was stipulated that the lands must be waste at the time of their survey, an indefinite future time rather than at the time of the Agreement to avoid the distribution of newly occupied and cultivated land. The county chiefs were to receive both private and official estates within their own counties. Subchiefs were to receive collectively some 3,000 square miles of waste land "inclusive of what they already possess" for their maintenance. Most important, each peasant (*mukopi*) was to be responsible for the payment of a tax of two rupees per annum or one month of labor service per annum to his county chief. Thus, the perpetuation of the dominance of the collaborators was assured. On 13 June 1906, the new Commissioner and soon to be Governor, Sir Hesketh Bell, signed the new arrangements into law. Not only did Toro become a unified kingdom by this act,[66] but the Toro elite led by Kasagama had succeeded in incorporating a far wider area than Toro had

---

[64] Ibid. Cf. Informal interview O. W. Furley, 4 March 1969.

[65] "Toro: Kasagama's Lubiri searched by Policy, inquiry re:" 25 March 1914, *ESA* C 186, refers to illicit ivory trade and hunting by Kasagama and Mugurusi (cf. *ESA* SMP 79/09).

[66] Uganda Protectorate, *Enquiry into the Grievances of the Mukama and People of Toro* (Entebbe, 1926). Appendix C contains the text of the final

ever been in the previous century into a political system in which the Toro monarch was to prove a far more powerful ruler than any in the country's history. From then on the Toro chiefs were to be clearly and unequivocally subordinate to a powerful monarch at the head of a centralized administrative system. With the unfaltering support of the British authorities and their police power, Kasagama had maneuvered himself into a position as king of a centralized and "easily governed" colonial protectorate. In power, prestige, and wealth, collaboration for king and chiefs had been a profitable exercise.

Before a year was out, Kasagama was exercising his new power derived from the seemingly formalistic constitutional adjustments. In December 1906, the Assistant Collector for Toro submitted a full list of all the chiefs, subchiefs, and notables of the Toro Kingdom, including 42 Babito headed by Vikitoria Kahinju, the queen mother, and Maliza Bagaya, Kasagama's royal sister. Ten county chiefs were listed as given in Table 7-1.[67]

Beyond the formal recognition of Kasagama's royal kinsmen in a government document, there were two chieftaincy changes that showed the reinforcement of Kasagama's power. First, the replacement of the recently deceased Kalyegera Rwakiomba in Kitagweta by his 14-year-old nephew, Lazaro Kiiza Basigara, enabled Kasagama to name his own followers as regents to rule during Basigara's minority.[68] Thus, a difficult and independent-minded chief was replaced with a malleable (and unwilling) youth and his appointive guardians. Second, the removal of Kwitakulimuki on charges of misappropriation of funds, with a possible hidden motive of his recent conversion from an early and leading member of the Protestant faith to Islam, opened the way for

---

Memorandum. Cf. D. A. Low, "Uganda: The Establishment of the Protectorate, 1894–1919," in V. Harlow and E. M. Chilver, eds., *History of East Africa*, II (Oxford: Clarendon Press, 1965), pp. 84–85, for a version that stresses Toro's constitutional unification.

[67] From "System of Chieftainship: Toro." List, pp. 1–15, *ESA* SMP 559/06.

[68] Interview C/8 Basigara, 15 January 1969.

Table 7-1

Toro Chiefs, December 1906

County	Title (Luganda)	Incumbant
Mwenge	Pokino	Nasanaeri Kagwahabi
Kitagwenda	Katambala	Edwadi Bulemu
Chaka (Kyaka)	Lukekula	Sirasi Kagoro
Kitagweta	Kitunzi	Lazaro Kiza
		(Basigara)
Nyakabimba	Chambalango	Samuiri Kato
Bunyangabo	Mukwenda	Maliko Dwakaikara
		(Rwakaikara)
Busongora	Kimbugwe	Mikaeri Lusoke
		(Rusoke)
Kibali (Kibale)	Sekibobo	Tito Kamarampaka
Bulahya (Burahya)	Kaima	Zakaliya Kibogo
Bwamba (provisional)	Kasuju	Nikodemu Kakurora

the appointment of Tito Kamarampaka on the recommendation of Kasagama alone.[69]

The other changes from the 1900 list of chiefs do not appear to be significant with regard to Kasagama's consolidation of power. Tibagwa, the leading Catholic chief, had been replaced by Rwakaikara, another strong Catholic supporter.[70] Tigwezire, removed for the incidents in Bwamba, had been replaced by the equally loyal Kakurora and was even then a first subchief to Rwakaikara on the way to rehabilitation and reappointment as county chief within three years.[71] Three names were missing. Korokoro and Rukambuza, whose counties had been eliminated in 1906, were both old, uncon-

[69] Galt to Commissioner, 12 May 1905, *ESA* A14/2. Cf. Interviews C/35 Kyamulesire, 31 January 1969, and C/33 Manyindo, 30 January 1969.

[70] Ormsby, Toro Report, December 1902; J. P. Wilson to Commissioner, 4 June 1903, *ESA* A12/3, and Interviews C/40 Binyomo, 12 February 1969, and C/34 Basigara, 31 January 1969.

[71] *ESA* SMP 559/06, p. 8; also, "Complete List of Chiefs of 1st Grade in Toro," 4 April 1910, *ESA* SMP 330 (Toro: Chiefs, deposition and appointment of). Cf. Interviews C/18 Mukidi, 21 January 1969; C/19 Tigwezire, 22 January 1969; C/16 Kibooga, 20 January 1969; C/21 Bamuroho, 23 January 1969.

verted, and had been pensioned off.[72] Tomasi Bamya, who also lost his county chief's status, was appointed as a regent for Basigara in Kitagweta along with the elderly Yoswa Rusoke, the former Katikiro to Kasagama. In fact, Bamya served as an acting county chief until such time as a new opening could be made for him.[73]

It did not take Kasagama long to create such an opportunity. In July 1907, Kasagama "verbally requested the removal of two saza chiefs."[74] The grounds cited were "general incompetence," and the removal of both Edwadi Bulemu from Kitagwenda and Sirasi Kagoro from Kyaka was approved by the Subcommissioner. Before the end of the month, both chiefs who had led their counties with a marked degree of independence before the 1906 "readjustments" were replaced by two chiefs who had shown consistent and devoted loyalty to the Toro monarch. Tomasi Bamya replaced Kagoro and Nasanaeri Mugurusi, the Katikiro, replaced Bulemu by order of the Toro Rukurato.[75]

More important than Kasagama's ability to put his own men in key positions as evidenced by the appointments of Bamya and Mugurusi, he had established a regular procedure for the deposition and appointment of chiefs at all levels and in all the counties (excepting always Bwamba, which was not regularly administered until after World War I). Recommendations from the Mukama as chief executive of the Toro kingdom went to the Rukurato and from there to the Collector, restyled District Commissioner. The D. C. would comment on the principals involved in each recommended change

[72] Interviews C/29 and C/38 Rwakiboijogoro, 29 January and 11 February 1969.

[73] *ESA* SMP 559/06, p. 8, lists Bamya as one of 14 Batangole under Rwakaikara in Bunyangabo.

[74] Knowles to Collector, Toro, 2 July 1907, *ESA* SMP 850/07 (Toro Chieftainships).

[75] "Lukiko measure," 26 July 1907, *ESA* SMP 850/07; Interview C/8 Basigara, 15 January 1969. Cf. Browning to Chief Secretary, 4 March 1912, and other items in *ESA* A/72 (Toro chiefs) for Mugurusi's performance in his dual role of saza chief and prime minister.

and forward recommendations and comments to the Chief Secretary in Entebbe for the approval of the Commissioner or, after 1908, of the Governor. The most frequent comments of the D.C.s of Toro on such changes were to second the recommendations for removal of chiefs for "being useless" and to support the intelligence of the new appointments.[76] There were occasions when a D.C. might initiate or recommend changes on his own. But seldom did the hierarchy in the Protectorate administration care to brook the hostility of their close collaborators at Kasagama's court by acting without reference to the wishes of the Rukurato, which Kasagama dominated.

What is ultimately most notable about the 1906 agitation is how little it has been noted. Colonial historians have tended to mention it exclusively in terms of the readjustment in the constitutional relations between the counties and in the status of the monarch.[77] Little attention has been paid to the political motives and impact of the changes nor to the major land resettlement that was very much the driving force behind the petition campaign. Perhaps more striking is the almost total lack of impact that the agitation had on the Toro populace or on the memories of Toro's local historians. It may be that the reason for the lack of concern evidenced by paucity of oral testimony on the events *per se* was, first, the failure of the agitation among the chiefs to penetrate to the common man and, second, that only minor inconveniences were caused to the bakopi by the relocation of county seats and the reallocation of titles and estates.[78] Indeed, "the spirit of restlessness" which George Wilson noted in 1905 in Ankole seems hardly

[76] "Toro: Chiefs, deposition and appointment of." *ESA* SMP 330 includes material on chieftainship changes from 1910 to 1921 as well as a complete list of chiefs and subchiefs (71 in all) for nine counties (excluding Bwamba) in April 1910.

[77] K. Ingham, *The Making of Modern Uganda* (London: Allen and Unwin, 1958), pp. 93–94 and Low, "Uganda, the Establishment," pp. 84–85.

[78] Interviews C2/1 Rwakiboijogoro and C2/2 Basigara, 13 June 1972. Cf. Uganda Protectorate, *Grievances of the Mukama and People of Toro*, pp. 3–4 and Appendixes.

to have affected more than a close circle of collaborating chiefs around the royal court in Toro.

Rebellion in Bunyoro: 1907

George Wilson had cautioned in 1905 that the spirit of unrest manifested in Ankole at the time of the Galt murder was bound to recur throughout the western kingdoms "unless the action of the government on this occasion leaves an indelible impression behind it."[79] He was clearly too sanguine about the efficacy of government action in quelling a spirit of discontent and disaffection that was gaining ground throughout the Protectorate. Nonetheless, his belief in the necessity of strong government action would persist as he came to confront the most serious threat to British hegemony in Uganda in the first decade of the twentieth century.

Early in 1907, various Nyoro chiefs and subchiefs began to evict other subchiefs who were ethnically Baganda from the positions they had come to occupy during the preceding five or six years. Ganda chiefs and evangelists had been used by the administration in a variety of capacities in Bunyoro and elsewhere from the first days of colonial penetration. It was in Bunyoro that their position became most onerous and where simmering resentment against them first came to a boil. By March, public refusal of cooperation or protection of the Baganda by the Nyoro chiefs led to the withdrawal of the Baganda to the protection of district headquarters in Hoima. The British officials issued direct orders to the Nyoro chiefs to allow the Baganda to return to their offices and duties. The Nyoro chiefs refused to reinstate them. "Nyangire Abaganda," as this act of disobedience is remembered, means "I refuse the Baganda."[80]

[79] Deputy Commissioner's Report, Introduction, *ESA* A12/6.

[80] The best vernacular accounts are found in J. Nyakatura, *Abakama ba Bunyoro-Kitara* (St. Justin's, P.Q., Canada: 1947), translated as *Anatomy of an African Kingdom*, G. N. Uzoigwe, ed. (New York: Anchor, 1973), p. 219; and O.L.O. Katyanku and S. Butera, *Obwomezi Bw'Omukama Duhaga II* (Kampala: Eagle Press, 1950), pp. 18–20.

And so they did refuse, persisting in the refusal for over two months, while gathering at Hoima to give voice to their grievances. Ultimately, British commitment to both the Baganda and to forceful government action in the face of unrest brought about the arrest of 54 of the demonstrating Nyoro chiefs. Although there were what Wilson described as "frenzied" demonstrations, no one was killed during the months of disobedience. Even violence against property was limited to the burning of some houses of the Ganda chiefs in the outlying areas. The intensity of the peaceful protest led Wilson to suggest that the "conspiracy had been marked with such able organization and recusancy for a long period so quietly and persistently sustained as to stamp it with the suspicion of non-native guidance."[81] Wilson's long experience in Uganda and his familiarity with the politics of collaboration make it difficult to dismiss this suggestion of "outside agitators" as mere racist or reactionary hallucinations. Yet there is no shred of evidence to suggest that anyone but Banyoro were involved in the protest. Wilson's back-handed compliment to Nyoro ability to organize and sustain the protest must be attributed to his blindness to their grievances and the justice of their cause. In examining the Nyoro grievances, we shall once again be able to look into the politics of collaboration, this time as practiced in Bunyoro after the establishment of a new regime in 1901.

Bunyoro's status as a conquered province and the British conviction that the Banyoro were hostile to progress and incapable of efficient self-government led to the creation of a regime of collaboration unlike those in Toro or Ankole.[82] Not only was there no agreement to fix the rights of the collaborating chiefs, but the "backward" position of the Banyoro led to the introduction of Ganda chiefs as tutors to those Nyoro chiefs who had entered into collaboration. Not only were the Baganda to come as teachers and preachers, clerks and interpreters in the colonial administration in Bunyoro, Ganda presence took the uniquely irritating form

[81] G. Wilson to Elgin, 25 June 1907, *ESA* SMP 710/07.
[82] Supra, Chapter 6, pp. 157–177.

of territorial and political authority over the Banyoro. Not only were vast areas of the former kingdom of Kitara lying between Bunyoro and Buganda severed from Nyoro control and annexed to Buganda, but even in the rump of territory left under the Nyoro monarch and his chiefs, Ganda chiefs were introduced beside them to teach the arts of government *à la* Buganda.

At the head of the Baganda in Bunyoro was Jemusi Miti,[83] brought to Bunyoro in 1901 on petition by the Nyoro chiefs for someone to teach them the arts of local administration. He and his small following of Baganda had a profound impact on Nyoro government in a very short time. At first they were well received by the Banyoro, or at least by the Nyoro chiefs with whom they had come to work. Miti was the main force in drafting and pushing through the Protectorate hierarchy a new territorial arrangement that regularized the chiefly authorities inherited from the turbulent decade of resistance. The chief virtue of the arrangement for the Banyoro was that it recognized the authority of the ruling Nyoro chiefs and subchiefs and provided for their support by means of tax rebates. Indeed, but for the absence of the grant of freehold tenure to the king and chiefs, the arrangements closely resembled the Agreement's provisions in Toro and Ankole. The absence of landed estates, however, should not be skipped over lightly, as it would emerge as an important grievance against the Ganda intruders and their British backers.

The power of the new chiefs was made manifest in late 1902 when they succeeded in petitioning the Protectorate authorities to remove from office the Mukama of Bunyoro himself. Mukama Kitahimbwa had been appointed as a young man in 1898 in an effort to break Kabarega's grip on the loyalty of his countrymen.[84] Despite his youth he had proven a difficult tool to handle, as he steadfastly held to the pastoral

[83] G. Wilson to Jackson, 14 August 1901, *ESA* A12/1. Cf. P.M.K. Lwanga, *Obulamu Bw'omutaka J. K. Miti Kabazzi* (Kampala: Friends Press, n.d.), pp. 1–11.

[84] G. Wilson to Salisbury, 16 March 1898, *P[arliamentary] P[apers]* C8941, and Bagnall to Commissioner, 3 April 1898, *ESA* A4/10.

lifestyle of his Huma supporters. Both Paulo Byabacwezi, the arch-collaborator, and Miti found him difficult to influence and impossible to work with on the Nyoro governing council. They initiated the petition that led to Kitahimbwa's replacement by his elder brother, who became Mukama Andereya Duhaga II. Duhaga, already a devout Christian, proved a far more suitable monarch in the eyes of his powerful subordinates. Miti especially was quick to gain the king's confidence and to utilize it to become the effective ruler of the council and country. His preeminence in government led directly to the increasing employment of Ganda agents, as amibitious Baganda came to enter government service in order to advance their careers as colonial administrators.[85]

The inevitable result of the influx of ambitious and often arrogant Ganda chiefs was the intensification of "the very bad feeling that exists between the Unyoro chiefs, and those who have been brought from Uganda and elsewhere, and put in charge of some of the counties."[86] A fear came to haunt the Nyoro chiefs and people: that the remnant of their kingdom would be whittled away by annexation or piecemeal appropriation by Ganda chiefs, as was the case in the "lost counties" of Bugangaizi and Buyaga. Even in 1902, the mistreatment and abuse of Nyoro peasants in the "lost counties" had led to large-scale movements of Nyoro cultivators from under the control of Ganda chiefs to the milder treatment of their Nyoro authorities.[87] Thus, the Ganda presence in both the "lost counties" and the rump kingdom served to unite the Nyoro chiefs and peasants in opposition to Ganda subimperialism, the main grievance of the brewing discontent.

Fear of the eventual loss of all of Bunyoro to the Baganda was not as far-fetched as may first appear. As late as December 1904, a colonial officer in Bunyoro recommended "the

[85] Tomkins to Commissioner, 16 October 1902, *ESA* A12/2. Cf. Interviews B/34 Komukyeya, 11 November 1968, and B/3 Mukidi, 13 October 1968.

[86] Tomkins to Commissioner, 16 June 1902, *ESA* A12/2.

[87] Bagge to Commissioner, 16 May 1902, *ESA* A12/2, and Interview B/10 Katuramu, 21 October 1968.

employment of carefully selected Waganda" as chiefs in Bunyoro, as they would "give more favourable results than are at present obtained by the apathetic, unreliable and untrustworthy Wanyoro."[88] This was especially true in the efforts to introduce the cultivation of cash crops by means of the authority of the chiefs. Indeed, the authority of the chiefs had already been the subject of some considerable controversy which bears upon the grievances of the Banyoro against colonial overrule.

In January 1904, the new district officer in Bunyoro took it on his own authority to cancel the labor services owed to the chiefs by the peasants, as he felt it interfered with the cultivation of their own gardens. Administrative action was necessary, argued the district officer, as the peasantry, who had "become little more than slaves ready to work for the chiefs when ordered," feared that their complaints would be cause for further prestations when they came before the governing council, dominated as it was by Miti.[89] There was an immediate outcry from among the chiefs, including Mukama Duhaga, at the arrogation of an important source of the wealth and power of the ruling elite. Despite the humanitarian impulse and the recognition of the legitimacy of some of the peasant grievances by the administration, the labor services were quickly restored. Deputy Commissioner George Wilson decided to uphold the "properly constituted authority" of the chiefs, who although lacking in education and discipline, were essential to effective control of the territory. Moreover, he commented, "the peasantry require discipline in even greater degree."[90] Some adjustments were made in the wake of the controversy, such as the keeping of labor rolls by chiefs and the right of appeal from the council to the local British officer. Nonetheless, the powers of the chiefs, both alien and Nyoro, were confirmed. The peasantry was obligated to work and pay taxes to whomever the British

[88] Fowler to Wilson, 31 December 1904, *ESA* A12/5.

[89] Prendergast to Commissioner, 10 January 1904, *ESA* A12/5.

[90] Wilson to Commissioner, 10 March 1904, *ESA* A12/5. Cf. Katyanku, *Duhaga II*, p. 18, where these events are described as a "rebellion."

government set over them. Peasant grievances, although not the precipitant of rebellion, were an important underlying factor in the discontent that erupted in 1907.

At the time of the dispute over labor services, the leading chiefs had intended to petition the colonial authority for salaries and estates like those obtained by the chiefs of Buganda. The dispute over labor prestations temporarily delayed their appeal. However, by 1905 new arrangements on the rights and responsibilities of chiefs were being made and were promulgated as the *System of Chieftaincy in Unyoro, 1906*. Although the Nyoro chiefs seem to have been satisfied with the arrangements at the time, they contained the seeds of some discord. First, no private estates were allotted under the new system. By this time the Nyoro chiefs were well aware of the differences between themselves and the chiefs of the neighboring kingdoms, but that did little to soften the resentment. By late 1906 the Banyoro had petitioned unsuccessfully for the grant of private estates to the incumbent county chiefs. Second, there was a marked increase in the territorial authority of both Jemusi Miti and Mika Fataki. Fataki, a Musoga by birth, was closely allied to Ganda influence in Bunyoro. The increase in their authority seems to have exacerbated the fears of the Nyoro chiefs and possibly heightened the incipient rivalry within the governing council between Byabacwezi, the leading Nyoro chief, and Miti, the acknowledged leader of the alien chiefs.[91]

Indeed, the growth of Miti's authority and his strong influence with the young Nyoro monarch, Duhaga, were important grievances among the Nyoro elite. In addition to creating the rivalry between himself and Byabacwezi, the Nyoro arch-collaborator, Miti's influence seems to have alienated a large number of the royal Bito dynasty from the rule of Duhaga. Criticism of Duhaga for allowing the Baganda to gain a foothold (although Miti himself was invited to Bunyoro before Duhaga was installed as Mukama) and for

[91] Wilson to Commissioner, 10 May 1904, *ESA* A12/5, and "Unyoro Chiefs, Grant of Estates to," *ESA* SMP 1019/06, for correspondence on the question of land grants.

granting too much power to his Ganda advisors was a prevalent complaint among Duhaga's numerous and important
Bito kinsmen. How much was sincere objection to Duhaga's
failure to exercise royal authority and how much was self-
seeking opportunism among potential candidates for Duhaga's throne is difficult to say. But there is evidence from the
Nyoro side to indicate that both forces were at work among
the Bito clansmen. Even British and Ganda suspicion of Bito
attempts to have Kabarega returned from exile and restored as
Mukama cannot be completely discounted.[92]

To this list of injuries must be added the insult of Ganda
cultural imperialism. The use of Luganda as the official language of state and church rankled from the onset of Ganda
influence. However, when the CMS missionary in Bunyoro,
A. B. Fisher, wrote a letter to the missionary in Toro, Henry
Maddox, on the subject of encouraging the use of Luganda,
he triggered more than he knew. In arguing for the retention
of Luganda in church affairs, the letter pointed up the growth
of Ganda influence sponsored by the Ganda chiefs in
Bunyoro. Maddox, a proponent of local language use, particularly by translating the Bible to make it as widely available
to the agricultural classes as possible, read the letter aloud to
the Toro Anglican Church Council. The council, composed
of many of the important Toro chiefs, had direct connections
to the Nyoro chiefly hierarchy. Word passed very quickly
from the Toro chiefs, who had fought a considerable struggle
to secure both their political and cultural independence from
Buganda, to the Nyoro chiefs, who were prompted to begin
their own struggle to rid themselves of Ganda influence.[93]

Thus, at every level of Bunyoro's political hierarchy—from
the peasant cultivators suffering under the sting of new taxes
and labor prestations to the royal dynasty itself—grievances

[92] Interviews B/3 Mukidi, 13 October 1968, and B/24 Winyi and Mugenyi,
2 November 1968. Cf. G. Uzoigwe, "The Kyanyangire, 1907," in *War and
Society in Africa*, B. A. Ogot, ed. (London: Frank Cass, 1972), pp. 179–214.

[93] Fisher to Maddox, Christmas 1905, Fisher Correspondence, microfilm,
Makerere Library, Kampala. Thanks to Dr. Louise Pirouet for bringing
Maddox's important role to my attention.

against the colonial system that had introduced the Baganda
to Nyoro politics were rampant. Among the Nyoro subchiefs, jealousy of the growing influence of the Baganda was
extreme. In February 1907, these Nyoro chiefs came forward
to express their protest at the unhappy state of affairs in the
kingdom and precipitated a rebellion against colonial authority.

The rebellion began in the absence of Jemusi Miti from the
Nyoro Rukurato. Through his "undue influence over the
Mukama and thus over the Lukiko [Rukurato] generally,"
Miti had become a force to reckon with at court.[94] It is of
some significance that the Nyoro chiefs raised a united voice
of protest while he was away in Buganda. Suspicion that Miti
had gone to Buganda to recruit more Ganda agents for service
in Bunyoro may lie behind the rumors of a Ganda conspiracy
to oust the Nyoro title-holders and explain the timing of the
protest.[95] In any case, Miti's absence provided "a much desired opportunity to speak out." At this stage, the protest remained strictly verbal and confined to the Rukurato. In this
parliamentary forum the major themes of the rebellion were
clearly articulated. According to the Collector, Cubitt:[96]

> the chief reason for this burst of feeling against the
> Waganda lies in the fact that the Mukama and chiefs
> asked H.E. the Commissioner if they could be given
> official and private miles [estates] and the Wanyoro are
> afraid that a lot of their land will be handed over to the
> Waganda.

Although Cubitt tended to dismiss such fears as groundless,
the fact that the leading chiefs, including the alien chiefs led
by Miti, had petitioned the government for extensive grants
of freehold land late in 1906 provided a major threat to the
Nyoro cultivators and minor chiefs. Cubitt's report speaks of
the protestors as "Batongole," a Ganda term whose colonial

---

[94] Cubitt to Deputy Commissioner, 21 February 1907, *ESA* SMP 267/07.
[95] Interview B/3 Mukidi, 13 October 1968, and Nyakatura, *Abakama*, p.
219.
[96] Cubitt to Deputy Commissioner, 21 February 1907, *ESA* SMP 267/07.

usage referred to subchiefs at the gombolola level. Although they were Rukurato councillors and chiefs, they would not have shared in the distribution of land grants if freehold tenure were introduced at this time. The introduction of mailo estates might well have created a class of landed oligarchs whose control of land and political power would reinforce each other as they did in Buganda.[97] The outcry in the Rukurato was intended to prevent the senior chiefs, especially the Ganda chiefs, from gaining a permanent foothold in Bunyoro and thus increasing their power by becoming landlords as well as chiefs.

It was the anti-Ganda theme that came to dominate the protests. Miti's position as both a Muganda and a top chief focused the resentments of both the Nyoro chiefs and peasantry. Originally, Miti had been invited to Bunyoro to teach the Nyoro chiefs how to rule, but in his wake had come an influx of other Baganda. As Miti's friends and followers they had found themselves comfortable, often lucrative, positions in the conquered province. They came as petty traders and evangelists, as well as minor chiefs and headmen, bringing with them a cultural arrogance, commercial and religious attitudes, and a desire for authority that was not calculated to win friends among the Nyoro population. They began turning out the "rightful landholders" and assuming power at a grass-roots level. A popular complaint was "that the Waganda have brought nothing into the country, and that all the profits that they get they send over to Uganda, thus impoverishing Unyoro and enriching Uganda."[98] It is not difficult to see the formation of a stereotype of the alien exploiters which fed the outburst of feeling against them. Both popular and chiefly protest could be symbolically united in the campaign against the 20 or so Ganda chiefs led by Jemusi Miti.

The groundswell of resentment against the chiefs stemming from the fear of extensive land grants to an oppressive ruling class was channeled into a protest against the alienation

[97] Cf. J. A. Rowe, "Land and Politics in Buganda, 1875–1955," *Makerere Journal* 10 (1964):1–13.

[98] Cubitt to Deputy Commissioner, 21 February 1907, *ESA* SMP 267/07.

of land and authority to the Ganda intruders. In this the Nyoro senior chiefs were able to rejoin their subordinate chiefs and peasants. Although the minor chiefs started the manifestations, it was the senior chiefs, Paulo Byabacwezi, Leo Kaboha, and Katalikawe, who organized the next stage of the protest: the expulsion of the Ganda chiefs. By siding with the dissidents, the senior chiefs were able to channel popular resentment away from themselves and into a xenophobic protest that struck a responsive chord among the Nyoro populace. By March 1907, the Baganda were being driven out of the countryside by the threat of violence from the Nyoro peasantry and were seeking refuge at Hoima.[99]

The administrative response to the expulsion of the Baganda was to treat it as a test of the British system of colonial rule. Cubitt initially felt that the protest might be viewed as an opportunity for allowing the Nyoro chiefs to govern under threat that any "regressive movement" would be handled by bringing the Baganda back. Wilson, to the contrary, insisted on upholding the letter of the law. As Deputy Commissioner, he advised the district officer to "nip in the bud any attempt to interfere with the scheme of chieftainships proposed by the Lukiko and confirmed by the Commissioner according to the book published" in 1906. Unhappy with the way Cubitt was handling the situation, Wilson dispatched another officer, Tomkins, who arrived in early April, bearing instructions to enforce strictly the system of chieftaincy "according to the book." Despite the statements of Byabacwezi that he and Kaboha had "only signed as they feared to do otherwise, and the Mukama did what Jemusi Miti told him," Tomkins was unable to adopt a flexible solution to the crisis.[100]

Tomkins called a *Baraza* of all the senior chiefs and reminded them of the system of chieftaincy that had been agreed to by the chiefs and the Protectorate government. To

[99] Nakiwefu to Jemusi (Miti) Kago, 6 February 1907, and Fataki to Apolo Kagwa Kitikiro, 7 March 1907, *ESA* SMP 267/07.

[100] Tomkins to Deputy Commissioner, 7 and 15 April 1907, and Wilson to Collector, Hoima, 13 March 1907, *ESA* SMP 267/07.

the pleas of duress in signing the agreement the Nyoro chiefs added a catalogue of complaints against the Ganda chiefs and Miti in particular. Tomkins reported that the "great point with the Bunyoro chiefs is that they should be allowed to rule their own country as the chiefs of Toro, Uganda, Ankole, &c. are allowed to do."[101] Although this was not "the great point" of the Nyoro peasantry or even of the lesser chiefs, it was a point that seems to have convinced Tomkins of the justice of the Nyoro cause.

By May, the administration could no longer tolerate delays in the return to order. The Ganda chiefs had been thoroughly driven out of their offices and were waiting at Hoima to be reinstated. Some huts had been burned, but no violence against persons had taken place. Wilson still insisted on a hard line. Eden, the third district officer in two months, called a Baraza and put an ultimatum to the chiefs: they must reinstate the Baganda or risk losing their own positions. It was suggested that the reinstatement might be only temporary, subject to the government's review of the Nyoro grievances, but immediate reinstatement of the Baganda was the only solution the Protectorate government would consider. On 7 May, the order to reinstate the Baganda was read to the assembled chiefs, who refused to cooperate, contending that, even if they were willing, the "*bakopi*" or peasants could not be persuaded and wanted the Baganda expelled. This the government considered an excuse. Apparently the absence of personal violence had already convinced them that this was a well-organized and controlled demonstration out of keeping with stereotypes of African emotionalism and peasant violence.[102]

Two more Barazas on 8 and 9 May saw the Nyoro chiefs remain adamant, but calm, in their refusal to allow the Baganda to return to their villages even on a temporary basis. On 9 May Eden announced a four-day moratorium, after which if the Nyoro chiefs persisted in refusing they would

[101] Ibid.
[102] Eden to Wilson, 11 May 1907; Wilson to Spires, 28 May 1907, and Wilson to Elgin, 25 June 1907, *ESA* SMP 710/07. Cf. Lwanga, *Miti*, pp. 50–51.

jeopardize their positions. But when Wilson's ultimatum was reiterated after the four-day period of grace had passed, the Nyoro chiefs not only refused but did so in loud and "passionate" terms. Two days later, on 16 May, the chiefs were again assembled, again refused, and this time, following the orders of George Wilson, 54 of the assembled rebels were arrested. This number included senior and minor chiefs and important personages, among them many members of the royal Bito clan.[103]

Throughout the disturbances, the Mukama had tried to remain neutral. He insisted that he personally did not want the Baganda to leave and that his chiefs were the motive force for expulsion. His failure to assume leadership in the protest has been laid to a weakness of character and the influence of the Baganda and missionary advisors. A more charitable view sees him in full support of the rebellion, but shrewdly avoiding a situation that would jeopardize his authority and his throne. In support of this contention, it is not unlikely that the Ganda leadership in Kampala coveted an even more direct subjugation of Bunyoro and might well have aimed at placing a member of the Ganda royal family on the Nyoro throne. In that light, Duhaga's neutrality may well have served to preserve not only his own position, but may have saved the Nyoro dynasty and the peace of the country as well.[104]

Paulo Byabacwezi, who was considered by Eden as the ring leader of the rebellion, was not present on the 16th and managed to escape arrest. In fact, Byabacwezi appears to have wavered in his support of the protest and to have been pushed into opposition to the British by his co-chief, Leo Kaboha, and particularly by his own subchiefs. Byabacwezi was prepared to surrender to British pressure were it not for fear of loss of popular support. It was reported that Byabacwezi had verbally agreed to the ultimatum on the 14th of May, but on telling his subchiefs was derided into continued resistance. It

[103] Wilson to Elgin, 25 June 1907, *ESA* SMP 710/07. Cf. Interview B/19 Bikundi, 30 October 1968, and Lwanga, *Miti*, pp. 51–52.

[104] Interviews B/3 Mikidi, 13 October 1968, and B/34 Komukyeya, 11 November 1968. Cf. Katyanku, *Duhaga II*, pp. 19–20.

was "better to suffer with the rest and have the good opinion
of others. Byabacwezi is said to have cried and to have decided to be a martyr rather than a turn-coat."[105]

It is the crucial role of the subchiefs that deserves further
notice. Ibrahim Talyeba, the first deputy (mumyoka) subchief under Miti, played a very prominent part in organizing
the disturbances and in persuading Byabacwezi to persist.
Daudi Bitatuli, the deputy to Byabacwezi, was also among
the prominent organizers arrested. Pressure from the leading
subchiefs may well have been motivated by jealousy at the
growth of Ganda title-holding, which narrowed their access
to the senior positions. The large number of Babito among
the subchiefs raises the question of the role of dynastic intrigue, possibly against Duhaga and favoring a restoration of
Kabarega, then in his eighth year of exile. In any case, it was
believed by the district officer, Eden, and it would appear
from the numbers of subchiefs arrested that it was the second
rank of Nyoro chiefs who initiated, organized, and sustained
the agitation and protest that Wilson could not believe was of
local African authorship. Although the British officials discounted the allegation by the chiefs that the bakopi were hostile to the Baganda and would kill them if they returned to the
villages, the role of both Bito and commoner subchiefs in the
agitation lends credence to the contention that popular discontent with the growth of alien influence and the resulting
social uncertainty was a powerful force in sustaining the "rebellion" by the chiefs.[106]

As a side note, the highly politically conscious nature of the
rebellion as a constitutional protest can be illustrated by a
unique maneuver by the Nyoro chiefs. During the disturbances envoys were sent to the neighboring kingdoms of Toro
and Ankole and to Busoga and the "lost counties" in the
hopes of finding allies there who might extend the anti-Ganda
rebellion throughout the Ganda-dominated provinces. Such
an attempt to increase the pressure on the British to remove

[105] Haddon to Collector, Unyoro, 19 May 1907, *ESA* SMP 267/07.
[106] Eden to Wilson, 11 May 1907, *ESA* SMP 710/07, and Interviews B/44
Kinimi, 3 December 1968, and B/12 Tibangwa, 22 October 1968.

the Ganda chiefs by seeking to generate a multitribal movement shows a political wisdom that we tend to identify only
with the more modern African protest movements.
Moreover, the agitation for the return of the "lost counties,"
which Wilson for one believed was the object of the entire
exercise, spread to those counties and required the presence of
a police force under Apolo Kagwa, the Prime Minister of
Buganda, to ensure the "Pax Britannica."[107] This too is
reminiscent of more modern acts of political protest.

Deputy Commissioner George Wilson arrived at Hoima on
22 May 1907 with police and military reinforcements to put
an end to the spirit of rebellion in Bunyoro. Unhappy at the
handling of the disturbances by the local officers, he felt that
prolonged confrontation even after the arrest of more than 50
agitators might well lead to violence against the Baganda still
at Hoima. A new round of Barazas was begun with Wilson
presiding.[108]

On 27 May, a judgment was handed down by Wilson,
which reflected both his prejudices and the necessities of
compromise to secure peaceful collaboration. The four
Nyoro senior chiefs implicated in the rebellion were most un-
evenly punished. Leo Kaboha was deposed from his chieftaincy and exiled to Buganda. Katalikawe was deposed and
forfeited one-third of his land holdings. Daudi Katongole lost
one-third of his estates and two years of tax revenues.
Byabacwezi, whom it was still believed was the prime mover
in the rebellion, lost a third of his estates and was fined £500
to be paid within two years. The fine was later reduced.
Moreover, whatever debts were due to him from the Protectorate government for a decade of service in establishing the
regime of collaboration were considered to be wiped out.[109]

[107] Isemonger to Wilson, 18 June 1907, and Haddon to Collector, Unyoro,
19 May 1907, *ESA* SMP 267/07. Cf. Uzoigwe, "Kyanyangire," pp. 194–195
and Lwanga, *Miti*, p. 53.

[108] Wilson to Elgin, 25 June 1907, *ESA* SMP 710/07.

[109] Wilson, "Award," 27 May 1907, *ESA* SMP 710/07, and Interviews
B/41 P. Kaboha, 25 November 1968; B/42 Wm. Kaboha, 26 November 1968,
and B/19 Bikundi, 30 October 1968.

All in all, Byabacwezi's penalties were not as harsh as one might have expected. Did leniency flow from Wilson's merciful qualities and the recognition of past services, or did they result from a calculated realization of the importance of Byabacwezi to the functioning of the regime of collaboration in Bunyoro?

All those arrested on 16 May when the Baraza threatened to erupt into violence were to be removed to Buganda. Twelve of the 54 arrested were eventually deported from Uganda entirely. This number consisted of Leo Kaboha and 11 of the most vocal agitators among the subchiefs. It was on these men that the penalties fell heaviest. Complaints were later received that their property was being confiscated and that their wives and children were being driven off their estates.[110]

Curiously, no blame was ever assigned to the peasantry who had driven the Baganda from office and threatened them with violence if they returned. Unlike the collective punishments imposed by Wilson on the peasants of Ibanda in Ankole following the Galt assassination in which they were not involved, Wilson appended a word of sympathy for the peasants of Bunyoro, whom he stated had "not been deeply implicated" in the rebellion.[111] The myth of a quiescent peasantry and the need to lay the blame for sedition on a handful of misguided leaders combined to exonerate the bakopi, whose grievances underpinned the entire campaign against colonial overrule.

The award issued by Wilson also restored the Baganda to their positions as chiefs in the Nyoro kingdom "with proper impressiveness and with a fitting force."[112] In this sense, the rebellion failed to achieve its primary objective, the removal of the Ganda chiefs. But the spirit of unrest did not vanish. Tensions continued high against the Baganda, and the houses of two Ganda chiefs were burned the following year. Eventually, the Ganda chiefs were retired in favor of Nyoro succes-

[110] Manara to Wilson, 7 June 1907, *ESA* SMP 710/07, and "Deportation of Unyoro Chiefs," *ESA* SMP 1367/07.
[111] Wilson, "Award," 27 May 1907, *ESA* SMP 710/07.
[112] Ibid.

sors, and no new Ganda chiefs were ever appointed to office in Bunyoro.[113] Thus, a delayed and disguised victory did attend the Nyangire rebellion, which is remembered with pride among the Banyoro.

Discussion

The period from the establishment of collaboration at the turn of the century to the crises of 1905–1907 should be seen as one of readjustment and reaction. The African collaborators only slowly came to realize that the loss of sovereignty brought in its train other losses. The power to tax, to allocate land, to demand labor services passed from the African rulers of the country to the colonial rulers. There might be consultation, advice, and consent, but the ultimate power to control the resources and manpower of the kingdoms had passed from African hands. The loss was not without compensation, at least, to those who helped to establish and maintain the new system. The collaborators were handsomely rewarded, but they came to realize that in order to enjoy the full exercise of their powers and to command their new-found wealth, they had to master the new political system. In each of the kingdoms, the attempts by the collaborating elite to adjust the terms of collaboration and improve their position in the regime led to a spirit of unrest which surfaced halfway through the first decade of colonial rule.

The spirit of unrest in each kingdom was conditioned by the temper and structure of local politics. In Ankole, two contending factions, which the British labeled progressive and reactionary, formed around Mbaguta and Igumira, respectively, and dominated the politics of court and council. The result was a crisis characterized by intrigue and political maneuver between the two factions over responsibility for an act of violence for which, in all likelihood, neither side was to blame. In Toro, where the royal party had firm control of all the new institutions and firm support of the colonial agents, it

[113] Leakey to Deputy Commissioner, 31 January and 24 April 1908, *ESA* SMP C10/08, and "Annual Report, 1911–1912," p. 56, *ESA* SMP 2135.

was possible for the king himself to stage-manage a campaign of petition and pressure through the colonial council and church for the consolidation and enrichment of his regime. In Bunyoro, where traditions of resistance persisted beneath the veneer of active collaboration, even the most ardent and committed of collaborators was forced into opposition to the agents of colonial overrule in a passionate, if symbolic, protest of the loss of sovereignty and power under the new order. For all the differences in tenor and tone created by variations in the politics of collaboration, the ultimate outcome was a course of political action well within the framework of acceptance and accommodation to the imposing realities of imperial power and colonial control. The collaborators might chafe, but none were prepared to challenge directly the colonialism that had set them in power over their fellows.

CHAPTER VIII

Conflict and Collaboration: Some Conclusions

B y the end of 1907, three kingdoms in western Uganda had made the difficult transition from independence and effective isolation to the status of remote dependencies within a worldwide empire. Some of the lesser kingdoms of the lacustrine region had disappeared in the course of the transition, others had emerged more powerful than at any time in their history. The key to a successful transition in each kingdom was the emergence of a collaborating elite who were willing to occupy the crucial roles and do the vital work of accommodating the once independent kingdoms to their new statuses. It is not surprising that similar groups came to power in what were historically and genetically related societies, sharing a great deal in the way of political culture and social structure. The fact of a common colonial overlord in addition makes possible a "controlled comparison,"[1] both implicit and explicit, in studying the events of the period from 1890 to 1907. By this comparative method, the responses of resistance and collaboration in western Uganda can be used to fill out a theory of colonial collaboration from the preliminary sketches already made.[2]

Any theory of collaboration must first clear away some of the debris of previous meanings and connotations of that highly evocative term. First of all, collaboration has generally been taken as the polar opposite of resistance, despite the fact that the two responses have historically been closely associated in a complex pattern of reaction to colonial intrusion. To speak of "resisters" as against "collaborators" or "resisting" as against "cooperating" societies[3] is to distort the often

---

[1] On the Method of "controlled comparison," See the Appendix.

[2] R. Robinson, "Non-European Foundations of European Imperialism: Sketch for a Theory of Collaboration," in *Studies in the Theory of Imperialism*, R. Owen and B. Sutcliffe, eds. (London: Longmans, 1972), pp. 117–140.

[3] T. O. Ranger, "African Reactions to the Imposition of Colonial Rule in

complex behaviors adopted by African political actors and to construe the history of Africa under colonial rule as a Manichaean melodrama. Instead, the two terms should be descriptive of a homogeneous pattern of responses operated in a subtle, sometimes violent, and often devious manner to admit to the local political arena a host of new, external, and imperial political forces. This pattern of response, in addition to the accommodation of imperial interests, served the dual role of simultaneously preserving a sphere of independent political action for the initiative of African leaders. Thus, collaboration should not be seen as a morally and politically bankrupt reaction to conditions beyond the control of the African actors. Removed from the context of World War II and the anti-Fascist resistance, collaboration with colonialism can be seen as a fluid and creative response by African ruling groups and individuals to a situation of inherent conflict and compromise. The response itself, dictated by the perceived needs and objectives of the collaborators, and the resultant accommodation of western political values and institutions occurred through a contentious process of political exchange, negotiation, and struggle, not from the mechanical imposition of those values by the colonizer or a judicious selection of preferred values by the colonized. In this view of collaboration as a political process, the African element of continuity, the gradual adaptation of local institutions and practices, emerges as the equal of the imperial element of administrative and economic exigencies in the creation of the collaborative mechanism of colonial rule.

The Emergence of Chiefly Collaboration

In western Uganda, where highly stratified social systems were paired with highly authoritarian political systems, the emergence of a collaborative mechanism involved the transformation of the "traditional" political elite and ruling class of those societies into a collaborating class. It was the chiefs, the

East and Central Africa," in *Colonialism in Africa*, 5 vols. L. H. Gann and P. Duignan, eds. (Cambridge: Cambridge University Press, 1969), 1:302–304.

territorial and military leadership of the African kingdoms, who had the most to offer as collaborators as well as the most to gain by seizing the opportunity to cooperate in the institution of a new regime. As a class, they possessed the skills and attitudes that made for effective cooperation and compromise with the British overlords. Once a class of collaborators had emerged, it also had the most to lose if it failed to make the essential compromises or refused cooperation with those who had the ultimate power to remove them from authority. In general, each of the three regimes of collaboration involved not just the creation of a collaborative mechanism in the form of a recognized and rewarded hierarchy of appointed chiefs; it also involved a continual renegotiation of the terms and conditions of chiefly cooperation. This renegotiation, often accompanied by conflict, might well be deemed "resistance" by those inclined to emphasize the heroic elements in African behavior. Whatever the label, the process was one of constant maneuver for political advantage: a politics of collaboration.

Neither the social nor the political systems of the three kingdoms of western Uganda were identical in 1890. The differences in the degree of stratification and class hostility as well as the degree of authoritarianism and political domination were manifested in each kingdom's reaction to intrusion. The range of the spectrum of response exhibited by each kingdom in its adoption of a policy of collaboration seems to have varied with the degree of stratification and domination in each system. Of course, other factors cannot be held constant in a historical study. It is therefore impossible to make categorical statements of the relationship of class domination to collaboration, but we can at least remark on what appear to be the propensities of the three systems under study.

I believe we can conclude from the examination of the responses of the three kingdoms that the more politically authoritarian and socially divided the society, the more likely a response of collaboration by the ruling elite and the less likely that elite is to mount a concerted and effective campaign of resistance. Thus, the most pastoral-dominant and class-based system—Ankole—was the most ready to adopt a policy of collaboration. The most national, least divided into hierarchical classes—Kabarega's Bunyoro—was correspondingly the most resistant to imposed changes and the slowest to develop a counterelite willing and able to make the compromises necessary to the establishment of a collaborationist regime. Toro, with its pastoral traditions and Bito dynasty, proved intermediate in its response. The schism created by rival dynastic claims in conjunction with the class division of Toro society provided the opening for the emergence not only of a collaborating elite, but of a collaborating monarch as well.

If the degree of social and political solidarity accounts for variations in the range of collaborationist response, what is the mechanism by which social statics are translated into historical dynamics? Although it is impossible to speak with certainty from the evidence of only three societies, the process that social science terms "elite recruitment" seems crucial to the understanding of the dynamics of emergent chiefly collaboration. In Ankole, where selection of the elite was highly restricted and intensely competitive within the class of potential rulers, a political culture of intrigue and factionalism for all the political offices tended to the perpetuation of those politics under a new sovereign. In Bunyoro and Toro, where the dynastic politics of the Bito clan were seen as being above the politics of competition for chiefly office, a moderating influence on factionalism seems to have operated. The wider range of eligibility for the chiefly elite including both pastoral and agricultural groups in Bunyoro as well as a smattering of talented aliens, particularly in military service, seems to have opened the recruitment patterns in Bunyoro and promoted a degree of solidarity between classes and status groups that, if not quite nationalist in its intensity, was a great improvement on the tensions and frictions of her southern neighbors. The system of recruitment of the political elite before the colonial intrusion thus emerges as a crucial variable in the expression of the social tensions and political frictions that facilitated the emergence of a response of active collaboration with the intruders. If we are to make sense of the African history of imperialism, it is such variables within African societies as these to which we must increasingly turn.[4]

The fact that previous patterns of elite recruitment persisted into the colonial era meant a continuation of many of the cultural and political practices of the old regime under the new. The largely self-selected elite that sought and gained recognition by the British suzerains only gradually moved away from the behaviors and practices on which their traditional authority rested. Much has been written about the conflicting values of traditional and bureaucratic chieftaincy under colonial rule. Far less has been said about the continuity of African values in relative harmony and accord with the performance of chiefly roles expected by the colonial powers. At least in the first years of colonial overrule, the most effective collaborators among the African elite were those who blended the two roles and represented in their person the collaborative mechanism that mediated the contact of two cultures, two political and economic systems. Thus Mbaguta could instigate the construction or roads and the system of regular tax collection and bookkeeping while remaining a devoted pastoralist who would ultimately retire to tend his extensive herds of cattle. He could similarly initiate a formal investigation into the assassination of a colonial official while simultaneously spreading the rumors and hatching intrigues that would cast suspicion on his political rivals and ensure his predominance in the court politics of Ankole. Like the members of the collaborating elite with a foot in both camps, the political practices of collaboration were to share elements of both the old and new regimes.

The Politics of Collaboration

The first feature of collaborationist politics to which we must draw attention is the creation of new divisions within

[4] Attempts to examine African views of the imperial encounter that stress these internal African variables is just beginning. Cf. T. Hodgkin, "Some African and Third World Theories of Imperialism," in *Studies in the Theory of Imperialism*, R. Owen and B. Sutcliffe, eds., pp. 93–114.

the society being ruled. We might at first attribute this to the
policy of divide and rule so widely practiced by the colonial
powers within their newly mapped territories.[5] In Uganda, as
elsewhere, the British used *inter*ethnic differences to their advantage. There is no evidence, however, to support the idea
that the British consciously sought to promote the existing *in-
tra*ethnic divisions of class, culture, or status of the Uganda
kingdoms in an effort to facilitate their takeover or administration of those societies. On the contrary, most attempts at
administering through the native authorities presupposed that
the divisions could be ignored or were at most minor hin-
drances to centralized and uniform administration. The new
binary divisions that did emerge during the first decades of
colonial rule must be traced to latent tendencies within the
African societies activated by the inherent proclivities of the
colonial system, not the conscious policy decisions made in
Entebbe or London.

In the western kingdoms, a marked tendency to form parties or at least factions around certain clusters of politicians
seems to have emerged quite clearly by the late 1890s. The
British tended to see and label these parties as either conservative or progressive, the latter term being reserved for the
group in most intimate association with the colonial rulers
and their ideas. Often, the parties took a name and identity
provided not by a set of policies, but by the religion or language of the missionaries who became their champions and
advisors. Thus, the progressive party in the administrator's
terminology came to be synonymous with the "English"
Protestant party of the CMS missionaries and their African
adherents. The conservatives accepted the designation and the
practice of "French" Roman Catholicism during the first
years of contact with the religion of the French-speaking
White Fathers Mission. It is of course tempting to view the
internal and inherent attributes of the competing religious
doctrines as the basis for this association of English Protestant
progressives as against French Catholic conservatives. After

[5] Cf. H. Brunschwig, "De la Résistance Africaine a l'Impérialisme Euro-
péen," *Journal of African History* 15, 1(1974):57–58.

all, Catholicism has frequently been closely associated with conservatism in politics, Protestantism with reform in Europe and elsewhere. Nonetheless, this obfuscates the far more important factor of the association of Protestantism with the English-speaking rulers of the country. The partisanship of the active collaborators for the religion of their partners should come as no surprise. The decision of the passively collaborating "opposition" to affiliate with the Catholic denomination stemmed from their desire to be less closely associated with the Anglophile "Protestant establishment." What this suggests is that the formation of a bipolar political system had little to do with the programs or ideology of the opposing parties. Rather bipolarity derived from a structural tendency of political competition under colonialism to channel itself into a relatively stable system of binary divisions.[6]

The question as to whether this tendency to binary division and bipolarity in politics under colonial rule derives from precolonial African political practices or from the conditions of political competition imposed by the new regime is difficult to answer. There is evidence from West Africa that bipolar party systems existed prior to colonial subordination.[7] But there is little to suggest such a stable and regular bipolar partisanship in the lacustrine area. Only the factionalism of barusura/military versus bakungu/territorial chiefs in Bunyoro approaches the bipolarity described for Ashanti and Dahomean politics, and even here the instability and cross-cutting membership of the factions would belie any real party system, bipolar or otherwise.

Thus it would seem that the Protestant versus Catholic partisanship that emerged in western Uganda following the prac-

[6] Cf. F. Barth, "Segmentary Opposition and the Theory of Games," *Journal of the Royal Anthropological Institute* 89, 1(1959):5–21.

[7] G. I. Jones, *The Trading States of the Oil Rivers* (Oxford: University Press, 1963), pp. 159–204; I. Wilks, *Political Bipolarity in Nineteenth Century Asante* (Edinburgh: Centre of African Studies, 1970); and J. Yoder, "Fly and Elephant Parties: Political Polarization in Dahomey, 1840–1870," *Journal of African History* 15, 3(1974):417–432.

tice in Buganda reflected conditions specific to the situation of collaboration with imperialism and colonial administration. Here the structural features of politics and patronage under conditions of a zero-sum majority game imposed by British expectations of African behavior led the previously segmentary and factional politics of chiefly competition to aggregate into a "persisting opposition" of named blocs under leaders of great stature. Initially there were no fundamental differences in policy or ideology between the Protestant/progressive and Catholic/conservative groupings. They had both accepted the general condition of alien suzerainty. Neither party envisioned a major transformation of the system of collaboration, nor were they very far apart about how forthcoming they were with their cooperation. The religious differences seem to have masked a fundamental agreement on the question of collaboration. The competition for British recognition of their status as chiefs and the associated rewards created a situation of bipolarity rather than a total monopoly of power by one faction. During the colonial era, the binary division and political bipolarity was accentuated as each party began to accumulate distinct cultural symbols and institutions associated with their religious denominations. By the late colonial era, religious differences between political groups had assumed fundamental importance in the political life of the entire Uganda Protectorate.[8]

Regardless of the party to which a member of the elite was affiliated, the entire elite operated so as to monopolize the advantages created by the colonial nexus. On any given issue involving tax rebates, land grants, or other emoluments of office under the colonial administration, the collaborators very clearly had an interest in maximizing their demands and did so with considerable finesse. There were few breaches of the limits placed on these demands by the British. Moreover, the financial and economic rewards allotted to the African collaborators by the Agreements were thoroughly concentrated

[8] Cf. D. A. Low, *Political Parties in Uganda*, 1949–1962 (London: Athlone, 1962).

in the hands of the narrow stratum of bakungu chiefs, royal dynasts, and courtiers. Indeed, a later study of the land settlements in the western region indicated that there was no cultivated land outside that land granted as estates to the kings, the royal family, and the chiefs.[9] The collaborators in fact "owned" the kingdoms from the ground up.

In addition to a monopoly of the economic rewards of collaboration, the ruling elite also obtained social benefits and new privileges of status. Chief among these were the rewards of educational privilege and judicial authority. The first schools were expressly designated as schools for the children and proteges of the elite. Intended to operate as a training ground for future junior and middle-level administrators, they were utilized by the elite to groom a future generation of political leaders. Instead of apprenticing a child or protege to another leading chief as a means of perpetuating one's influence in the traditional manner of the pastoral class, the collaborating elite sent selected individuals to school in order to accomplish the same political purpose. The payment of school fees by a father or patron became a new form of clientage contract establishing and perpetuating networks of loyalty and partisanship. The purposes of the British were served by the spread of literacy to a generation of future colonial employees, whereas the collaborators managed to turn that same mechanism to their advantage as a political instrument. The development of parallel Protestant and Catholic school systems reflects as much the partisan lines of African politics as the denominational deferences between the missionary bodies that created them.[10]

The fact that every chief presided over a court, licensed by the colonial power to hear civil and criminal cases and administer justice, is another example of elite's monopoly of advantages. Not only did court fees and a percentage of the

[9] Uganda Protectorate, *Reports of the Committee appointed to consider the question of Native Land Settlement in Ankole, Bunyoro, Busoga, and Toro* (Entebbe, 1913), pp. 14–16.

[10] O. W. Furley, "Education and the Chiefs in East Africa," Conference Paper, University of East Africa (Kampala, 1968–1969).

fines imposed by the courts provide additional and important revenues to the chiefs, but it made their position as privileged individuals palpable to the African populace who were subjected to their jurisdiction. As important as was the establishment of a system of justice to the administration of a colonial dependency,[11] it was equally important to the collaborators to be part of that system which represented, at the local and most immediate level, the power of the new authorities in the land. Titles and estates might make the collaborators rich, but their regular exercise of judicial authority is what made them tangibly and manifestly powerful in the eyes of their subordinates. The fact that the same men who controlled the land also controlled the courts was a further indication of the total monopoly exercised by the collaborating elite.

In pressing for the advantages made possible by the acceptance of an alien sovereignty, the collaborating elite demonstrated what was probably the most important political trait of the collaborative mechanism: the constant struggle for leverage on the part of the African collaborators vis-à-vis both their subordinate African subjects and the superordinate European rulers. In this struggle, Africans were quick to recognize European weaknesses and press their advantages. They were also usually quick to recognize a point beyond which the colonial authorities would not be pushed. The example of *Nyangire* in Bunyoro can be seen as a test of those limits. A wide area was left open within these limits to the initiative of the men who were so essential to the maintenance of colonial rule on a local basis. By extending and testing the limits of their initiative, the African elite succeeded in making the imperial nexus a stormy channel rather than an open sea of cooperation. In the process of negotiating and stretching the margins of African initiative, new areas were opened for the emergence of the new elites who would ultimately challenge the entire structure of colonial rule in Uganda as elsewhere in

[11] E. Hopkins, "The Politics of Crime: Aggression and Control in a Colonial Context," *American Anthropologist* 75, 3(1973):731–742.

Africa.[12] In 1907, however, this was a distant and generally unforeseen consequence of the still emerging politics of collaboration.

The Failure of Resistance and Rebellion

It may seem irrelevant to try to come to any conclusions regarding the failure of the African societies of western Uganda to mount effective armed struggles against the imposition of colonial rule. The overwhelming technological superiority of Britain expressed in terms of military firepower and potential manpower made the outcome of virtually any armed resistance, no matter how well organized and led, a foregone conclusion. In the end it would have been the Maxim gun, if it had gone that far. But outside of Bunyoro's struggle under Kabarega, the question was never put to the acid test of firepower. Indeed, the failure of resistance and rebellion is really a question of the failure to raise a significant movement among the populace in that direction. It is a question of the failure of political leadership and popular support, not of military strategy or tactics.

Put in political terms, the failure of resistance must be seen as a function of the success of an alternative strategy by the African political leadership. Once a significant number of the political elite of each kingdom had opted for a policy of active collaboration with the imperial forces, the schisms within African society made resistance a futile and costly alternative. The divisions between the elite and the masses could not be bridged by an effort to secure popular support for armed struggle once the leadership itself was fractionated. More important, the emergence of divisions within the ruling class would have made civil war of some sort an inevitable outcome of attempts at resistance. Ultimately the successes of the collaborators in securing British support for their authority within the African kingdoms meant the demise of the initial

[12] Brunschwig, "De la Résistance," pp. 59–63. Cf. Ranger, "African Reactions," pp. 300–302.

attempts at mounting armed opposition to British intrusion in local affairs.

The successful application of a policy of collaboration goes a long way toward explaining the near total absence of immediate "postpacification" rebellions. With a locally respected and traditionally legitimate elite to administer the new systems of taxation, courts, and public works, no effective leadership could be found to champion any serious attempts at the overthrow or radical modification of the colonial system. Where opposition to colonial rule did border on rebellion, as in Bunyoro, it was focused on the participation of non-natives in the colonial system, which threatened both the loyalty of the masses and the elite's position of authority. But the very style of political confrontation represented by Nyangire brings into focus some of the deeper underlying bases for the failure of rebellion.

The politics of confrontation themselves seemed to have been contrary to African cultural and political traditions. The tendency of Africans to avoid or deflect hostility by verbal and cultural stratagems—by joking, deception, or "signifying" one thing when meaning something else—was often noted by observers of African (and Afro-American) behavior.[13] Often what was misunderstood as a propensity to lying and trickery was in fact a propensity to indirection, aimed at avoiding confrontation and rupture by preserving the semblance of amicability and agreement. For example, a European's demand for a contract of blood brotherhood would seldom be refused by an African host. Instead, the exchange of gifts that accompanied the ritual exchange of blood would be intentionally insulting or the ritual itself marred, making clear to all but the European communicant that the contract was a sham. By such cultural devices, contracts and solemn agreements were made that Europeans believed were in earnest, but that Africans felt free to ignore. Unfortunately, when the Europeans took such agreements seriously

[13] Cf. M. J. Herskovits, *The Myth of the Negro Past* (Boston: Beacon Press, 1958), pp. 150–158.

and acted upon them, the Africans often found that the cultural misunderstanding had generated a political reality that could not be ignored. By such stratagems, confrontation was deflected until it was too late to find the means to oppose openly what had come to be the reality of European dominance. Perhaps, then, at the deepest level, the root cause of the failure of African resistance and rebellion in western Uganda can be located, not in the inadequacy of their arms or martial virtues, but in the propensity within African society to schism and within African culture to pacific and indirect accommodation to potentially disruptive and explosive situations.

Discussion

A few speculations are in order on the impact of the era of conflict and collaboration on the development of colonial rule and independence in western Uganda after 1907. First, the establishment of regimes of collaboration based on a hierarchy of titled chiefs adapted from Buganda precedents meant that despite the wide differences in social and political systems in what became the Uganda Protectorate, a common system of administration was established on a territorywide basis. The predominance of Ganda agents in western and eastern Uganda, and later Ganda, Nyoro, and other Bantu speakers in northern Uganda, did not alter the fact that the structure of government that they served and maintained was uniform and national. Thus, despite the granting of federal status and certain privileges of autonomy in the southern kingdoms,[14] a national political culture was promoted by the establishment of similar collaborative regimes in each area of the country.

Second, the training, education, and status offered to the members of the collaborating elite led to the emergence of a new class with a modernizing and oligarchic ideology. This ruling class was especially entrenched in the monarchical areas

[14] G. Ibingira, *The Forging of an African Nation* (New York: Viking Press, 1973), pp. 144–174, 222–234, and 274–281.

and provided a single and homogeneous class capable of administering the country as a whole upon the departure of the
colonial rulers. However, this class often had little or no interest in hastening that departure. Where in most African colonies the educated and westernized elites served as the vanguard of nationalist political activity, in Uganda the effective
preoccupation of the "modernizing oligarchy" with operating the local regime of collaboration and securing the rewards
offered by participation in politics made them as resistant to
the appeal to nationalist solidarity as any class within colonial
society.[15] Successful collaboration at an early stage of colonial
rule may have acted as a brake on the democratic and nationalist reaction that colonial rule seems to have triggered
elsewhere in colonial Africa. Perhaps even the neocolonial
and authoritarian tendencies of the nationalist elite may be
traceable to a collaborationist heritage. Certainly much research on the role of this neotraditional elite in colonial politics remains to be done.

In summation, the period from 1890 to 1907 in western
Uganda seems to have been crucial in a number of ways. Certainly, it is remembered as a time of great importance in the
history of the kingdoms, far overshadowing any other period
of colonial or even precolonial history in the richness of its
remembered events and the stature of its heroes. Those turbulent decades set a course for the future development of the colonial system, which in turn established the conditions for the
emergence of an independent Uganda. Indeed, the recent and
regrettable history of military rule and the resignation of the
populace to tyranny may sadly reflect some of the marks left
on Ugandan politics during those early days of conflict and
collaboration.

[15] D. Apter, *The Political Kingdom in Uganda* (Princeton, N.J.: Princeton
University Press, 1967).

A Note on Method

For the purpose of this study, which is intended to be interpretive rather than comprehensive, I adapted a comparative methodology developed in ethnographic and sociological research. The adaptation of this comparative technique to a historical research project stems from a particular attempt to identify certain regularities in the history of the lacustrine area during the period of early colonial contact. I proposed to isolate by this method those factors that produced these regularities and the systematic variations in the historical responses of the three kingdoms studied. Of course, comparison is always a feature of the study of a society, and the conscious application of a comparative method is meant merely to make explicit the elements of comparison and thus make the examination of the evidence more systematic.[1] The method then was intended as an aid to analysis, not a substitute for it.

The particular method used in this study was suggested by the work of two anthropologists among North American Indians.[2] Known as "controlled comparison" or "concomitant variation," this method seeks to compare societies that are fundamentally similar yet display variations in the phenomena under examination. By finding societies that are closely, if not genetically, related, we can limit the number of independent variables that are relevant to explaining the divergencies that exist between those societies.[3] If, for in-

[1] R. Marsh, *Comparative Sociology* (New York: Harcourt, Brace and World, 1967), chap. 1 and 2.

[2] F. Eggan, *The Social Organization of the Western Pueblos* (Chicago: University of Chicago Press, 1950); and E. Spicer, *Potam, a Yaqui Village in Sonora, American Anthropologist Memoir #77*, Vol. 56 (1954).

[3] F. Eggan, "The Method of Controlled Comparison," *American Anthropologist* 56 (1954):743–763, and R. Clignet, "A Critical Evaluation of Concommitant Variation Studies," in *A Handbook of Method in Cultural An-*

stance, the societies were similar in kinship, language, and political structure, yet varied in their religious beliefs, we would try to isolate the factors that co-varied with religion in these societies, holding constant the elements of culture and social organization they shared in common. By identifying these correlates we open new channels for the investigation of change in these societies.

The societies of the lacustrine area present a nearly ideal "laboratory" for controlled comparison. Because of the basic structural and cultural similarities (such as in language, kinship, and economy) that we described in Chapter 1,[4] the three western lacustrine kingdoms fulfill the primary condition for this comparison. Recently a comparison of this sort was done in a study of the systems of social stratification of two lacustrine societies, Bunyoro and Buganda. This study by Melvin Perlman[5] explicitly used the technique of controlled comparison on societies that are less closely related than the three being compared here.

A second condition for the application of a controlled comparison is the existence of divergence in the phenomena studied. The societies being studied should show a range of variation in those phenomena that we hope to explain by making the comparison. Thus, if, for instance, the religious beliefs of our sample societies were the subject of our examination and did *not* vary, this method would bring us no closer to understanding the determinants of the religious systems of such societies. In the case of the western kingdoms, the condition of variance in our dependent variable is fulfilled by the divergent initial responses to colonial impact and the establishment of a colonial regime during the 1890s. The range of variation of our dependent variable moves from armed resistance on the one side to active collaboration on the other. The

---

thropology, R. Naroll and R. Cohen, eds. (Garden City, N.Y.: Natural History Press, 1970).

[4] See supra, pp. 5–7.

[5] "The Traditional Systems of Stratification Among the Ganda and Nyoro of Uganda," in *Social Stratification in Africa*, A. Tuden and L. Plotnicov, eds. (New York: The Free Press, 1970).

application of this method to the historical evidence of variation against the background of anthropological evidence of similarity should help illuminate the basis for resistance and collaboration responses to British rule in western Uganda.

Because we are confronted with a welter of anthropological and historical data on the lacustrine area, there is a difficult problem in selecting those independent variables that we believe are relevant to explain the divergencies in response among the three kingdoms. Despite the similarities that limit the number of variables as well as ensure a certain uniformity of categories being compared, we still find a superabundance of possible independent variables. This problem calls for an exercise of critical judgment by the researcher, who must interpret the evidence so as to isolate those factors considered relevant from those that we must somewhat arbitrarily hold constant. Because such a comparison is by its nature a limited exercise in analysis and not a synthesis of all the available evidence, certain factors were selected for examination in detail. Other factors that were judged to be of less explanatory value in the comparison have not been ignored in the description, but were defined as constants for reasons of comparison although they might be crucial factors in the wider scheme of the historical description. For instance, the imperial factor in the conquest and colonization of western Uganda is profoundly important to understanding the evolution of colonial status.[6] The question of British policy, attitude, and capacity cannot be ignored. However, for the purposes of explaining divergencies among the three kingdoms, it has been convenient to treat colonial policy and other "external" factors as constants.

How, then, did we decide what factors will bear the weight of examination and explanation in our study of resistance and collaboration? Because our purpose was to illuminate the internal political histories of the three kingdoms rather than the diplomatic relations between these states and the alien powers, it was necessary to choose a subject for detailed

[6] A. Roberts, "The Evolution of the Uganda Protectorate," *Uganda Journal* 27,1 (1963):95–106.

examination that we hoped would expose the underlying premises of political life (e.g., the structure of competition for office and the exercise of authority) as they came under external pressures. We particularly sought to examine independent variables within the internal structure of the African political systems represented in the sample that have been the concern of sociological research, but that historians have tended to ignore.

Following Peter Lloyd's theoretical model for the study of African kingdoms,[7] I decided to focus on the recruitment and tenure of the political elite in conducting archival and field research and for framing hypotheses for testing. I interpreted Lloyd's political elite of "titled office-holders" to include the monarchs and the top rank of territorial and military chiefs, who we believed were the holders of the distinctly political authority within each kingdom. The development of the political role of the chiefs has been the subject of extensive study in the lacustrine area,[8] and we considered that their role would be vital to the determination of any policy in response to the advent of colonial pressures. Due to the high degree of political centralization, the chiefly hierarchy, which became the leading tool of colonial administration during the twentieth century, stood out as the likely locus for both acts of organized resistance and political accommodation. Careful examination of recruitment and tenure of this chiefly hierarchy would, it was hoped, provide the data for systematic comparison of the politics of transition to colonial rule.[9]

With this method in mind, problems of data collection were also systematized. Although the history of the royal dynasties of the kingdoms has been collected and archival material on the political life at the capital particularly in relation to the colonial authorities was available, material on the chiefs

[7] P. Lloyd, "The Political Structure of African Kingdoms," in ASA monograph #4, *Political Systems and the Distribution of Power*, M. Banton, ed., (London: Tavistock, 1965), pp. 63–112.

[8] A. Richards, ed., *East African Chiefs* (London: Faber and Faber, 1960).

[9] Cf. M. G. Smith, *Government in Zazzau, 1800–1950* (London: Oxford University Press, 1960), chap. 2.

during the period of this study was not readily accessible. The archives provide some data on recruitment, often in the form of chief lists and passing references to individual chiefs. Still, it was necessary to collect oral information in order to supplement the spotty evidence of the archives on elite recruitment. By interviewing the living relatives of the important chiefs of the 1890s, a fuller picture of the process of elite recruitment, and through it of the African side of the politics of collaboration, could be drawn. The children, kinsmen, and occasionally the contemporaries of the chiefs who governed the western kingdoms were sought and questioned about their illustrious forebears and associates.[10] Memories were often flattering; they were also often vivid and generally willingly transmitted for preservation by anyone who wanted to help record the place of the important men of the past. It was also hoped that by collecting a variety of viewpoints from members of the families and factions of the different African political camps, we might gain insights into the structure of political factions and activity during the two decades of crisis and remedy some of the bias toward dynastic history that comes so readily in working on the history of the kingdoms.

Such were some of the methods, preconceptions, and anticipations with which this study was conducted. If the method used is to be justified further, it must be by the preceding historical narrative and analysis. The purpose of the method in this essay was to help interpret what I believe to be important problems in the history of these societies and of colonialism. If the method provides new insights or a new dimension to our understanding of the problems illustrated by the histories of these kingdoms and does not obscure other possible views and analyses, it will have succeeded in achieving its purpose.

[10] See Bibliography of Interviews.

Primary Sources

Entebbe Secretariat Archives

The government archives are located at the Ministry of Foreign Affairs at Entebbe. They contain correspondence to the Company and Protectorate officials in Kampala from the first military and civilian officials to visit and stay in western Uganda. Their evidence is virtually the only government material dealing with local political problems. The files used are listed below; those most relevant and useful are marked with stars.

Class A1 General, 1890–1892.
Class A2 Staff inward, 1893–1894.★
Class A3 Staff outward, 1893–1894.
Class A4 Staff inward, 1895–1900.
Class A6 Miscellaneous inward, 1895–1903.★
Class A7 Miscellaneous outward, 1895–1904.
Class A12 Bunyoro inward, 1900–1906.★
Class A13 Bunyoro outward, 1900–1906.
Class A14 Toro, 1900–1906.★
Class A15 Ankole, 1900–1906.★
Class A21 H. H. Johnston, May 1900.
Class A22 Church Missionary Society correspondence.
Class A33–35 and 38 Foreign Office, 1895–1905.
Class A36 and 39 Colonial Office, 1905–
Class A42–45 Minute papers, 1906–1909.
Class A46 Confidential correspondence, 1901–1909.

District Archives

The District Headquarters in each former kingdom houses the archives for that district. Fort Portal, a former provincial headquarters for the western province, contains provincial archives as well. However, little of value for this early period is available in any of these three locations. Ankole's archives contain no material earlier than the 1920s, and that consists mostly of tax and real estate records. Fort Portal's large and disorganized collection is similarly void of early material. It was explained that all such material had been sent to Entebbe. Bunyoro was worst of all. I was informed by Mr. Odwori, Assistant District Commissioner, that no files prior to 1914 were available and that he believed that the last colonial official had burned many of those papers before turning over the headquarters at Independence.

Church Missionary Society Archives

I consulted microfilmed editions available at both the Northwestern and the Makerere University Libraries. The missionaries' letters to the society proved to be full of material on the politics of the palace and were extremely useful in providing data for the early formation of factions at the capitals of each kingdom. The relevant files are listed below:

G3 A5/013 1897.
G3 A7/01 1898–1899.
G3 A7/02 1900–1901.
G3 A7/03 1902–1903.
G3 A7/04 1904–1905.
G3 A7/05 1906–1907.
G3 A7/06 1908–1909.
G3 A7/07 1910.

Official Publications

Great Britain, Parliamentary Papers:
    C6817 Africa No. 4 (1892) Papers relating to the Mombasa
        Railway Survey and Uganda.
    C6817 Africa No. 8 (1892) Papers relating to Uganda.
    C6847 Africa No. 1 (1893) Further Papers relating to
        Uganda.
    C6848 Africa No. 2 (1893) Further Papers relating to
        Uganda.
    C6853 Africa No. 3 (1893) Further Papers relating to
        Uganda.

C7109 Africa No. 8 (1893) Further Papers relating to Uganda.

C7303 Africa No. 2 (1894) Reports relating to Uganda by Sir Gerald Portal.

C7708 Africa No. 7 (1895) Papers relating to Uganda.

C7924 Africa No. 1 (1896) Report on Military Operation against Kabarega, King of Unyoro.

C8718 Africa No. 2 (1898) Papers relating to Recent Events in the Uganda Protectorate.

C8941 Africa No. 7 (1898) Papers relating to Recent Events in the Uganda Protectorate.

C9123 Africa No. 1 (1899) Papers relating to Recent Events in the Uganda Protectorate.

C9232 Africa No. 4 (1899) Papers relating to Events in the Uganda Protectorate and Lieut. Colonel Macdonald's Expedition.

Uganda Protectorate. *Enquiry into the Grievances of the Mukama and People of Toro*. Entebbe, 1926.

————. *Enquiry into land Tenure and the Kibanja System in Bunyoro, 1931*. Entebbe, 1932.

————. *Reports of the Committee appointed to consider the question of Native Land Settlement in Ankole, Bunyoro, Busoga and Toro, with appendices*. Entebbe, 1913.

————. *System of Chieftainships in Ankole, 1907*. Entebbe, 1907.

Unpublished Papers

Clayton, Rev. H. Extracts from Letters from Uganda, 1897–1901. Microfilm. Makerere University Library.

Clayton, Hilda (*née* Turnbull). Letters. Microfilm. Makerere University Library.

Fishers, A. B. Diaries. Microfilm. Makerere University Library.

Kasagama, Daudi. Diary entitled "Toro Notes." Makerere University Library.

Kivebulaya, Apolo. Diary. Namirembe Cathedral, Mengo. Selection translated by Mr. J. Bukenya. Cyclostated.

Mbaguta, Muwa. Papers and Letters. In the possession of Mr. James Mugyerwa, Kampala.

Sitwell, Captain C. H. Diary for May 1895–May 1899. Secretarial Library, Entebbe. Manuscript photocopy made available by Dr. John Rowe, Department of History, Northwestern University.

Willis, Rev. J. J. Letters and Journals, 1900–1912. Microfilm. Makerere University Library.

Periodicals

Bunyoro Church Magazine, 1931–1940. Cyclostated selections translated by Father A.B.T. Byaruhanga-Akiiki, 1968. Made available by Dr. L. Pirouet, Department of Religion, Makerere University.

Church Missionary Intelligencer, Volumes 28–31, 1903–1906.

Mengo Notes (later *Uganda Notes*), Volumes 1–2, 1900–1901.

Interviews

The form for these entries is as follows: class/number, subject's name, date of interview (language of interview); year of birth of subject; clan of subject. Textscriptions are available on microfilm through the Center for Research Libraries, Chicago, Illinois.

SERIES A–ANKOLE

A/1 A. G. Katate, 24 July 1968 (English); b. 1910; Bayangwe.

A/2 John C. Macwa, 25 July 1968 (English); b. 1916; Bahinda.

A/3 Kazekia Katukura, 25 July 1968 (Runyankole); b. 1895; Bateizi.

A/4 George Nathan Kirindi, 30 July 1968 (English); b. 1918; Bashari.

A/5 Ananyas Murumba, 27 July 1968 (English); b. 1910; Babito.

A/6 Samwiri Rwabushongo, 30 July 1968 (Runyankole); b. 1910; Bashari.

A/7 Ernest Mugoha, 26 July 1968 (English); b. 1902; Bahinda.

A/8 Ernest Mugoha, 31 July 1968 (Runyankole and English); follow-up interview.

A/9 Lazaro Kamugungunu, 2 August 1968 (Runyankole); b. reign of Ntare; Bagahe.

A/10 Miriamu Kabyibara, 5 August 1968 (Runyankole); b. reign of Ntare; Banonsi.

A/11 Canon Yoweri Buningwire, 5 August 1968 (Runyankole); b. 1881; Bashambo.

A/12 Canon Yoweri Buningwire, 6 September 1968 (Runyankole); follow-up interview.

A/13 Andereya Rugangura, 7 August 1968 (Runyankole); b. 1886; Mwitera.

A/14 Esau Khunyirano, 9 August 1968 (English); b. 1930; Balsia.

A/15 Ernest Katungi, 10 August 1968 (Runyankole); b. 1889; Basheigyi.

A/16 Cristofa Kafureeka, 13 August 1968 (English and Runyankole); b. 1905; Beneishemunrari Bashambo.

A/17 Zekeria Mungonya, 14 August 1968 (English); b. 1900 (or 1901); Mugahe.

A/18 Edisa Kagaga and Miriamu Nyabayangwe, 20 August 1968 (Runyankole); b. 1892 and 1898, respectively; Bahinda.

A/19 Alfred Rwahaiguru, 21 August 1968 (English); b. 1936; Bashambo.

A/20 Verenika Munyashumju, 22 August 1968 (Runyankole); b. 1910; Bahweju.

A/21 Georhe Biyindi, 23 August 1968 (Runyankole); b. 1919; Bateizi.

A/22 Arthur Murari, 24 August 1968 (English); b. 1929; Beneishemurari Bashambo.

A/23 Daniel Kanduhho, 24 August 1968 (English); b. 1935–1936; Henerukari Bashambo.

A/24 Henry Barah, 25 August 1968 (English and Runyankole); b. 1920; Balisa.

A/25 Eryasafu Rukunyu, 26 August 1968 (Runyankole); b. 1924; Benemafundo Bashambo.

A/26 Eriya Rwakanaigisa, 27 August 1968 (Runyankole); b. circa 1896; Benekihondwa Bashambo.

A/27 Erinesti Kigaza, 28 August 1968 (Runyankole and English); b. 1904; Beneishemurari Bashambo.

A/28 Rev. E. Kamujanduzi and Y. Katundu, 28 August 1968 (Runyankole and English); b. ?; "Bairu." (Both men were leaders of the Bairu movement, Kumanyana.)

A/29 Alfred Mutashwera, 29 August 1968 (English); b. 1905; Bagahe.

A/30 Irene Mbanga, 29 August 1968 (Runyankole); b. 1905; Benemuganda Bashambo.

A/31 Lazaro Kamugungunu, 31 August 1968 (Runyankole); follow-up interview.

A/32 A. G. Katate, 1 September 1968 (English); follow-up interview.

A/33 Yosiya Kabikyira, 2 September 1968 (Runyankole); b. 1905; Bagahe (Bairu branch).

A/34 Erifazi Kyatuka, 3 September 1968 (Runyankole); b. 1917; ?.

A/35 Mary Berwanamu, 3 September 1968 (Runyankole); b. post-1911; Baitara.

A/36 Surumani Rutabindwa, 3 September 1968 (Runyankole); b. 1905; Bahinda.

A/37 Benoni Karugaba, 4 September 1968 (Runyankole and English); b. 1938; Bahinda.

A/38 William Kantayomba, 5 September 1968 (Runyankole); b. 1930; Basingo.

A/39 Samwiri Zororwa, 5 September 1968 (Runyankole); b. year of Ntare's burial at Kaigoshora (1910?); Beneishekatwa.

A/40 Alozio Kabuhaya, 7 September 1968 (Runyankole); b. 1907; Banito.

A/41 George H. Mbata, 9 September 1968 (Runyankole); b. 1921; Bahinda.

A/42 Violoti Bananka, 9 September 1968 (Runyankole); b. 1905; Bahinda.

A/43 Miriamu Muhindi, 9 September 1968 (Runyankole); b. circa 1905 in Somalia; Bahinda.

A/44 Erika Mukindo, 10 September 1968 (Runyankole and English); b. 1927; Balisa.

A/45 Anatoli Katebalirwe, 10 September 1968 (Runyankole); b. 1926; Basheigyi.

A/46 Samwiri Rwabushongo, 12 September 1968 (Runyankole); follow-up interview.

A/47 Sir Charles G. Gasyonga, 12 September 1968 (Runyankole); b. 1910; Bahinda.

A/48 James Mugyerwa, 10 September 1968 at Kampala (English); b. 1941; Beneishemurai Bashambo.

A/49 Agostino Kaniola, 27 September 1968 (Runyankole, administered by A. Katate); b. time of Ganda Christians (1888?); Banzira.

Informal interview, Jeremy Bamunoba, 12 August 1968.

Informal interview, Ananyas Murumba, 13 August 1969.

SERIES B—BUNYORO

B/1 L. M. Muganwa, 3 October 1968 (Runyoro and English); b. 1904; Bafumambogo.

B/2 Simon Kyamanywa, 7 October 1968 (English); b. 1913; Bahinda.

B/3 Martin D. Mukidi, 13 October 1968 (English); b. 1899; Basingo.

B/4 Kosia Rwebembera, 14 October 1968 (Runyoro); b. 1913; Bairuntu.

B/5 Samwiri Nyamayarwo, 16 October 1968 (Runyoro); b. 1889; Basambo.

B/6 John Nyakatura, 18 October 1968 (Runyoro); b. 1895; ?.

B/7 Alikanjeru Isoke, 19 October 1968 (Runyoro); b. 1904; Babito.

B/8 George Rwakaikara, 20 October 1968 (Runyoro); b. 1912; Bacubo.

B/9 Festo Mugenyi, 20 October 1968 (English); b. 1910; Basingo.

B/10 Metushera Katuramu, 21 October 1968 (English); b. 1922; Bafumambogo.

B/11 H. B. Kakooko, 22 October 1968 (English and Runyoro); b. 1924; Bamoli.

B/12 Nebayosi Tibangwa, 22 October 1968 (Runyoro); b. 1928; Balisa.

B/13 Sebastiano Mukoto, 23 October 1968 (Runyoro); b. 1901; Bahamba.

B/14 A. N. W. Kamese, 27 October 1968 (English); b. 1908; Bahamba.

B/15 Sulemani E. N. Katongole, 28 October 1968 (English); b. 1906; Basaigi.

B/16 Marko Rwanga, 28 October 1968 (English and Runyoro); b. 1901; Basira.

B/17 Kosia Labwoni, 28 October 1968 (English and Runyoro); b. 1900; Babito.

B/18 Yeremia Byarufu, 29 October 1968 (Runyoro); b. circa 1897; Balisa.

B/19 Isaya Bikundi, 30 October 1968 (Runyoro); b. circa 1867; Basaigi.

B/20 Ezekieli Muchwa, 30 October 1968 (English); b. 1912; Bapina.

B/21 Zakayo Munubi, 31 October 1968 (Runyoro); b. 1901; Banyuagi.

B/22 Zakariya Birihanyomyo, 31 October 1968 (Runyoro); b. circa 1870; Basambo.

B/23 Sir Tito Winyi, 31 October 1968 (Runyoro and English); ?; Babito.

B/24 Z. K. Winyi and Z. K. Mugenyi, 2 November 1968 (Runyoro); b. 1914 and 1926, respectively; Babito.

B/25 Bihogo Byabo and Fenehansi Rwanubitoke, 2 November 1968 (Runyoro); b. 1905 and 1914, respectively; Balebeki and Basita, respectively.

B/26 Ibrahim Isingoma, 3 November 1968 (Runyoro); b. 1921; Basita.

B/27 Samsoni Baseka, 3 November 1968 (Runyoro); b. 1907; Bachwa.

B/28 Samsoni Ireeta, 4 November 1968 (Runyoro and English); b. 1907; Basaigi.

B/29 Abisagi Kabajunuka, 5 November 1968 (Runyoro); b. pre-1902; Babito.

B/30 John Rukayi and Sulemani Kanira-Fataki, 11 November 1968 (Runyoro and English); b. 1896 and 1895, respectively; Babito.

B/31 John Kaparaga, 11 November 1968 (Runyoro); b. 1878; Muganda.

B/32 Abedenego Gafwaki, 11 November 1968 (Runyoro); b. circa 1899; Bamoli.

B/33 Abimereki Kabyemera, 11 November 1968 (English and Runyoro); b. 1903; Banyonza.

B/34 Princess Alexandria Konukyeya, 11 November 1968 (Runyoro); b. 1905; Babito.

B/35 Yulam Kihika, 12 November 1968 (English); b. 1928; Bachwa.

B/36 Zakayu Jawe, 14 November 1968 (Runyoro); b. ?; Bamoli.

B/37 Mohammed Byamboijana, 14 November 1968 (Runyoro); b. reign of Kamurasi (?); Bagahya-nchobe.

B/38 Francois Kyahurwa, 15 November 1968 (Runyoro); b. circa 1886; Bakurungu.

B/39 Isaya Bikundi, 16 November 1968 (Runyoro); follow-up interview.

B/40 Gasaki Erigi, 16 November 1968 (Runyoro); b. circa 1886; Bagahya-nchobe.

B/41 Pancras Kaboha, 25 November 1968 (English); b. 1941; Baitira.

B/42 William Kaboha, 26 November 1968 (English); b. 1928; Baitira.

B/43 L. Rubangoya and F. Katabarwa, 26 November 1968 (English); A special interview on linguistic problems with Radio Uganda vernacular language experts for western Uganda.

B/44 Yesse Kinimi, 3 December 1968 (English and Rutoro); b. 1905; Babito Bachake.

B/45 Solomon Mbabi-Katana, 25 April 1969 (English); b. 1922; ?.

SERIES C—TORO

C/1 Moses Nyakazingo, 20 March 1968 (English); b. 1931; ?.

C/2 Samsoni Rwakabuguli, 23 March 1968 (Rutoro); b. circa 1890; ?.

C/3 Asanasio Byairungu, 8 January 1969 (Rutoro); b. 1895; Bagwere.

C/4 Selevasta Ruhume, 9 January 1969 (English); b. 1925; Basita.

C/5 Samuel W. Rububi, 10 January 1969 (English); b. 1946; Bagwere.

C/6 Hosea Nkojo, 11 January 1969 (English); b. 1905; Bagaya.

C/7 Bishop Aberi Balya, 13 January 1969 (Rutoro); b. circa 1881; Balisa.

C/8 Lazaro Kiiza Basigara, 15 January 1969 (Rutoro); b. 1900; Babito.

C/9 Princess Ruth Komuntali, 15 January 1969 (Rutoro); b. 1900.

C/10 Susana Rusoke; 16 January 1969 (Rutoro); b. circa 1895; Basita.

C/11 Evalyn Kasamba, 16 January 1969 (Rutoro); b. ?; Babito Batwara.

C/12 Antwani Mujasi, 17 January 1969 (English and Rutoro); b. 1907; Babito.

C/13 Eseri Mugurusi, 17 January 1969 (Rutoro); b. 1898; Basumbu.

C/14 Ernesto Isingoma and Erasto Kato, 18 January 1969 (Rutoro); b. 1912; Babito Matwara.

C/15 Zakaliyo Okwiri, 20 January 1969 (English and Rutoro); b. 1924; Bagwere.

C/16 Eseri Kibooga, 20 January 1969 (Rutoro); b. 1898; Bagumba.

C/17 Enoch Kaberinde, 21 January 1969 (English); b. 1918; Basita.

C/18 Adam Mukidi, 21 January 1969 (Rutoro); b. 1911; Bayaga.

C/19 Miriam Tigwezire, 22 January 1969 (Rutoro); b. circa 1884; Basumbi.

C/20 Eseri Nyakabwa, 22 January 1969 (Rutoro); b. circa 1889; Basita.

C/21 Yowas Bamuroho, 23 January 1969 (Rutoro and English); b. 1902; Bagumba.

C/22 Airosi Kabaziba, 27 January 1969 (Rutoro); b. 1923; Babito Batwara. Also present were Nasanaeri Kaliba, b. 1921, Babito Batwara; Stanley Njumba, b. 1933, Babito Batwara; and Jeska Kalegera, b. circa 1905, Basita.

C/23 Yafesi Bitamazire, 27 January 1969 (Rutoro); b. 1908; Babito Batwara.

C/24 Sulemani R. Mpaka, 28 January 1969 (Rutoro); b. 1916; Bagwere.

C/25 Kalyegera, 28 January 1969 (Rutoro); b. circa 1895; Bagwere.

C/26 Samsoni Katemba, 28 January 1969 (English and Rutoro); b. 1904; Babopi.

C/27 Maria Kanihire, 29 January 1969 (Rutoro); b. 1917; Bacwezi.

C/28 John Tinkaboine, 29 January 1969 (Rutoro); b. 1918; Bafumambogo.

C/29 Danieri Rwakiboijogoro, 29 January 1969 (Rutoro); b. 1890; Basambu.

C/30 Tefilo Kagoro, 30 January 1969 (Rutoro and English); b. 1922; Babopi.

C/31 Ezeroni Mugungu, 30 January 1969 (Rutoro); b. circa 1885; Baitera.

C/32 Alikanjeru Kutambaki, 30 January 1969 (Rutoro); b. 1887; Bafumambogo.

C/33 Erasto Manyindo, 30 January 1969 (Rutoro); b. circa 1885; Basambu.

C/34 Lazaro Basigara, 31 January 1969 (Rutoro); follow-up interview.

C/35 Efraim Kyamulesire, 31 January 1969 (Rutoro); b. 1932; Babito.

C/36 Emmanuel Kakete, 10 February 1969 (English); b. 1905; Basita.

C/37 Blasio Karamagi, 11 February 1969 (Rutoro); b. 1902; Babito.

C/38 Danieri Rwakiboijogoro, 11 February 1969 (Rutoro); follow-up interview.

C/39 Alikanjeru Mubirigi, 11 February 1969 (Rutoro); b. 1926; Babito.

Bibliography

Bibliography

Bibliography

Bibliography

Bibliography

Bibliography

Bibliography

Bibliography

Bibliography

Bibliography

Bibliography

Bibliography

Bibliography

Bibliography

Bibliography

Bibliography

Bibliography

Bibliography

Bibliography

Bibliography

Bibliography

Bibliography

Bibliography

Bibliography

Bibliography

Bibliography

Bibliography

Bibliography

Bibliography

Bibliography

Bibliography

Bibliography

Bibliography

Bibliography

C/40 Rev. Ezekyeri Binyomo, 12 February 1969 (Rutoro); b. 1888; Bayaga.

C/41 Emmanuel Mutazindwa, 17 February 1969 (English); b. 1916; Babito Batwara.

C/42 Erasto Mpisi, 17 February 1969 (Rutoro); b. circa 1888; Basambu.

C/43 Samuel Mutooro, 18 February 1969 (English); b. 1932; Basu Bakonjo.

C/44 Joseph Winyi, 19 February 1969 (Rutoro); b. 1901; Babito Batwara.

C/45 Kosia Mukonjo, 19 February 1969 (Rutoro); b. 1901; Babopi.

C/2/1 Danieri Rwakiboijogoro, 13 June 1972 (Rutoro); follow-up interview.

C/2/2 Lazaro Kiiza Basigara, 13 June 1972 (Rutoro); follow-up interview.

Contemporary Published Accounts

Ansorge, W. J. *Under the African Sun*. London: Heinemann, 1899.

Ashe, R. P. *Chronicles of Uganda*. New York: A. D. F. Randolph & Co., 1895.

———. *Two Kings of Uganda*. London: Sampson Low, Marston, Searle and Rivington, 1889.

Baker, Samuel. *The Albert Nyanza*, new ed., London: Macmillan & Co., 1883.

Bell, Hesketh. *Glimpses of a Governor's Life*. London: Sampson Low, 1950.

Bovill, Mai, and Askwith, G. R., comps. *"Roddy" Owen*. London: John Murray, 1897.

Chaille-Long, Charles. *Central Africa: Naked Truths of Naked People*. New York: Harper and Bros., 1877.

Colvile, Col. Sir Henry. *The Land of the Nile Springs*. London: Edward Arnold, 1895.

Cunningham, J. F. *Uganda and Its Peoples*, reprint. New York: Negro Universities Press, 1969.

Decle, Lionel. *Three Years in Savage Africa*. New York: M. F. Massfield, 1898.

Fisher, Ruth B. *On the Borders of Pygmy Land*. New York: Fleming H. Levell Co., 1905.

——. *Twilight Tales of the Black Baganda*. London: Frank Cass, 1970.

Gessi, Romolo. *Seven Years in the Soudan*. London: Sampson Low, 1892.

Gregory, J. W. *The Foundation of British East Africa*. London: Horace Marshall and Son, 1901.

Jackson, Sir Frederick. *Early Days in East Africa*. London: Edward Arnold, 1930.

Johnston, Sir Harry. *The Uganda Protectorate*, 2 vols. London: Hutchinson, 1904.

Junker, Wilhelm J. *Travels in Africa*, 3 vols. London: Chapman and Hall, 1890–1892.

Kitching, Rev. A. L. *On the Backwaters of the Nile*. London: T. Fisher Unwin, 1912.

Lloyd, Albert B. *In Dwarf Land and Cannibal Country*. London: T. Fisher Unwin, 1899.

——. *A Life's Thrills*. London: Lutterworth Press, 1948.

Lugard, Frederick D. *The Diaries of Lord Lugard*, 2 vols., Margery Perham, ed. Evanston, Ill.: Northwestern University Press, 1959.

——. *The Rise of Our East African Empire*, 2 vols. Edinburgh: William Blackwood and Sons, 1893.

——. *The Story of the Uganda Protectorate*. London: Horace Marshall and Son, n.d.

MacDonald, Major James R. L. *Soldiering and Surveying in British East Africa 1891–1894*. London and New York: Edward Arnold, 1897.

Portal, Sir Gerald. *The British Mission to Uganda in 1893*. London: Edward Arnold, 1894.

Roscoe, John. *Twenty Five Years in East Africa*. Cambridge: Cambridge University Press, 1921.

Schweinfurth, G., Ratzel, F., Felkin, R. W., and Hartlaub, G., comps., *Emin Pasha in Central Africa*. London: George Philip and Son, 1888.

Schweitzer, Georg, comp. *Emin Pasha*, 2 vols. New York: Negro Universities Press, 1969.

Speke, John A. *Journal of the Discovery of the Source of the Nile*. New York: Harper and Bros., 1864.

Stanley, Henry M. *In Darkest Africa*, 2 vols. New York: Scribner, 1890.

————. *The Story of Emin's Rescue as Told in Stanley's Letters*, J. Scott Keltie, ed. New York: Negro Universities Press, 1969.

————. *Through the Dark Continent*, 2 vols. New York: Harper and Bros., 1878.

Ternan, Trevor. *Some Experiences of an Old Bromsgrovian*. Birmingham: Cornish Bros., 1930.

Thruston, Brevet Major Arthur B. *African Incidents*. London: John Murray, 1900.

Tucker, Alfred. *Eighteen Years in Uganda and East Africa*, 2 vols. London: Edward Arnold, 1908.

Vandeleur, Lieutenant Seymour. *Campaigning on the Upper Nile and Niger*. London: Methuen and Co., 1898.

Secondary Sources

Books

Apter, David. *The Political Kingdom in Uganda*. Princeton, N.J.: Princeton University Press, 1967.

Attwater, Donald. *The White Fathers in Africa*. London: Burns, Oates and Washbourne, 1937.

Austen, Ralph. *Northwest Tanzania Under German and British Rule*. New Haven, Conn.: Yale University Press, 1968.

Banton, Michael, ed. *Political Systems and the Distribution of Power*. London: Tavistock, 1965.

Beattie, John. *Bunyoro, An African Kingdom*. New York: Holt, Rinehart and Winston, 1960.

————. *The Nyoro State*. Oxford: Clarendon Press, 1971.

Bikunya, Petero. *Ky'Abakama ba Bunyoro*. London: Sheldon Press, 1927.

Burke, Fred G. *Local Government and Politics in Uganda*. Syracuse, N.Y.: Syracuse University Press, 1964.

Davis, M. B. *A Lunyoro-Lunyankole-English and English-*

Lunyoro-Lunyankole Dictionary. Kampala: Uganda Bookshop, 1952.

d'Hertefelt, M., Trouwborst, A., and Scherer, J. *Les Anciens Royaumes de la Zone Interlacustrine Meridionale*. London: International African Institute, 1962.

Doornbos, Martin. *Regalia Galore*. Nairobi: East African Literature Bureau, 1976.

Dunbar, A. R. *A History of Bunyoro-Kitara*. Nairobi: East African Institute of Social Research, 1965.

Edel, May M. *The Chiga of Western Uganda*. New York: Oxford University Press, 1957.

Eggan, Fred. *The Social Organization of the Western Pueblos*. Chicago: University of Chicago Press, 1950.

Fallers, Lloyd A. *Bantu Bureaucracy*. Cambridge: Heffer and Sons, 1956.

————., ed. *The King's Men*. London: Oxford University Press, 1964.

Fallers, Margaret C. *The Eastern Lacustrine Bantu*. London: International African Institute, 1960.

Gorju, Julien. *Entre le Victoria, l'Albert et l'Edouard*. Rennes: Imprimeries Obarthur, 1920.

Harlow, V., and Chilver, E. M., eds. *History of East Africa*, Vol. 2. Oxford: Clarendon Press, 1965.

Henige, David. *The Chronology of Oral Tradition*. Oxford: Clarendon Press, 1974.

Herskovits, Melville J. *The Myth of the Negro Past*, Boston: Beacon Press, 1958.

Ibingira, G. S. K. *The Forging of an African Nation*. New York: Viking Press, 1973.

Iliffe, John. *Tanganika Under German Rule, 1905–1912*. Cambridge: Cambridge University Press, 1969.

Ingham, Kenneth. *The Kingdom of Toro in Uganda*. London: Methuen, 1975.

————. *The Making of Modern Uganda*. London: Allen and Unwin, 1958.

Jones, G. I. *The Trading States of the Oil Rivers*. Oxford: Oxford University Press, 1963.

Jones, Herbert G. *Uganda in Transformation, 1879–1926*. London: Church Missionary Society, 1926.

Kagwa, Apolo. *The Customs of the Baganda*, Ernest B. Kalibala, trans. New York: Columbia University Press, 1934.

Karubanga, H. K. *Bukya Nibirwa*. Kampala: Eagle Press, 1949.

Karugire, Samwiri Rubaraza. *A History of the Kingdom of Nkore*. Oxford: Clarendon Press, 1971.

———. *Nuwambaguta*. Kampala: East African Literature Bureau, 1973.

Katate, A. G., and Kamugungunu, L. *Abagabe B'Ankole*, 2 vols. Kampala: East African Literature Bureau, 1967.

Katyanku, Omubitokati Lucy Olive, and Bulera, Semu. *Obwomezi Bw'Omukama Duhaga II*. Kampala: Eagle Press, 1950.

Kittler, Glenn D. *The White Fathers*. New York: Harper and Bros., 1957.

Kiwanuka, M. S. M. Semakola. *A History of Buganda*. London: Longmans, 1971.

———. *The Kingdom of Bunyoro-Kitara—Myth or Reality?* Kampala: Longmans of Uganda, 1968.

Krader, Lawrence. *Formation of the State*. Englewood Cliffs, N.J.: Prentice-Hall, 1968.

Low, D. Anthony. *Buganda in Modern History*. Berkeley: University of California Press, 1971.

———. *Lion Rampant*. London: Frank Cass, 1973.

———. *Political Parties in Uganda 1949–1962*. London: Athlone Press, 1962.

———. *Religion and Society in Buganda 1875–1900*. Kampala: East African Institute of Social Research, 1956.

———, and Pratt, R. C. *Buganda and British Overrule*. London: Oxford University Press, 1960.

Luck, Anne. *African Saint*. London: SCM Press, 1963.

Lwanga, P. M. K. *Obulamu Bw'omutaka J. K. Miti Kabazzi*. Kampala: Friends Press, n.d.

Mair, Lucy. *An African People in the Twentieth Century*. London: George Routledge and Sons, 1934.

————. *Primitive Government*. Harmondsworth: Penguin Books, 1962.

Maquet, Jacques J. *The Premise of Inequality in Ruanda*. London: Oxford University Press, 1961.

Marsh, Robert. *Comparative Sociology*. New York: Harcourt, Brace and World, 1967.

Maxse, Col. F. I. *Seymour Vandelour*. London: National Review Office, 1905.

Morris, Henry F. *The Heroic Recitations of the Bahima of Ankole*. Oxford: Clarendon Press, 1964.

————. *A History of Ankole*. Kampala: East African Literature Bureau, 1962.

Moyse-Bartlett, Lieutenant-Colonel H. *The King's African Rifles*. Aldershot: Gale and Polden, 1956.

Mungeam, Gordon H. *British Rule in Kenya 1895–1912*. Oxford: Clarendon Press, 1960.

Naroll, R., and Cohen, R., eds. *A Handbook of Method in Cultural Anthropology*. Garden City, N.Y.: Natural History Press, 1970.

Nyakatura, John. *Abakama ba Bunyoro-Kitara*. St. Justin, P.Q., Canada, 1947.

————. *Anatomy of an African Kingdom*, G. Uzoigwe, ed. New York: Anchor Books, 1973.

Ogot, Bethwell A. *History of the Southern Luo I*. Nairobi: East African Publishing Company, 1967.

————. *War and Society in Africa*. London: Frank Cass, 1972.

Oliver, Roland. *The Missionary Factor in East Africa*, 2nd ed. London: Longmans, Green and Co., 1965.

————, and Mathew, Gervase, eds. *History of East Africa*, Vol. 1. Oxford: Clarendon Press, 1963.

Owen, Roger, and Sutcliffe, Bob, eds. *Studies in the Theory of Imperialism*. London: Longmans, 1972.

Perham, Margery. *Lugard: The Years of Adventure, 1958–1898*, 1st of 2 vols. London: Collins, 1956.

Ranger, Terence O., ed. *Emerging Themes in African History*. Nairobi: East African Publishing House, 1968.

Richards, Audrey, ed. *East African Chiefs*. London: Faber and Faber, 1959.

Robinson, Ronald, and Gallagher, John. *Africa and the Victorians*. New York: St. Martin's, 1961.

Roscoe, John. *The Baganda*. London: Macmillan, 1911.

———. *The Bakitara or Banyoro*. Cambridge: Cambridge University Press, 1923.

———. *The Banyankole*. Cambridge: Cambridge University Press, 1923.

———. *The Northern Bantu*. Cambridge: Cambridge University Press, 1915.

———. *The Soul of Central Africa*. London: Cassell, 1922.

Rotberg, Robert I., ed. *Africa and Its Explorers*. Cambridge, Mass.: Harvard University Press, 1970.

Rowe, John A. *Lugard at Kampala: A Reappraisal*. Kampala: Longmans of Uganda, 1969.

Seal, Amil. *The Emergence of Indian Nationalism*. Cambridge: Cambridge University Press, 1968.

Smith, Iain R. *The Emin Pasha Relief Expedition, 1886–1890*. Oxford: Clarendon Press, 1972.

Smith, Michael G. *Government in Zazzau, 1800–1950*. London: Oxford University Press, 1960.

Southwold, Martin. *Bureaucracy and Chieftainship in Buganda*. Kampala: East African Institute of Social Research, 1961.

Spicer, Edward H. *Potam, A Yaqui Village in Sonora*. American Anthropologist *Memoir* #77, Vol. 56, #4, Part 2, 1954.

Stock, Eugene. *The History of the Church Missionary Society III*. London: Church Missionary Society, 1899.

Taylor, Brain K. *The Western Lacustrine Bantu*. London: International African Institute, 1962.

Thomas, H. B., and Scott, Robert. *Uganda*. London: Humphrey Milford, 1935.

Tuden, Arthur, and Plotnicov, Leonard, eds. *Social Stratification in Africa*. New York: The Free Press, 1970.

Uzoigwe, G. N. *Revolution and Revolt in Bunyoro-Kitara*. Kampala: Longmans, 1970.

Vansina, Jan. *L'evolution du royaume rwanda des origines a 1900*. Bruselles: Academie Royale des Sciences d'Outre-Mer, 1962.

Welbourn, Frederick B. *East African Rebels*. London: SCM Press, 1961.

――――. *Religion and Politics in Uganda 1952–1962*. Nairobi: East African Publishing House, 1965.

Wild, J. V. *The Story of the Uganda Agreement*. London: Macmillan, 1955.

――――. *The Uganda Mutiny, 1897*. London: Macmillan, 1954.

Wilks, Ivor. *Political Bipolarity in Nineteenth Century Asante*. Edinburgh: Centre of African Studies, 1970.

Wilson, C. J. *Uganda in the Days of Bishop Tucker*. London: Macmillan, 1955.

Winter, Edward H. *Bwamba*. Cambridge: Heffer, 1956.

Wright, Michael. *Buganda in the Heroic Age*. Nairobi: Oxford University Press, 1971.

Articles

Baker, John R. "Baker and Ruyonga." *Uganda Journal* 25, 2(1961):214–16.

Baker, S. J. K. "Bunyoro: A Regional Appreciation." *Uganda Journal* 18, 2(1954):101–112.

――――. "The Geographical Background of Western Uganda." *Uganda Journal* 22, 1(1958):1–10.

Barth, F. "Segmentary Opposition and the Theory of Games." *Journal of the Royal Anthropological Institute* 89, 1(1959):5–21.

Beattie, John. "Aspects of Nyoro Symbolism." *Africa* 38, 4(1968):413–442.

――――. "Bunyoro: An African Feudality?" *Journal of African History* 5, 1(1964):25–35.

――――. "Democratization in Bunyoro." *Civilisations* 11, 1(1961):8–20.

――――. "A Further Note on the Kibanja System of Land Tenure in Bunyoro, Uganda." *Journal of African Administration* 4(1954):178–185.

――――. "The Kibanja System of Land Tenure in Bunyoro, Uganda." *Journal of African Administration* 1(1954):18–28.

――――. "The Nyoro." In *East African Chiefs*, A. Richards, ed. London: Faber and Faber, 1960.

Brunschwig, Henri. "De la resistance Africaine a l'Im-
    perialisme Europeen." *Journal of African History* 15,
    1(1974):47–64.
Clignet, Remi. "A Critical Evaluation of Concommittant
    Variation Studies." In *A Handbook of Method of Cultural An-
    thropology*, R. Naroll and R. Cohen, eds. Garden City,
    N.Y.: Natural History Press, 1970.
Codere, Helen. "Power in Ruanda." *Anthropologica* Ser. 2, 4,
    1:45–83.
Cohen, D. W. "The Cwezi Cult." *Journal of African History* 9,
    4(1968):651–657.
Cox, A. H. "The Growth and Expansion of Buganda."
    Uganda Journal 14, 2(1950):153–159.
Davidson, A. B. "African Resistance and Rebellion Against
    the Imposition of Colonial Rule." In *Emerging Themes in
    African History*, T. O. Ranger, ed. Nairobi: East African
    Publishing House, 1968.
d'Hertefelt, M. "Stratification Sociale et Structure Politique
    au Ruanda." *Le Revue Nouvelle* 31, 5(1960):449–462.
Doornbos, Martin R. "Kumanyana and Rwenzururu: Two
    Responses to Ethnic Inequality." In *Protest and Power in
    Black Africa*, R. Rotberg and A. Mazrui, eds. New York:
    Oxford University Press, 1970.
———. "Land Tenure and Political Conflict in Ankole,
    Uganda." *Journal of Development Studies*, 12, 1(1975):54–74.
Dunbar, A. R. "The British and Bunyoro-Kitara, 1891–
    1899," *Uganda Journal* 24, 2(1960):229–241.
———. "European Travellers in Bunyoro-Kitara 1862–
    1877." *Uganda Journal* 23, 2(1959):101–117.
———. "Emin Pasha and Bunyoro-Kitara, 1877–1889."
    Uganda Journal 24, 1(1960):71–83.
Eggan, Fred. "The Method of Controlled Comparison."
    American Anthropologist 56(1954):743–63.
Fallers, Lloyd. "Despotism, Status Culture and Social Mobil-
    ity in an African Kingdom." *Comparative Studies in Society
    and History* 2 (1959–1960):11–32.
———. "Ideology and Culture in Uganda Nationalism."
    American Anthropologist 63, 4(1961):677–686.

————. "The Predicament of the Modern African Chief." *American Anthropologist* 57, 2(1955):290–305.

Furley, O. W. "Kasagama of Toro." *Uganda Journal* 25, 2(1961):184–198.

————. "The Origins of Economic Paternalism in a British Territory: Western Uganda." *Social and Economic Studies* (Kingston, Jam.) 2, 1(1962):57–72.

————. "The Reign of Kasagama in Toro from a Contemporary Account." *Uganda Journal* 31, 2(1967):183–190.

Gravel, Pierre, B. "Life on the Manor in Gisaka (Rwanda)." *Journal of African History* 6, 3(1965):323–331.

Gray, Sir John Milner. "Anglo–German Relations in Uganda, 1890–1892." *Journal of African History* 1, 2(1960):281–297.

————. "Early Treaties in Uganda, 1888–1891." *Uganda Journal* 12, 1(1948):25–42.

————. "Kabarega's Embassy to the Mahdists in 1897." *Uganda Journal* 19, 1(1955):93–95.

————. "The Suspension of the Ankole Agreement in 1905." *Uganda Journal* 22, 1(1958):86–87.

————. "Toro in 1897." *Uganda Journal* 27, 1(1953):14–27.

————. "The Year of the Three Kings of Buganda, Mwanga-Kiwewa-Kalema, 1888–1889." *Uganda Journal* 14, 1(1950):15–52.

Hodgkin, T. "Some African and Third World Theories," in *Studies in the Theory of Imperialism*, R. Owen and B. Sutcliffe, eds. London: Longmans, 1972.

Iliffe, John. "The Organization of the Maji-Maji Rebellion." *Journal of African History* 8, 3(1967):495–512.

Ingham, Kenneth. "Some Aspects of the History of Western Uganda." *Uganda Journal* 21, 2(1957):131–149.

Karugire, Samwiri R. "Relations Between Bairu and Bahima in Nineteenth Century Nkare." *Tarikh* 3, 2(1970):22–33.

————. "Succession Wars in the Pre-Colonial Kingdom of Nkare." In *War and Society in Africa*, B. A. Ogot, ed. London: Frank Cass, 1972.

Kiwanuka, M. S. M. "Bunyoro and the British: A Reappraisal of the Causes for the Decline and Fall of an African Kingdom." *Journal of African History* 9, 4(1968):603–619.

Lanning, E. C. "Kikukule: Guardian of Southeast Bunyoro." *Uganda Journal* 32, 2(1968):119–147.

LeMarchand, Rene. "Power and Stratification in Rwanda: A Reconsideration." *Cahiers d'Etudes Africaines* 6, 4(1966): 592–610.

Lloyd, Peter C. "The Political Structure of African Kingdoms: An Exploratory Model." In *Political Systems and the Distribution of Power*, ASA Monograph #4. London: Tavistock Publishers, 1965.

Low, Anthony D. "The Advent of Populism in Buganda." *Comparative Studies in Society and History* 6 (1963–1964):424–444.

————. "Lion Rampant." *Journal of Commonwealth Political Studies* 2, 13(1964):235–252.

————. "Warbands and Ground-Level Imperialism in Uganda, 1870–1900," *Historical Studies* (Melbourne) 16, 65(1975):584–597.

Mair, Lucy. "Clientship in East Africa." *Cahiers d'Etudes Africaines* 2, 6(1961):315–325.

Maloney, M. T. "The Suicide of Musinga." *Uganda Journal* 22, 1(1958):85–86.

Maquet, Jacques J. "The Problem of Tutsi Domination." In *Cultures and Societies of Africa*, S. and P. Ottenberg, eds. New York: Random House, 1960.

Mbabi-Katana, Solomon. "Bunyoro's Grand Old Man." *Uganda Herald*, 25 July 1953, p. 5.

Meldon, J. A. "Notes on the Bahima of Ankole." *Journal of the Royal African Society* 6, 22 and 23 (1907):136–153 and 234–249.

Morris, H. F. "The Making of Ankole." *Uganda Journal* 21, 1(1957):1–15.

————. "The Murder of H. St. G. Galt." *Uganda Journal* 24, 1(1960):1–15.

Mungeam, G. H. "Masai and Kikuyu Responses to the Establishment of British Administration in the East African Protectorate." *Journal of African History* 11, 1(1970):127–143.

Needham, Rodney. "Right and Left in Nyoro Symbolic Classification." *Africa* 37, 4(1967):425–452.

Oberg, Kalvero. "A Comparison of Three Economic Organizations." *American Anthropologist* 45, 4(1943):572–587.

———. "The Kingdom of Ankole in Uganda." In *African Political Systems*, M. Fortes and E. E. Evans-Pritchard, eds. London: Oxford University Press, 1940.

———. "Kinship Organization of the Banyankole." *Africa* 11, 2(1938):129–159.

Odhiambo, E. S. Atieno. "The Paradox of Collaboration: The Uganda Case." *East Africa Journal* 9, 10(1972):19–25.

Oliver, Roland. "A Question About the Bachwezi," *Uganda Journal* 17, 1(1953):135–137.

———. "Some Factors in the British Occupation of East Africa." *Uganda Journal* 15, 1(1951):49–64.

———. "The Traditional Histories of Buganda, Bunyoro and Ankole." *Journal of the Royal Anthropological Institute* 85(1955):111–117.

Perlman, Melvin. "The Traditional Systems of Stratification Among the Ganda and Nyoro of Uganda." In *Social Stratification in Africa*, A. Tuden and L. Plotnicov, eds. New York: The Free Press, 1970.

Posnansky, Merrick. "Kingship, Archaeology and Historical Myth." *Uganda Journal* 30, 1(1966):1–12.

Pratt, R. C. "Nationalism in Buganda." *Political Studies* 9, 2(1961):157–178.

Ranger, Terence O. "African Reactions to the Imposition of Colonial Rule in East and Central Africa." In *Colonialism in Africa*, Vol. 1, L. H. Gann and P. Duignan, eds. Cambridge: Cambridge University Press, 1969.

———. "The Role of Ndebele and Shona Religious Authorities in the Rebellions of 1896 and 1897." In *The Zambesian Past*, E. Stokes and R. Brown, eds. Manchester: Manchester University Press, 1965.

Roberts, Andrew. "The Evolution of the Uganda Protectorate." *Uganda Journal* 27, 1(1963):95–106.

———. "The 'Lost Counties' of Bunyoro." *Uganda Journal* 26, 2(1962):194–199.

———. "The Sub-Imperialism of Buganda." *Journal of African History* 3, 3(1962):435–50.

Robinson, Ronald. "Non-European Foundations of Euro-
pean Imperialism: Sketch for a Theory of Collaboration."
In *Studies in the Theory of Imperialism*, R. Owen and B.
Sutcliffe, eds. London: Longmans, 1972.

Rothchild, D., and Rogin, M. "Uganda." In *National Unity
and Regionalism in Eight African States*, G. Carter, ed. Ithaca,
N.Y.: Cornell University Press, 1966.

Rowe, John A. "Land and Politics in Buganda, 1875–1955."
Makerere Journal 10(1964):1–13.

———. "The Purge of Christians at Mwanga's Court." *Journal of African History* 5, 1(1964):55–71.

———. "The Western Impact and the African Reaction:
Buganda, 1880–1900." *Journal of Developing Areas* 1
(1966):55–65.

Southwold, Martin. "The Ganda of Uganda." In *People of Africa*, J. Gibbs, ed. New York: Holt Rinehart and Winston,
1965.

Steinhart, Edward I. "The Kingdoms of the March: Speculations on Social and Political Change." In *Chronology in African History*, J. F. Webster, ed. Dalhousie Series in African
Studies. Halifax: Longmans, 1977.

———. "The Nyangire Rebellion of 1907." In *Protest Movements in Colonial East Africa*, Eastern African Studies XII.
Syracuse, N.Y.: Program of Eastern African Studies, 1973.

———. "Royal Clientage and the Beginnings of Colonial
Modernization in Toro," *International Journal of African Historical Studies* 6(1973):265–285.

———. "Vassal and Fief in Three Lacustrine Kingdoms."
Cahiers d'Etudes Africaines 7 (1967):606–623.

Stenning, Derrick J. "Salvation in Ankole." In *African Systems
of Thought*, M. Fortes and G. Dieterlen, eds. London: Oxford University Press, 1965.

Tamuno, Takena N. "Some Aspects of Nigerian Reaction to
the Imposition of British Rule." *Journal of the Historical Society of Nigeria* 2 (1965):271–294.

Thomas, H. B. "Capax Imperii—The Story of Semei
Kakungulu." *Uganda Journal* 6, 3(1939):125–136.

————. "Gordon's Farthest South in Uganda in 1876." *Uganda Journal* 5, 4(1936):284–288.

————. "Imperatrix v. Juma and Urzee." *Uganda Journal* 7, 2(1939):70–84.

————. "The Rev. A. B. Fisher in Uganda: A Memoir." *Uganda Journal* 21, 1(1957):107–110.

Tosh, John. "The Northern Lacustrine Region." In *Pre-Colonial African Trade*, R. Gray and D. Birmingham, eds. London: Oxford University Press, 1970.

Trouwborst, A. A. "L'Organization politique et l'Accord du Clientele au Burundi." *Anthropologica* 4, 1(1962):9–43.

Twaddle, Michael. "The Bakungu Chiefs of Buganda Under British Colonial Rule, 1900–1930," *Journal of African History* 10, 2(1969):309–322.

Uzoigwe, Godfrey. "Kabarega and the Making of a New Kitara," *Tarikh* 3, 2(1970):5–21.

————. "Pre-Colonial Military Studies in Africa," *Journal of Modern African Studies* 13, 3(1975):469–481.

Vansina, Jan. "Notes sur l'histoire du Burundi," *Aequatoria* 24, 1(1961):1–10.

————. "Les Regimes fonciers Ruanda et Kuba-Une Comparison." In *African Agrarian Systems*, D. Biebuyck, ed. London: Oxford University Press, 1963.

————. "The Use of Process Models In African History." In *The Historian in Tropical Africa*, J. Vansina, R. Mauny, and L. V. Thomas, eds. London: Oxford University Press, 1964.

K. W. (pen name of Winyi, Sir Tito). "The Kings of Bunyoro-Kitara, Part I." *Uganda Journal* 3, 2(1935):155–160.

————. "The Kings of Bunyoro-Kitara, Part II." *Uganda Journal* 4, 1(1936):78–83.

————. "The Kings of Bunyoro-Kitara, Part III." *Uganda Journal* 5, 2(1937):53–69.

Weekes, D. "John Macallister and the Town of Mbarara, 1898–1900," *Uganda Journal* 37 (1973):29–54.

————. "The Journey of Cunningham Through Ankole in 1894," *Uganda Journal* 37 (1973):55–62.

Williams, F. Lukyn. "Blood Brotherhood in Ankole." *Uganda Journal* 2, 1(1934):33–41.

———. "Early Explorers in Ankole." *Uganda Journal* 2, 3(1935):196–208.

———. "The Inauguration of the Mugabe to Office." *Uganda Journal* 4, 4(1937):151–155.

———. "Nuwa Mbaguta, Nanzi of Ankole." *Uganda Journal* 12, 2(1946):124–135.

Wilson, James. "The Foundation of the Toro Kingdom," in *The History of Uganda*, Vol. 2, D. J. N. Denoon, ed. Nairobi: East African Publishing House, forthcoming.

Wrigley, C. C. "The Christian Revolution in Buganda." *Comparative Studies in Society and History* 2(1959–1960):33–48.

———. "Some Thoughts on the Bacwezi," *Uganda Journal* 22 (1958):11–17.

Yoder, J. "Fly and Elephant Parties: Political Polarization in Dahomey, 1840–1870." *Journal of African History* 15, 3(1974):417–432.

Unpublished Sources

Theses

Glennon, John P. "Uganda 1890–1901." Doctoral diss., Clark University, 1955.

Kalibala, Ernest B. "The Social Structure of the Baganda Tribe of East Africa." Doctoral diss., Harvard University, 1946.

Low, D. Anthony. "The British and Uganda, 1862–1900." Doctoral diss., Oxford University, 1957.

Maquet, Jacques J. "The Indigenous Political Organization of the Kingdom of Rwanda." Doctoral diss., University of London, 1952.

Pirouet, M. M. Louise. "The Expansion of the Church of Uganda (N.A.C.) from Buganda into Northern and Western Uganda between 1891 and 1914, with Special Reference to the Work of African Teachers and Evangelists." Doctoral diss., University of East Africa, 1968.

Taylor, Brian K. "The Social Structure of the Batoro." Doctoral diss., University of London, 1957.

Seminar and Conference Papers

Arap Ng'eny, Samuel K. "Nandi Resistance to the Establishment of British Administration (1893–1906)." Research paper, Kabianga School, Kenya, n.d.

Des Forges, Alison. "The Impact of European Colonization on the Rwandan Social System." Paper presented at the African Studies Association Meetings, Bloomington, Ind., 1966.

Doornbos, Martin. "Protest Movements in Western Uganda: Some Parallels and Contrasts," Makerere Institute of Social Research Conference Paper, 1967.

Furley, O. W. "Education and the Chiefs in East Africa." University of East Africa Social Science Council Conference Paper, Kampala, 1968–1969.

———. "The Sudanese Troops in Uganda: From Lugard's Enlistment to the Mutiny, 1891–1897." Research paper, East African Institute of Social Research, 1959.

Kamuntu, E., Kamurari, F., Mbojana, S. Turyagyenda, E., and Rukwira, D. "Mbaguta and the Administration of Ankole," Joint research paper, Ntare V History Society, Ntare V Senior Secondary School, Mbarara, 1967.

Karugire, Samwiri. "The Foundation and Development of Western Kingdoms." Seminar paper, Makerere University, 1972.

———. "The Kingdom of Nkore." Seminar paper, University of London, 1967.

Low, D. Anthony. "The Anatomy of Administrative Origins: Uganda, 1890–1902." East African Institute of Social Research Conference Paper, 1958.

Nyakazingo, Moses. "Kasagama of Toro—A Despotic and Missionary King." Research paper, Makerere University College, 1968.

Policeapuuli, Isaac. "The History of Busongora County," Research paper, Makerere University College, 1967.

Rukidi III, Omukama, Sir George Kamurasi. "The Kings of

Toro," Joseph R. Muchope, trans. Cyclostated, Makerere University College, 1969.

Steinhart, Edward I. "The Collapse of Bunyoro: 1891–1899." Seminar paper, University of California, Los Angeles, 1965.

———. "An Outline of the Political Economy of Ankole." Western Association of Africanists Conference Paper, Laramie, Wyo., 1973.

———. "Primary Collaboration in Ankole: 1891–1901." University of East Africa Social Science Council Conference Paper, Kampala, 1968–1969.

———. "The Seed-Bed of Christianity in Ankole." Seminar paper, Northwestern University, 1966.

Stenning, Derrick J. "Preliminary Observations on the Balokole Movement Particularly Among Bahima in Ankole District." East African Institute of Social Research Conference Paper, 1958.

Twaddle, Michael. "The Politics of Collaboration in Uganda, 1900–1930." Seminar paper, Institute of Commonwealth Studies, University of London, 1966.

Wilson, James. "The Clans of Toro." Seminar paper, Makerere University, 1972.

———. "The Eighteenth Century Background to the Secession of Toro." Seminar Paper, Makerere University, 1972.

———. "Kaboyo's Sons Struggle for the Throne of Toro, 1860–1878." Seminar paper, Makerere University, 1972.

———. "Omukama Kaboyo Olimi I and the Foundation of the Toro Kingdom." Seminar paper, Makerere University, 1971.

Index

abangonya, 135, 138. *See also* military
  forces and operations, Ankole
Acholi, 20, 89-90
Achte, Père, 113-14, 117, 186
administration, 10, 205-209, 263-66,
  268-69, 273; of Ankole, 191-205,
  216-18; of Bunyoro, 159-77,
  239-54; Ganda model of, 166, 171,
  194, 226, 241, 268; of "lost counties," 70, 161; of Toro, 49, 113-14,
  129-32, 177-90, 224-39
Agreements, 157, 171, 206, 263,
  267-68; Ankole Agreement of
  1900, 199, 202-204, 219; Buganda
  Agreement of 1900, 191, 231;
  Toro Agreement of 1900, 178-90,
  225-38
agricultural class, 6, 16, 25, 35, 72,
  161-65, 203, 243-49, 253, 259. *See
  also* Bairu
Amara, 75, 90, 163, 166, 173
Ankole, 5, 6, 28, 29-30, 36-37, 38,
  53, 70, 100, 106, 128, 130, 135,
  171, 189, 240, 251, 254, 259, 260;
  class structure, 6-7, 9-10, 34-35;
  collaboration in, 133-56, 157,
  191-209, 211-24; Lugard in,
  39-41, 46, 56; political system,
  7-13, 15-18, 151; religion in,
  14-15; succession crisis, 141-48,
  165
Ashburnham, Lieutenant Cromer,
  80, 109-114, 132
assassination, 152, 186; of Galt,
  211-24, 232, 239, 253

Baamba, 4, 184, 226. *See also*
  Bwamba

Babito, 18, 19, 23, 35, 101-102, 118,
  123, 125, 162, 165, 169, 175, 182,
  184, 209, 235, 245, 250, 259;
  Baboyo, 26, 43, 182; Baitwara,
  101, 122, 181
Bacwezi, 5, 10, 14, 18
Bagaya, Maliza, 124-25, 235
Bagge, Stephen, 98, 127-29
Bagyendanwa, 14, 133, 140
Bahinda, 8, 10, 16-17, 35, 133, 136,
  141, 148, 155, 199-200, 203, 214,
  222, 224
Bahuma (Bahima), 6, 41, 56-57,
  133, 170; in Ankole, 7-14, 134-35,
  148, 191, 200, 202, 211, 218, 224;
  in Bunyoro, 19, 23, 161, 242; in
  Toro, 25, 117
Bairu, 6; in Ankole, 7-14, 135, 136,
  139, 141, 200, 203, 212-13, 224;
  in Bunyoro, 19; in Toro, 116,
  118
bajwara Kondo, 20
Baker, Sir Samuel, 3, 22, 31-33, 69,
  162
Bakonjo, 4, 105. *See also* Bukonjo
Bakora, 193, 199, 204
bakungu, see chiefs
Balisa, 195-96
Bamuroga, 20
Bamya, Tomasi, 180, 185, 237
Bantu (languages), 4, 268
"Banubi," 99. *See also* Sudanese
  troops
Banyonza, 54, 175
barusura, 21-22, 42, 50, 51, 53, 54,
  62, 65, 70-71, 73, 80, 88, 96, 107,
  158, 160, 168, 172, 173, 176-77,
  208. *See also* military forces,
  Bunyoro

Library of Congress Cataloging in Publication Data

Steinhart, Edward I.
  Conflict and collaboration.
  Bibliography: p.
  1. Uganda—History.   2.   Uganda—Colonization.
3. Bunyoro, Uganda—History.   4.   Toro, Uganda—His-
tory.   5.   Ankole, Uganda—History.   I.   Title.
DT433.27.S73   967.6'103   77-72136
ISBN 0-691-03114-2